The
Polish
Campaign
1939

The Polish Campaign 1939

by Steven Zaloga & Victor Madej

HIPPOCRENE
BOOKS, INC.

For information, address: Hippocrene Books, Inc., 171 Madison Avenue, New York, N.Y. 10016

Manufactured in the United States of America.

ISBN 0-88254-994-4

Contents

Foreword

The invasion of Poland in 1939 by Germany and the Soviet Union initiated World War II. While the political roots of the conflict are well known, little attention has been paid to the actual conduct of the Wehrmacht's first battles or to the struggle of the Polish Army. Indeed, most of the short accounts of the campaign focus on popular German propaganda myths, such as the tales of Polish cavalry charges against German tanks, or the notion of the "two-week war." That many serious historians still believe these myths is a sad indication of the lack of scholarship in English on this fascinating subject.

The aim of this book is to examine the September Campaign from the perspective of the Polish Army. While there are many accounts of the actions of the Wehrmacht during this period, there is a lack of comparable studies of its smaller opponent. Although this subject has been dealt with in extensive depth by Polish authors, the language barrier has prevented much access to this material for most English-reading scholars and historians.

Contrary to the popular myths, the September Campaign was by no means an easy campaign for the Wehrmacht. In view of its overwhelming superiority in men and machines, it suffered surprisingly high equipment losses. Nor was the campaign without its blunders by the German side. The lack of tactical experience with mechanized units was quite evident in several of the major battles of the campaign. Against a much weaker enemy, the Germans could develop needed experience and make the necessary changes before confronting their more equal French and British foe. While the Soviet intervention in the second week of the war did not change the inevitable outcome of the campaign, it did relieve the Wehrmacht of the risk of protracted small-scale partisan warfare in the hinterlands of eastern Poland.

Assessments of the Polish Army's performance in 1939, in contrast, have tended to focus on its outdated strategy and equipment. There has been a general tendancy to overestimate the size of the Polish Armyand to deprecate the quality of its troops and military leaders. Some of these mistaken impressions have been brought about by lack of access to Polish documents dealing with actual Polish operational doctrine, as well as a general unfamiliarity with details of the Polish Army's organization, order of battle, or conduct in the September fighting. The authors hope that this more detailed appraisal will refocus attention on these subjects and make other historians more aware of the wealth of material available on this forgotten war.

The photographs appearing in this book were provided by the Pilsudski Institute (New York), National Archives (Washington, D.C.), Sikorski Institute (London), the author's collections, and the collections of friends in Poland. The authors would like to express their thanks to these sources for their kind help.

Although the Polish Army was more famous for its cavalry troops, its heart in the 1939 campaign was the infantry. Here, a company of infantry exercises outside Warsaw before the outbreak of the fighting.

The Polish Campaign 1939

1. The Polish Army, 1918–1939

After 123 years of foreign subjugation, Poland regained its independence in 1918. Poland's independence was won by the actions of its fledgling army which in the first three years of its existence was obliged to fight against German, Lithuanian, Ukrainian, and Soviet forces in an effort to redefine Poland's amorphous boundaries.

The Polish Army was initially an amalgam of small political militias, regional defense forces, and units formed with the assistance of foreign governments. Numerically, the most important of the forces raised with foreign assistance was the Polish Army in France, under Gen. Jozef Haller, totaling some six divisions. Poland had a traditional relationship with France in military affairs, harking back especially to the numerous Polish troops who formed the cream of Napoleon's cavalry a century before. Polish units were formed in 1915 as part of the French Foreign Legion, and a major expansion took place in 1917 as an adjunct to French foreign policy, which had decided to support an independent Polish state after the war. The troops for the new Polish Army came primarily from Polish prisoners-of-war who had been drafted into the German and Austro-Hungarian armies and who were captured on the French or Italian fronts. In addition, about 25,000 Polish-American volunteers were recruited and initially trained in Canada due to American neutralist policies. The Haller Army was transferred to Poland in the spring of 1919. In 1914, the tsarist government had allowed the formation of a Polish Legion, sometimes called the Pulawy Legion. Although quashed in 1915 because of anxiety over swelling Polish nationalism, the Polish units were gradually expanded due to a shortage of manpower in the Russian Army. With the revolution and the arrival of the liberal Kerensky regime in the spring of 1917, the Poles were allowed to form an army on Russian soil, and the 1st Polish Eastern Corps was transferred to Byelorussia. Byelorussia was occupied by German forces in February 1918 and the Polish units disbanded and returned to Poland. Nevertheless, they formed an important reserve of trained soldiers for recruitment by local defense forces. Although numerically one of the smaller forces, the Polish Legions raised by the Austro-Hungarian Army in 1914 proved to have a disproportionate influence on the later Polish Army. The Polish Legions were led by the erstwhile socialist, Jozef Pilsudski, on the basis of paramilitary sporting and rifle clubs formed in Austrian Poland. Two brigades were formed and fought against the Russians through 1917. In 1917, the Kerensky government in Russia declared its support for Polish independence on the heels of an Austro-Hungarian declaration of the restitution of the Kingdom of Poland. Pilsudski's troops were obliged to take an oath swearing their allegiance to the Austro-German vassal state, which they refused and the Legion was disbanded. It was replaced by the Royal Polish Army, derisively called the Polnische Wehrmacht. Besides these formal units, a large number of local defense groups were formed on Polish soil after the October revolution in Russia and after the collapse of the Central Powers at the end of 1918.

In February 1919, the infant Polish parliament (Sejm) passed the Army Law, appointing Jozef Pilsudski as the commander-in-chief of the ragtag Polish Army. The bulk of the army at first came from troops of Pilsudski's disbanded legions and formed a loyal core around which a regular army could be built. Added to this were the Polnische Wehrmacht and the Poznanian regiments of the regular German Landwehr which came over to the Polish side in December 1918. The army was bolstered by the arrival of the Haller Army in April 1919, and by various Polish forces which had been formed by Polish troops serving in the Russian Army. Also, a number of small armies were formed in outlying Polish cities like Wilno and Lwow.

The source of the ensuing border wars is not hard to trace. In the wake of the defeat of the Austro-Hungarian and German empires in World War I, and the disintegration of the Russian empire after the two revolutions, there was a relative power vacuum in east-central Europe which permitted the resuscitation of the Polish state. Although all three empires still claimed much of the territory they had wrested from the old Polish-Lithuanian Commonwealth at the end of the eighteenth century, they were in no position in 1919 to hold on to it. The question was who could control the borderlands of the empires. The Western Powers showed little interest in defining the amorphous borders in eastern Europe, though they all supported an independent Polish state. The shape of this state was in some dispute, both in Poland and in the West. Roman Dmowski, head of the Polish delegation at the Versailles Peace Conference and head of the right-wing National Democratic Party, was an ardent integral nationalist. Dmowski believed that the future Poland should be relatively small within

Polish ethnic boundaries. Dmowski did not believe that Poland should absorb a significant section of the Byelorussian and Ukrainian borderlands, beyond those which contained important Polish communities like Lwow. Dmowski also hoped that the future Poland could reach an amicable understanding with whatever Russian state eventually emerged from the Russian civil war. Pilsudski, a former socialist and leader of the Polish Army, was an ardent federalist who hoped that a future state containing a significant Ukrainian and Byelorussian minority could serve as a Central European bastion against the encroachments of the neighboring empires. The central problem in most of these conceptions was that there were no clearly definable ethnic frontiers. The Western Ukraine (Malopolska) and Western Byelorussia (Polesie) were a checkerboard pattern of small Polish villages intermixed with small Byelorussian and Ukrainian villages and an occasional town or city. The towns and cities tended to be of mixed Polish and Jewish population. Western suggestions for frontiers frequently overlooked the complexity of the ethnic landscape in the region.

The initial fighting began in sporadic outbursts. Wilno was contested by the Poles and Lithuanians. Although the city was clearly Polish (and the birthplace of Pilsudski), many of the surrounding villages were Lithuanian

The dominant force in the development of the Polish Army was Josef Pilsudski, seen here reviewing his victorious forces at the conclusion of the 1920 war.

and the Lithuanians planned to make Wilno their new capital. In the Ukraine, an independent state had been declared, and its forces began to lay siege to Lwow. The Lwow fighting was the heaviest in the initial round, with the Poles emerging victorious. An uneasy truce settled on the ill-defined Polish-Russian frontier. The Soviets were too busy with the Whites to bother with the Poles, and Pilsudski was reluctant to assist the Whites against the Soviets. The Soviets at least mouthed platitudes about Polish independence while most of the Whites insisted on a return of Poland to the Russian empire. After a year of fruitless negotiations, Pilsudski decided in April 1920 to join with the Ukrainian nationalist forces under Petlura and invade the Ukraine. The Kiev operation was a startling success, with Polish cavalry ranging far into the Ukraine. The Polish invasion sparked a Soviet reply. With the bulk of the White armies defeated, the Red Army could turn much of its force against the Poles. The Polish Army suffered an equally stunning setback as the Red Army pushed it back to the gates of Warsaw by the end of the summer of 1920. The seesaw war had another swing, and a brilliant counterstroke engineered by Pilsudski sent the Red Army hurtling back in a complete rout to the Russian frontier. The Soviets were forced to sue for peace, and the eastern frontiers were formalized in 1921 in the Riga treaty. During the course of the 1920 Russo-Polish War, Czechoslovakia had taken advantage of the distraction of the Polish Army and seized a contested strip of territory centered around the city of Teschen (Cieszyn). This action deeply embittered the Poles and served as a permanent wedge between the two neighbors for the next two decades. The Wilno question was finally settled when Polish forces, ostensibly against Pilsudski's commands, seized the city. Lithuania remained in a state of war with Poland for the next two decades as a result. The final demarcation of the Polish-German border was supposed to be settled by plebiscites in the industrial region of Silesia (Slask). Both sides used paramilitary forces in attempts to nudge the plebiscites in their favor, and Polish militias were involved in several uprisings during the course of the border demarcations.

The outcome of the border wars of 1920–22 defined the geographic shape of Poland as well as its foreign and military policies. The disputes with Lithuania and Czechoslovakia so badly poisoned relations between these otherwise natural allies that no politicians in any of the three states were able to transcend these territorial squabbles and form a necessary defensive alliance against the encroachments of their German or Soviet neighbors. Polish successes in Silesia and the eastern borderlands left both Germany and the Soviet Union with festering revanchist ambitions that envisioned the crushing of the upstart Polish state.

The military experiences of the Russo-Polish war had important domestic and defense implications for the revived Poland. Pilsudksi showed little affection for assuming a role of responsibility in the peacetime government, although he continued to exert influence in military affairs. In some respects, this mirrored the experiences of Marshal Karl Mannerheim in Finland at the time. On the other hand, Pilsudski's central role in defending and shaping the new Polish state made him one of the few leaders with any broad national support. The central role played by the military, rather than by political figures, in assuring the independence of Poland made the army one of the few national institutions having the respect of Poland's heterogeneous population. Although the Catholic Church had the allegiance of the vast majority of ethnic Poles, over 30 percent of the population was of non-Polish origin.

The new Poland was a land beset with severe economic and social problems. Poland had been exploited as an agricultural preserve by the German, Russian, and Austro-Hungarian empires and economic and industrial development had not been fostered. The agricultural economy was little removed from the feudal past, and millions of small peasant farms existed at a subsistence level. What few industrial products were manufactured such as textiles from the Lodz area or coal and steel from Silesia had lost their natural markets in Russia and Germany due to vengeful import restrictions in these countries. Most of the fighting on the Eastern Front in World War I had taken place on Polish soil with the resultant loss of property and livestock. Furthermore, the century of division between the three empires had left Poland saddled with three sets of laws and three administrative organizations, speaking three official languages. Poland was ethnically heterogeneous with about 69 percent being Polish, 14 percent being Ukrainian, 8 percent being Jewish, 3 percent Byelorussian, and 2 percent German. Of the minority populations, the Germans were viewed as being totally opposed to the new Polish state, while the Ukrainian population was undergoing a major revival of Ukrainian nationalism which occasionally spilled over into outright terrorism against Polish officials and institutions.

The effects of the borderland wars were mixed for the armed forces. On the one hand, the exemplary performance of the army in the fighting had ensured it a central position in the postwar state, enjoying both widespread public support and status, and a generous portion of the nation's gross national product. On the other hand, it forged an alliance with France which tended to undercut Polish interest in forming alliances with neighboring states in favour of reliance on its Western mentor. France had an enormous impact on the Polish military, not only being the primary source of military equipment, but also providing much of the training and military theory upon which the Polish Army would be based. French officers were the main instructors at the Higher Military Academy where future Polish staff officers were taught until the late 1920s, when Pilsudski requested their departure to lessen their influence.

Nevertheless, the French influence should not be exaggerated to imply that Polish military doctrine imitated French predilections toward static attrition warfare. The Russo-Polish War of 1920 differed enormously from the trench warfare of the Western Front of the 1914–18 period. The wars in the east were mobile wars fought across vast plains and marshes where cavalry often proved to be the dominant arm. Newer forms of warfare including tanks, aircraft, motor transport, and radio communication were present in quantities too small to affect the outcome of the campaigns or to have a comparable impact on Polish military thinking. Even machine guns and modern artillery were not available in quantities to dispatch the cavalry as a viable maneuver force. The Poles appreciated these differences, and sought to modify French teaching by the incorporation of their own experiences in 1920–26.

The 1920 war between Poland and the Soviet Union was highly mobile and the last major European conflict in which cavalry played a dominant role. Here, a Polish sabre charge.

To add to Poland's problems, the experiment in parliamentary democracy between 1920 and 1926 was hardly successful. The Sejm was divided not only into ethnic blocs, but each of the ethnic blocs was in turn subdivided into a confusing array of ideological parties. In many cases, the parties themselves were divided into factions based on the old imperial divisions of the previous century. The Polish parties included the right-wing National Democrats, drawing their strength from both traditional aristocratic conservatives and the radical right of the urban middle class, the centrist Peasant Party and the leftist Socialist Party. The Jewish parties were even more badly fragmented, not only between the ideological divisions, but the Zionist and assimilationist trends and between the religious and secular parties. The Ukrainians were also divided between politicians who advocated accommodation with the Poles as a lesser evil than the Russians and extreme nationalist elements who continued to seek an independent Ukraine.

The political culture of the new state was immature and led to anarchic conditions which threatened civil war. In 1926, Jozef Pilsudski, with the backing of some of the political parties, and the backing of much of the army, staged a coup d'etat which wrested control of the country from the Sejm. Although Pilsudski refused to openly control the country in the wake of the coup, contenting himself with leadership of the armed forces, he remained the national leader until his death in 1935. The new government ostensibly permitted the continued existence of the various political parties, but Pilsudski showed little compunction in moving against the parties, as he did with the political leadership in 1930. Pilsudski's enormous public prestige and a public disaffection with the Sejm allowed Pilsudski to rule Poland without recourse to the extremities of fascism, Nazism, or communism.

Pilsudski's leadership ensured the armed forces of continued vigorous support. Pilsudski was able to fashion a well-integrated national army from the disparate, ragtag forces that had been under his command in 1920. In 1920, staff discussions could be heard in three or four languages, and there was considerable animosity between the political loyalists of the legions and the professional military officers who had served in the Russian, Prussian, or Austrian armies. Pilsudski would not tolerate these divisions and accepted the professional officers due to the need for their skills and a belief in their allegience to Poland.

In spite of his fondness and support for the armed forces, Pilsudski's role was often stifling. Pilsudski was not a trained military officer, nor were many of his closest associates. His patience for the details of peacetime military organization was very limited, as was his appreciation for the newer techniques of war. Following the 1926 coup, he reorganized the leadership of the armed forces in a fashion that would eventually prove detrimental, and he showed very little sympathy for the modernization of the armed forces in such areas as aircraft, armored vehicles, and communications. Moreover, like many strong national leaders, Pilsudski tailored the organization of the government and military to suit himself. The leaders who followed him were not able to fill his shoes, lacking the enormous prestige which had enabled him to exert his influence in spite of his lack of formal national office.

THE ORGANIZATION OF THE ARMED FORCES

The Polish Armed Forces (Polskie Sily Zbrojne, PSZ) consisted of the Polish Army and the Polish Navy. The Polish air force was part of the Polish Army, though it enjoyed more autonomy than the other service arms, for example, having its own uniforms and command structure. The PSZ after 1926 was organized along a peculiar two-track system devised by Pilsudski. The peacetime track was the responsibility of the War Ministry, which was subordinate to the President's Council of Ministers. The Minister for Military Affairs was responsible for the peacetime support of the armed forces, for example, in maintaining bases, providing supplies and equipment and the like. For this purpose, the country was divided into ten administrative regions (DOK, Dowodztwa okregow korpusow). These had no relation to the disposition of Polish military units on war footing.

The war track was the responsibility of the GISZ (Glowny Inspektorat Sil Zbrojnych, General Inspectorate of the Armed Forces), which Pilsudski strengthened in 1926 to take over direction of the Army from the General Staff in 1926–29. The General Staff was subordinated to the GISZ. Pilsudski was the original head of the GISZ, and the baton passed to Gen. Edward Rydz-Smigly in 1935. The GISZ was responsible for promulgating operational and strategic plans and for coordinating national economic activity to support the armed forces and to oversee the state of the armed forces through the General Inspectorate. Coordination between the "war track" and the "peace track," that is, between the War Ministry and the GISZ, was the responsibility of the KOR (Komitet Obrony Rzeczypospolitej, Committee for the Defense of the Republic) which was a civilian-military body having both political and military leaders. During wartime the organizations were subordinated to the High Command, the head of which was the peacetime head of the GISZ.

The subordination of the General Staff to the GISZ and the division of power between separate bureaucratic organizations created distinct problems, especially in regard to the modernization of the armed forces. Whereas under the German General Staff system doctrinal studies advocating the expansion of the armored force would be channeled directly to subordinate ranks in the command structure, under the Polish system studies from the emasculated General Staff had to pass through the upper ranks of the GISZ and be coordinated with the KOR and War Ministry before implementation. This complicated situation tended to delay tactical or technical innovation and stifled a number of attempts at army modernization, notably the attempts by General Daniel Konarzewski and others to gradually mechanize the cavalry beginning in 1929.

Nevertheless, in spite of the organizational shortcomings of the Polish armed forces, the main handicap in modernization was financial rather than doctrinal. Poland was a small, impoverished agricultural nation surrounded by two of Europe's largest states. It is worth noting that although Poland spent a larger percentage of its gross national product on the armed forces than any other state but the Soviet Union, the Polish defense budget from 1935 to 1939 was only about 10 percent of the German Luftwaffe's 1939 budget alone! The figures in Table 1–1 show comparable defense expenditures during this period.

TABLE 1–1
DEFENSE EXPENDITURES
(Billions of Dollars)

	Germany	Poland
1935	$3.0	$0.14
1936	$3.0	$0.14
1937	$3.5	$0.14
1938	$4.7	$0.16
1939	$9.7	$0.18

The financial problems were compounded by the lack of military industries in Poland. The Polish armed forces had adopted a conscious policy since the 1920s of manufacturing as many of its own weapons as possible. This policy stemmed from the experiences in the 1920 Russo-Polish War when arms shipments to Poland were halted in England, Czechoslovakia, and Danzig by pro-Soviet labor unions. Indigenous production circumvented potential future problems of this sort. However, indigenous military production was more costly than import of foreign weapons and required major capital investment to develop or expand factories capable of producing military equipment. In the 1936–39 period, capital investment in military industries absorbed 70 percent of all capital investment in industry in Poland. This investment was heavily concentrated in the Central Factory Region (COP, Centralny Okreg Przemyslowy), an industrial triangle stretching southward from Lublin which was selected because of its distance from the German and Soviet frontiers as well as the rampant poverty in the region. Industrialization of the region aimed both at curing the economic ills of this densely populated area as well as providing the Polish armed forces with a firm industrial base for the design and production of military equipment.

The small size of the national defense budget as well as the heavy drain imposed by the industrialization effort severely limited the procurement policies of the Polish armed forces. For example, in the case of fighter aircraft, the Polish armed force began acquiring the excellent P.7 and P.11 fighters in the early 1930s. These were superior to the German He-51 or Soviet I-15 fighters of the period. However, budget limitations precluded the Poles from buying a new generation of fighters in the last half of the 1930s, while at the same time the Luftwaffe had acquired the more modern Bf-109 fighter and the Soviets had acquired the I-16 in large numbers, both of which were superior to the P.11.

The death of Pilsudski in 1935 was followed by considerable agitation within the Polish armed forces for modernization. In 1936, the GISZ formed a special committee, the KSUS, under the direction of the very able Gen. Kazimierz Sosnkowski, to begin examining a program for modernization of the armed forces. The KSUS rearmament program aimed at expansion of Poland's military industries, production of new weapons to overcome various deficiencies, and expansion of neglected arms of service, notably the air force, armored force, antitank, transport, and communications units. The KSUS program was significantly bolstered when agreement was reached with the French government at Rambouillet in September 1936 for a substantial loan of 2.6 billion francs over a five-year period. This added about 12 percent to the annual Polish military budget and provided an important margin for the acquisition of new weapons. Other sources of funding for the KSUS program were a successful national bond drive and the proceeds from export of Polish weapons. There was considerable incentive for Poland to export weapons since such exports helped to fund military industrialization, reduced the cost of production of similar equipment for the armed forces, and assisted in maintaining a favorable trade balance during the difficult Depression years. By the end of the decade, the Poles were beginning to have considerable success in this field, notably in aircraft exports to such countries as Romania, Bulgaria, Greece, and Turkey. The Poles had also reached a number of agreements for the export of tanks and other equipment, but many of these contracts were never acted upon when war broke out.

The Polish defense budget for 1938–39 amounted to 800 million zloty, not counting the supplementary KSUS program additions (Table 1–2). The supplementary funding in 1938–39 amounted to over 300 million zloty, the bulk of which was used to acquire new weapons.

The KSUS rearmament program was not entirely successful. The plan was overly ambitious, given Poland's very modest industrial resources, and much of the procurement had been postponed to the later years of the

TABLE 1–2
POLISH DEFENSE BUDGET, 1938–1939
(Millions of Zloty)

Service	
Military administration	100.0
Infantry	225.0
Cavalry	58.0
National Guard	7.0
Artillery	16.0
Armored force	13.7
Engineers	8.9
Communications	5.1
Quartermaster	1.8
Air force	46.3
Navy	21.7
Industrial preparations	6.0
Research and training	30.0
Reservist stipends	8.0
Rail and road transportation	15.0
Construction	22.0
Reserve supplies	197.0
Salaries	16.0

program, from 1940 to 1942, and obviously had no impact on the situation in 1939. For example, Poland was producing barely 50 tanks annually, whereas Germany in 1938 alone was producing in excess of 1100 armored vehicles. There were a few bright spots. Poland began licensed production of the Swedish Bofors 37mm antitank gun and the 40mm antiaircraft gun. Both these excellent weapons were being produced in significant quantities by 1939. They considerably enhanced the fighting abilities of the Polish Army for a very modest investment. In addition, an indigenously developed antitank rifle was introduced; it added considerably to the antitank defense of infantry and cavalry units. In the air, a small number of the excellent P.37 Los bombers were produced, but production of a new generation of fighters and ground-attack planes was delayed, leaving the Polish air force a generation behind in these key areas. Two battalions of excellent 7TP light tanks were added to the inventory, though this could hardly compare to German or Soviet efforts. The KSUS plan fell considerably short of expectations in this critical field. However, two cavalry brigades were converted over to mechanized brigades, although the Warsaw Mechanized Brigade was not entirely formed at the time of the war's outbreak. Both units proved exceptionally valuable in the 1939 fighting.

As it became increasingly evident that Polish industry could not entirely fulfill the requirements of the rearmament program, Polish military delegations began discussing the purchase of equipment from France and Britain. The French proved unwilling to sell the excellent S-35 Somua tank to Poland due to shortages in the French Army, but permitted the purchase of a battalion of R-35 infantry tanks with additional battalions to follow. Discussions were held with Britain for the purchase of Matilda infantry tanks. France agreed to the sale of Ms.406 fighters, and pledged to dispatch to Poland on the outbreak of war a number of Amiot 143 bomber squadrons which would operate from Polish fields. Britain agreed to the sale of Fairey Battle light bombers and some fighter aircraft. A single Spitfire was on the way to Poland for evaluation when the war broke out. The outbreak of the war put an end to most of these plans. The R-35 battalion arrived just weeks before the outbreak of the war, and much of the other equipment was at sea or in transit through Romania in September 1939.

Pilsudski's passing from the scene in 1935 left control of the country in the hands of General Rydz-Smigly and a group of military officers commonly called the "colonel's regime." The military dictatorship ruled the country with less success than Pilsudski, lacking his prestige or popularity. Rydz-Smigly and his clique tried to mobilize popular support for their policies by the formation of transparty organizations but they were not successful in supplanting the traditional political parties. Ethnic tensions were exacerbated by the regime's turn from the federalist ethnic policy that Pilsudski had insisted upon to a more stridently nationalistic policy. This was done in the vain hope of attracting the radical right, but was unsuccessful as the radical right did not feel that the suppression of the Ukrainian nationalist movement or the anti-Semitic policies were vigorous enough. The politicization of the army distracted many key officers from their principal roles at a key time. Fortunately, it did not substantially affect the popularity or prestige of the army on the eve of war.

Following Pilsudski's death, command of the army fell to Marshal Edward Rydz-Smigly.

2. The Strategic and Operational Doctrine of the Polish Army

Initiation of Polish strategic planning was the responsibility of the General Inspectorate of the Armed Forces (GISZ), with the actual studies being undertaken by the General Staff. The central element in Polish strategic planning was its foreign policy in general, and its military relations with France in particular. In February 1921 Poland signed a defensive alliance with France, and this was followed in March 1921 by a military convention providing details of the mutual Franco-Polish alliance. The principal aim of the pact was to ensure military cooperation in the event of a war with Germany. The pact did not obligate the French to become directly involved in a Soviet-Polish war unless Germany allied itself with the Soviets. In the event of German involvement against Poland, the French were obligated to attack Germany. An important adjunct to the Franco-Polish military pact was the Romanian-Polish military alliance, also signed in 1921 with French blessing. In contrast to the Franco-Polish pact, the Romanian-Polish alliance was directed against the Soviet Union. Under the terms of these alliances, the Polish Army began studying a number of strategic plans in cooperation with the French Army. These included Plan R, directed against the Soviet Union, Plan N, directed against Germany, and a two-front war, sometimes called Plan R + N. The joint Polish-French plan directed against Germany called Plan Foch was studied in 1923 and envisioned a strategic drive in two directions on Berlin.

Polish strategic planning for a war against Germany in this period included three main variations, called Plan Silesia, Plan Baltic, and Plan East Prussia. Each plan offered different options for the Polish Army, some stressing a restricted drive against East Prussia with defensive provisions against German-Lithuanian cooperation, and others envisioned a westward orientation toward Berlin. The Franco-Polish and Romanian-

Polish military conventions pledged the Poles to commit a minimum of 20 divisions against Germany and 17 divisions against the Soviet Union. The problem with these commitments was that the Polish Army of the time was prepared to raise only 34 divisions, and so in the event of a two-front war would be unable to honor its treaty obligations. As a result, with the French agreement, the terms were modified, with the Poles committing themselves to a minimum of 11 divisions against Germany, 17 divisions against the Soviet Union, and 4 divisions in High Command Reserve.

In 1925 the Polish Army began general discussions with the French about an ambitious military rebuilding plan to better satisfy strategic commitments in the event of an eventual war with Germany. The plan envisioned raising Polish strength to a total of 60 infantry divisions, 9 cavalry divisions, 30 tank battalions and 180 to 200 aircraft squadrons. This plan presumed extensive French support for the effort. The aim of the rebuilding plan was to permit the commitment of a minimum of 20 divisions to the German front, 20 divisions to the Soviet front, and 20 divisions in High Command Reserve. Studies connected with this plan by the Polish General Staff found it to be grossly unrealistic, given Poland's very limited industrial and economic resources, and the unlikelihood of extensive French credits.

In 1926–27 a new scheme, called Plan S, was studied. This envisioned raising Polish Army strength over the next ten years to 30 infantry divisions, 9 reserve infantry divisions, 3 national defense brigades, 3 cavalry divisions, 4 independent cavalry brigades, and 5 light mixed divisions. The light mixed division was a combination of two cavalry regiments, two rifle battalions, and a cyclist company. Plan S envisioned a far less extensive technical modernization of the army than the 1925 plan, with only 3 tank battalions, 28 aircraft squadrons and 6 armored train troops.

By 1926, the General Staff had concluded that the two-front concept was unrealistic. With the accession of Jozef Pilsudski to power in 1926 following his coup d'etat, the orientation of Polish strategic planning shifted decidedly toward a concentration on the Soviet Union. Pilsudski felt that the German Reichswehr, limited to a hundred thousand men and threatened by a far more massive French Army on its western border, would pose no serious threat to Poland in spite of remaining tensions between Poland and Germany over a variety of territorial issues. In contrast, the Soviet Union harbored paranoid suspicions of Anglo-Polish designs—as was all too clear from the 1927 Soviet war scare—and entertained revanchist ambitions against Poland's eastern provinces lost in the 1920 Russo-Polish War. Although the II Department (Intelligence) of the General Staff was aware of German-Soviet military cooperation under the terms of the Rapallo Treaty, Pilsudski believed the main threat was the Soviet Union. As Inspector General of the Armed Forces, and head of GISZ from 1926 to his death in 1935, Pilsudski directed that nearly all strategic planning be aimed against the Soviet Union, so the "Germany Study" was allowed to languish.

The strategic plan for war with the Soviet Union was labeled Plan W (Plan Wschod, or Plan East). The plan was essentially defensive in nature, since by the late 1920s the Poles realized they would never again face a Red Army as weak as the one encountered in 1920. For example, the 1933 study of Red Army strength estimated that the Red Army could direct 60

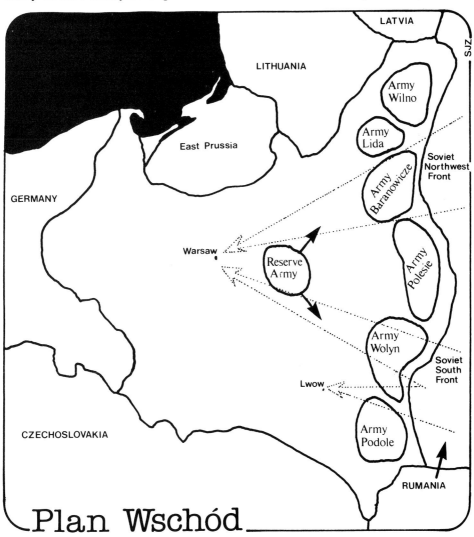

Plan Wschód

to 70 divisions against Poland by D-Day plus 22–30. The alliance with Romania was expected to contribute twenty-five divisions to the front, and to divert a portion of the Red Army to deal with this threat. The orientation of Polish strategic doctrine toward the east had significant impact on Polish military construction. With the exception of modest fortified belts on the periphery of the Upper Silesian industrial basin, and defense works at Mlawa, practically all Polish fortifications were constructed on the Soviet frontier. However, because of Polish commitments to an operational doctrine stressing maneuver, the fortifications were not comparable to Czech fortifications or to the French Maginot Line.

Of equal importance to the Plan W were Polish efforts to build an extensive railroad network into eastern Poland. Tsarist Poland had employed a different rail gauge than that used in Western Europe, so existing lines had to be modified when Poland began standardizing the nation's vital rail lines. In addition, many rail lines had to be added. The Poles expected that in the event of war, only about a third of the army would be available in garrisons near the Soviet front, and so nearly two-thirds of the army would have to be moved to concentration points.

Commitment to Plan W also affected the structure of the Polish armed forces. The costly construction of Poland's small Navy can be attributed primarily to the needs of Plan W, since in the event of a war with Germany, the naval base at Gdynia could be quickly overrun by German land forces or smothered by air attack. The uselessness of the Polish Destroyer Flotilla in a war with Germany became even more evident with the reconstruction of the Kriegsmarine after 1933. The length of the Polish-Soviet front, as well as the experiences of the 1920 Russo-Polish War, was a major factor in the prolonged retention of a significant and expensive horse cavalry force in the Polish Army. While the Poles had experimented with motorized infantry in the 1920 war, the extreme backwardness of the Polish-Soviet borderlands severely limited the use of motor transport in the region through much of the year. What few roads existed became clutching mud trenches during spring and fall rains and impassible in the snows of winter. The types of automobiles available in the early 1930s were not suited to cross-country travel, especially in the swampy terrain of the Pripyat Marshes that dominated the central Polesian front. In primitive conditions and with a meager defense budget, the Poles relied on the proven combat utility of their horse cavalry regiments for tactical mobility. The situation might have been different had Polish strategic doctrine in the 1930s paid more attention to the demands of the German front; the dry plains of western Poland were better suited to motorized and mechanized operations.

In 1933, Marshal Pilsudski secretly proposed to the French that the terms of the 1921 treaty be put into effect and that Plan Foch or a variant be put into action to crush the rise of Hitler. The French did not treat this suggestion seriously, and in 1934, the Poles signed a non-aggression pact with Nazi Germany marking the beginning of four years of tense detente. Nevertheless, while these actions may have cooled Franco-Polish relations, they did not change the basic dependence of Polish strategy on the French Army for dealing with Germany. The death of Pilsudski in 1935 and the gradual usurpation of his mantle by General Edward Rydz-Smigly as head of the GISZ did not lead to any immediate changes in Polish strategic planning. However, it did lead to the beginning of critical reappraisals of Polish Army tactical doctrine and war planning once the army was free of Pilsudski's well-intended but stifling control. By 1936, the international situation also had grown far more threatening and complex.

The rise of Hitler to power was marked as well by the rebirth of the German armed forces and more forceful assertion of German territorial claims. German remilitarization of the Rhineland in 1936 was accomplished without French counteraction. This not only meant that French Army action could no longer be easily conducted without concern for German border fortifications, but it seriously undermined the critical Polish assumption that France could be relied upon as Poland's bulwark against Germany. Nor did Poland see eye-to-eye with France on her policies in Central Europe. Poland's foreign policy after Pilsudski's death was dominated by Foreign Minister Jozef Beck, without close coordination with the Polish General Staff. Beck was firmly opposed to French schemes to unite France, Czechoslovakia, and the Soviet Union in a mutual defense pact directed against Germany. Moreover, Beck was in a position to scuttle any such alliance. The military conventions of this alliance would have required the Poles or Romanians to accede to the transit of Soviet troops through their territory to Czechoslovakia. Both Poland and Romania viewed such an event as little less threatening than an actual Soviet invasion and so would not agree. Although the Poles would not cooperate with this plan, and in spite of Polish anxieties over French unwillingness to confront Germany militarily, the Franco-Polish alliance remained the cornerstone of Polish foreign policy and strategy. It was again reconfirmed in 1936 when the French agreed to provide major credits as part of the 1936 KSUS plan to modernize the Polish Army. The alternatives were unsatisfactory. Although the Germans at various times made overtures for the formation of an anti-Bolshevik front, Beck was unwilling to permit Poland to become a German satellite that would probably be forced into serious territorial concessions as part of an alliance. Any coop-

A Polish infantry platoon on maneuvers in the 1930s. These troops still wear the French Adrian helmet, which was replaced in most of the infantry by a new Polish helmet in the mid-1930s.

eration with the Soviet Union was viewed as out of the question due to likely Soviet territorial demands and a profound distrust of Stalin's totalitarian regime. Polish plans for a Central European "Third Europe," while very tempting, were impossible, given lingering tensions between Poland, Czechoslovakia, and Lithuania over grievances stemming from the 1919–1920 wars.

Reassessments of Plan W in 1938 drew chilling conclusions. The General Staff concluded that in the event of a war with the Soviet Union, the Red Army could readily direct 77 divisions against the Polish front, consisting of 44 active and 28 reserve infantry divisions. The II Department of the General Staff estimated total Red Army strength at 100 infantry divisions, several cavalry divisions and 5 mechanized corps with the possibility of mobilizing up to 180–200 divisions in the long run. Against this were pitted 37 Polish infantry divisions, 11 cavalry brigades, 1 mechanized brigade, and 25 Romanian infantry divisions. The situation was unlikely to get any better in terms of modern weaponry, as the massive Soviet army buildup was clearly outstripping the modest Polish effort. However, there were two factors which somewhat brightened the picture from the Polish perspective. In 1938, Stalin embarked on a bizarre and grotesque slaughter of the Red Army's officer ranks as part of his horrific purges. The Red Army was being weakened not only by this madness, but its attention was being diverted eastward by Japanese actions on the Mongolian frontier. Nor was Soviet action against Poland deemed likely due to understandable Soviet concern over the rise of the German Wehrmacht. Nevertheless, the poisonous aftereffects of the 1919–20 fighting in East Central Europe prevented any effective alliances in the region to combat Hitler's aggressive designs.

An important first step in redressing the imbalance in Polish strategic planning came in 1938 when the General Staff began to modernize army mobilization plans. Under Pilsudski, these plans had languished. The new mobilization Plan W differed from earlier schemes in that it was a universal plan suitable in the event of either a war with Germany or the Soviet Union. The plan contained two basic elements, a secret mobilization method and a conventional public announcement of mobilization. The secret method involved the use of color-coded cards that would be sent through the regular mail during a time of crisis to bring all reservists back into service in waves. This method was to be used to avoid the provocative effects of a general public mobilization in times of diplomatic crisis. The mobilization plan, and the amended Plan W2 for speedier mobilization, assumed that general mobilization could be accomplished in seventy-two hours, and that the army could be mobilized and concentrated in twelve to fourteen days.

Revival of work on a strategic plan to confront Germany was initiated by Marshal Rydz-Smigly in 1935. The General Staff team assigned to the task of revising the Germany Study was led by Gen. T. Kutrzeba. An initial draft report was completed for the GISZ in the spring of 1936. It envisioned committing the whole Polish Army to the German front, leaving the Soviet front covered only by KOP units and perhaps a few "eastern" divisions. Polish forces would be organized into four armies: Army Warsaw, concentrated below East Prussia; Army Pomorze, centered on Torun; Army Poznan, concentrated east of Poznan, and Army Lodz-Czestochowa, concentrated in a line to the east of the Lodz-Czestochowa axis. A Reserve Army would be based between Kutno and Warsaw and formed from those elements of the Polish Army slowest in reaching full mobilization. The plan assumed that the main German blow would be directed from the northwest, radiating down from Bydgoszcz toward Kutno and Deblin. A supporting attack of smaller size was expected from Silesia toward Czestochowa and Deblin. A third and minor German thrust was expected to emanate from East Prussia southward to Warsaw. The plan called for Polish preemptive attacks on the East Prussia assault, with

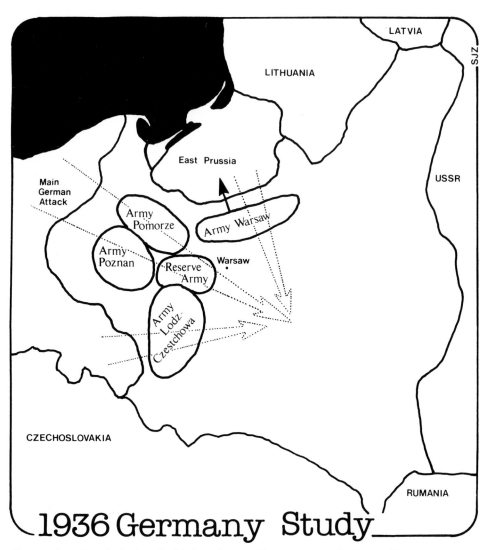

1936 Germany Study

the main attack being held by Army Pomorze and Army Poznan, supported by the Reserve Army. Army Lodz-Czestochowa was expected to hold the German Silesia attack, with elements of the Reserve Army later assisting in a counterattack from the Lodz area south.

The GISZ discussed the general aspects of the plan with Gen. Maurice Gamelin of the French General Staff in the summer of 1936. The plan assumed that the German rearmament program would be completed in the 1942–43 period, and that Poland would be the first target of German aggression. It also assumed that the German actions would result in the formation of a coalition of France, the Soviet Union, Czechoslovakia,

Romania, and Poland. The Polish 1936 plan was heavily influenced by studies of the German actions against the Tsarist army in 1914 in Prussia, especially the battle at Tannenburg.

The updated Germany Study was succeeded by initiation of studies of Plan Z (Plan Zachod, or Plan West) by the Polish General Staff. The initial version of Plan Z was turned over to the GISZ at the beginning of March 1939. Its general strategic outlook reflected the earlier studies, and contained several alarming warnings. Plan Z assumed that the Germans would be able to deploy 110 division-sized units, of which about 70 could be expected to be directed against Poland, and the remainder retained in western Germany along the Westwall to serve as a screen against the French until Poland could be knocked out of the war. The plan warned that German numerical and qualitative superiority was liable to increase rather than decrease in spite of the KSUS rearmament plan, and that while German forces in 1939 would be double in size and strength to the Polish Army, by 1942 they would be at least triple.

No sooner had the plan been submitted to Marshal Rydz-Smigly than events overtook it. The German seizure of the remainder of Czechoslovakia beginning on 15 March 1938 had disastrous consequences for Polish defense plans. It seriously undermined Polish confidence in its western allies, and gravely worsened Poland's position vis-à-vis Germany. Bohemia and Moravia were absorbed into Germany as a "protectorate," and a rump Slovak fascist state was set up on Poland's southern frontier. On 23 March 1939 Poland began a secret mobilization of a portion of its army, bringing its cavalry brigades and some infantry divisions up to wartime strength. Britain finally began to make gestures to Poland assuring British support in the event of war.

In May, meetings were held with the French General Staff to lay down details of French commitments in the event of a German invasion of Poland. The French gave assurances that upon declaration of war, mobilization would begin, followed by border skirmishes along the Westwall in three days' time, and a major offensive in the west two weeks after the declaration of war. The French also promised the dispatch of bomber squadrons to operate from Polish fields in support of the Polish Army, and the British made commitments to use the Royal Air Force in bombing German industrial areas.

The altered strategic situation forced a major reconsideration of the March version of Plan Z. To begin with, the Poles now found it necessary to contend with the likelihood of German attacks all along the southern periphery of their country. The General Staff developed a new assessment which reoriented the balance of the likely German attack. The new assessment argued that with Czechoslovakia in German hands, the main German thrust would not come in Pomerania, but rather would be directed against the Katowice-Czestochowa industrial basin and aimed at Warsaw, and that the attack toward Poznan would become only the secondary German axis of attack. German strategy in dealing with Czechoslovakia and her Western protectors also raised the alarming possibility that the Germans might not launch a full-scale war, but might instead try to seize disputed Polish territory to test Western and Polish resolve. Such a seizure might include absorption of the Pomeranian corridor, or areas west of Poznan or in Upper Silesia. Since involvement of France and Britain in the war was a major element of Polish strategy, operational plans had to be formulated to insure that Polish troops became immediately involved in any German incursion, triggering Western military commitments.

There were two principal strategic plans examined by the Polish General Staff for fielding the Polish Army. Gen. Maxime Weygand of the French Army suggested fielding the Polish Army behind the river barriers using the old Russian fortification line, which encompassed the rivers Nieman, Biebrza, Narew, Vistula, and San. This meshed well with Polish operational doctrine, as any more extensive deployment of the small number of divisions would overextend the units beyond prudent limits. However, this plan of action was rejected. The basic shortcoming of the plan was its presumption that the Polish Army would be mobilized and concentrated. The basic tenet of Plan Z was that the Germans could be expected to launch a surprise attack that would not permit the full mobilization of the Polish Army. Furthermore, the Poles expected that concentration of the Polish units would take twelve to fifteen days. The fear was that if the river-defense strategy was selected and the Germans launched a surprise attack, the Polish Army would be caught only partially prepared. Since it was expected that the Polish Army would be outnumbered by two to one

TABLE 2–1
ETHNIC COMPOSITION, ACTIVE INFANTRY DIVISIONS

Division	Percent Polish	Division	Percent Polish	Division	Percent Polish
1L	75	11	75+	21 Mtn	60
2L	60	12	70+	22 Mtn	60
3L	60	13	90	23	60
4	60	14	60	24	60
5	60	15	60	25	60
6	60	16	60	26	60
7	60	17	60	27	75
8	60	18	60	28	60
9	60	19	80	29	75
10	60	20	83	30	80

in the best of circumstances, such a strategy would inevitably mean that the Poles would face the Germans with even poorer odds. Central to all this was the fact that a sizable proportion of the Polish population lived in areas that would have been readily surrendered to the Germans, thereby depriving the Polish Army of many of these reservists. The General Staff was especially concerned because surrender of these areas would deprive the army of ethnic Polish troops, possibly undermining the narrow majority of Polish troops in the army. (See Table 2–1.) Added to these problems were concerns over the loss of key industrial areas as well as the image that Polish sacrifice of these regions might have in foreign capitals. The other risk was that the Germans might indeed adopt "salami tactics" by seizing portions of disputed territory without significant Polish military forces to contest these actions. The river strategy also overlooked the fact that many of the rivers look better on a map for defensive purposes than in actuality. During the summer, they begin to dry up and are easily fordable in many places. The Poles were aware that an early full-scale mobilization of the Polish Army could possibly make this plan feasible, but such an action would be regarded as a provocation to the French and British. Indeed, even as late as 30 August 1939 the French were pressuring the Poles not to declare general mobilization.

The second option was a slightly amended version of the original Plan Z with an additional army to protect the Carpathians and reinforcement of the vital Silesian front. The bulk of the army would be concentrated relatively far forward since the plan assumed that the Germans would launch a surprise attack and that the Army would not be fully mobilized or concentrated. The role of the frontier armies would be to wage a fighting withdrawal while the remainder of the army was mobilized and concentrated. These other forces, once concentrated, would be used to form reserve armies to counterattack any penetrations by the Wehrmacht past the defensive cordon on the frontier armies. The armies were expected to fall back into southeastern Poland, pivoting on Army Krakow in the south. This variant assumed that the army could be fully concentrated in two weeks, and that the French would abide by their May 1939 commitments to launch a full-scale counteroffensive two weeks after the start of hostilities. It fully expected that the Polish Army could not single-handedly resist the Wehrmacht but assumed that at least a portion of the Polish Army would survive until the French and British intervened. It was this variant that was selected for the final Plan Z. This plan has been widely misinterpreted as intending to create a static, linear defense line along the frontier. This was not the case, as is evident from the lack of Polish frontier fortifications in the west. Rather, the plan envisioned the frontier armies as a screen permitting the completion of army mobilization, and a gradual retreat until French intervention.

The plan had several fatal flaws. It violated Polish operational doctrine by spreading Polish forces much too thin. The initial defensive cordon was so long that the frontier armies were obliged to drain their reserve to hold the initial defense lines even before the fighting had broken out. The plan wasted the cavalry brigades by committing them in the initial defensive lines, where their mobility had no value at all but where their relative defensive weaknesses became all too clear. Although Polish operational doctrine foresaw the advantages of holding cavalry brigades in army reserve to provide mobile counterattacks against enemy breakthroughs, the paucity of Polish forces allotted to the armies under Plan Z forced their static use in the initial defense perimeter. As if this situation was not bad enough, Plan Z inevitably meant that armies would be obligated to give their infantry divisions and cavalry brigades excessive frontages to cover. This dilution of the force densities of the armies would prove especially serious when the armies were faced by German mechanized divisions. The dilution of forces made it virtually impossible for Polish units to break off engagements in order to withdraw to later defensive belts as was planned. German forces, with adequate reserves, could easily keep in unrelenting contact with Polish divisions until they were exhausted and destroyed.

Plan Z seriously misunderstood the likely pace of the fighting by underestimating the speed and capabilities of German mechanized units. This failure was hardly unique to the Poles, as many German, French, and British generals were also skeptical about the value of panzer divisions until they so stunningly proved themselves for the first time in the Polish campaign. Although the Poles planned to wage a war of maneuver, they failed to appreciate the bankruptcy of this operational conception when they faced an army having a markedly greater maneuvering ability made possible through motorization and mechanization. Not only were there inadequate reserves for the frontier armies, but the Wehrmacht could exploit breakthroughs much more quickly than the Polish Army could move forward its reserves. The tragic predicament of Polish strategic planning was that the Polish Army was in a hopeless position if it was fighting the Wehrmacht alone. The river-defense variant would have denied the Polish Army a significant portion of its already impoverished strength while at the same time being politically unacceptable. The forward-defense variant was politically acceptable and seemed to offer the prospect of permitting the Polish Army to concentrate its full, albeit meager, strength against the Wehrmacht even if in so doing it violated Polish Army operational doctrine. Neither option offered any hope of success unless the French Army intervened as promised, and the Polish General Staff grasped this unpalatable truth.

The defeat of Poland in 1939 was the culmination of two decades of shortsightedness in Polish and European foreign policy. Poland was obliged to depend on French assurances in spite of repeated French vacillation in the face of German military provocations since 1933. While Poland's unwillingness to subjugate itself by military alliance to its untrustworthy German or Soviet neighbors was understandable, insufficient efforts were made to forge an alliance with Czechoslovakia and Lithuania in 1938 and 1939. The leadership of all three countries allowed their thinking to be clouded by grudges and minor territorial disputes instead of focusing on the greater threat posed by Germany and the Soviet Union. The Lithuanian Army, though small, could have threatened East Prussia and taken pressure off a German drive on Warsaw from the north. An allied Czechoslovakia would have protected Poland's long southern flank, and added the strength of a small but well-equipped army that could have diverted considerable German forces. Their folly was equaled by that of France and Britain when they failed to live up to treaty commitments to Poland. The French Army passed up an unprecedented strategic opportunity to strike at Germany while the bulk of its forces was tied down in Poland. France would pay for this shortsightedness in 1940.

THE DISPOSITION OF THE POLISH ARMY IN 1939

On 23 March 1939, Marshal Rydz-Smigly in his role as head of the GISZ handed executive orders to the officers chosen to lead the armies and operational groups of the initial Polish defense line. These orders were not provided to commanders of the reserve armies or operational groups, since they had not been completed. In fact, Polish strategic planning beyond the initial assignments of the frontal forces was never satisfactorily examined by the General Staff, which instead felt it could improvise solutions to strategic questions as they arose during the fighting. During deliberations in the spring and summer of 1939, various changes were made in the disposition of Polish forces on the basis of estimates of German aims prepared by the II Department (Intelligence) of the General Staff. By then the II Department had successfully located and identified about 36 of the 55 German divisions subsequently used in the initial attacks. Although General Staff planning was done on the basis of earlier estimates of a German attack eventually involving about 70 divisions, Marshal Rydz-Smigly and some other national leaders tended to clutch at straws when assessing the German dispositions. Some of the assessments prepared by II Department were regarded as too pessimistic, as Rydz-Smigly was not altogether willing to believe that the Germans would risk denuding their western dispositions against the French in order to throw so large a force against Poland.

Army Modlin, commanded by General Emil Krukowicz-Przedrzymirski, was assigned two infantry divisions and two cavalry brigades. This army was meant to delay German attacks along the shortest route to Warsaw, that is, a southward attack emanating out of East Prussia. The resources allotted to Army Modlin for this task were inadequate because of Polish misperception of German plans. While the Poles expected only to face the German Third Army, German plans in fact called for portions of the Fourth Army to transit the Pomeranian Corridor to reinforce the southward drive on Warsaw. The Poles did not anticipate this.

Special Operational Group Narew (SGO Narew), commanded by Gen. Czeslaw Mlot-Fijalkowski, was assigned to protect the right flank of Army Modlin as well as cover northeastern Poland. Its two infantry divisions and two cavalry brigades were clearly inadequate to hold its assigned front of two hundred kilometers, but the Poles correctly assumed that this region would not receive major German attacks, and so planning revolved around the defense of more limited objectives.

The two units of the Polish northern front would screen the concentration of the Wyszkow Reserve, which consisted of three infantry divisions. Once mobilized and concentrated, Operational Group Wyszkow would cover the junction between SGO Narew and Army Modlin, and serve as High Command reserve in the region to counterattack any German breakthroughs toward Warsaw.

Army Pomorze, commanded by Gen. Wladyslaw Bortnowski, was assigned the defense of Pomerania. Plan Z assumed that the Germans would immediately attempt to isolate the Polish port and naval facilities on the Baltic, and Army Pomorze was not expected to engage in the hopeless task of preventing this. Defense of the seacoast positions was to be undertaken by a modest force of army and navy units under navy command with its aim being to delay and harass German forces in the area.

Army Pomorze was expected to bear the brunt of German attacks from northern Germany toward Warsaw. In fact, as mentioned earlier, the Poles misunderstood the aims of the Fourth Army, which planned to fight its way across the Pomeranian Corridor, allowing some of its units to support the drive of Third Army along a shorter route from East Prussia. As a result of Polish perceptions, Army Pomorze was allotted five infantry divisions and a cavalry brigade. Under the original study plans for Plan Z, Army Pomorze was to be placed outside of the Pomeranian Corridor because a force within the corridor was vulnerable to attack from both Germany on the left flank and East Prussia on the right. However, the actual dispositions in 1939 were further forward; the Polish were concerned that the Germans might attempt to make an uncontested seizure of the Pomeranian Corridor if there were no Polish forces present. The General Staff was concerned about possible parallels to the German seizure of the Sudetenland. The Germans might seize the Pomeranian Corridor and other contested regions in Upper Silesia and the Poznan area as a first step, thereby weakening Poland before launching an all-out war. As a result, General Bortnowski was ordered to form an "Intervention Corps" of two infantry divisions to be stationed inside the corridor to prevent the Germans from making an uncontested seizure. In the event an all-out war broke out, these units were to withdraw immediately to more defensible positions to the south. However, the positioning of units so far north had deleterious effects on the disposition of Army Pomorze. Their location in the corridor forced Bortnowski to position much of the rest of the army further northward than originally planned to cover their retreat. The revised dispositions increased the frontage of the army and forced the commitment of the reserves in the frontal positions.

Army Poznan, commanded by the highly capable Gen. Tadeusz Kutrzeba, was allotted four infantry divisions and two cavalry brigades. Like Army Pomorze, it was moved closer to the frontier than anticipated in earlier variants of Plan Z in order to prevent German seizure of contested territory along the frontier. The aim of this army was to threaten the flanks of German thrusts through Pomerania to the north or through Upper Silesia to the south. Behind Army Poznan was the small Kutno Reserve. This was not intended to form a later operational group, but rather would be used to reinforce Army Poznan or Pomorze, depending upon circumstances.

Army Lodz, commanded by Gen. Juliusz Rommel, was allotted five infantry divisions and two cavalry brigades. Army Lodz was given the vital task of preventing the interruption of the main High Command reserve, Army Prusy, while stubbornly defending the hard German blows expected against Lodz. Because Army Lodz was expected to cover the flank of Army Krakow to the south, and Army Krakow was expected to be located close to the frontier defenses of Upper Silesia, Army Lodz likewise was positioned well forward. Because of these dispositions, no substantial reserve was left. It was expected that other reserve units would arrive. This never happened.

Army Krakow, commanded by Gen. Antoni Szylling, was originally assigned to the defense of the densely populated Upper Silesian industrial basin. This was the only area on the western front with any significant fortifications, covering the Katowice area. It was expected that the main blow of the Wehrmacht would fall in this region and to the north against Army Lodz. It was hoped that the presence of the fortifications would help to protract defense of the region and provide a vital pivot point allowing the bulk of the whole Polish Army to gradually withdraw into the south-eastern portion of the country. It was gradually perceived that, in addition to the main attack against Upper Silesia, the Germans were also planning to launch a subsidiary attack from Slovakia up through the mountain passes. However, this was one of the few areas of Poland where the terrain favored the Polish forces, so the bulk of Army Krakow remained committed to the Silesian front. The only reserve for the army was the 10th Mechanized Brigade, Poland's only fully formed mechanized unit, and two more infantry divisions could not be expected until six to fourteen days after the 31 August general mobilization announcement.

The principal High Command reserve was to be Army Prusy, forming to the east of Army Lodz. It was expected to consist of seven infantry divisions, one cavalry brigade, and two independent tank battalions. Once concentrated, it was expected to be used in a major counterattack against the principal German thrusts in Silesia in the Piotrkow-Radomsko direction.

The last army to be formed was Army Karpaty, commanded by Gen. Kazimierz Fabrycy. The forces allotted to Fabrycy were modest, as the steep mountains of the Carpathian region were not very suitable for attack by the German and Slovak forces massing on their other side. However, in the event of stronger-than-anticipated attacks, a Southern Reserve was planned in the Tarnow area consisting of two infantry divisions which would be mobilized and concentrated in the two weeks after general mobilization.

Executive orders for the air force were not handed over to Gen. Jozef Zajac until 28 July 1939. They were entitled "General Guidelines for the Use of the Air Force." In fact, Zajac's forces did not consist of the entire air force, but rather the so-called dispositional air force and air defense units. The air force was divided between air units directly assigned to the armies for direct support and the dispositional air force, which was assigned independent tasks. The dispositional air force consisted of the Bomber Brigade, which had Poland's only modern medium bombers, and the Pursuit Brigade, which was assigned to defend Warsaw from air attack. The Bomber Brigade was to be employed to attack major German troop movements. The bulk of Zajac's air defense forces were antiaircraft units scattered throughout the country. Although equipped with very modern equipment, these antiaircraft units were very small in number, and so could be assigned only to key cities, mobilization areas, and industrial regions. Polish air units directly assigned to the armies were for use mainly in scouting and ground attack. The lack of sufficient fighter aircraft prevented Zajac from preparing a coordinated plan of national air defense except in the Warsaw area.

The Polish Navy realistically foresaw that the Destroyer Flotilla could not survive in Polish waters due to the proximity of the bases at Gdynia and Hel to German air and naval bases. As a result, the navy planned Operation Pekin. This plan foresaw the transfer of the Destroyer Flotilla to British bases as soon as war seemed imminent. The only surface warships to remain in Polish waters, aside from minor auxiliaries, were to be the ORP *Grom* and ORP *Wicher,* which would conduct minelaying operations to prevent German reinforcement of East Prussia from the sea. The Submarine Flotilla was to remain in the Baltic to harass the Kriegsmarine and to prevent the sending of reinforcements to East Prussia. The navy, in cooperation with the army, also planned a defense of Polish positions on the Hel Peninsula and at Westerplatte to harass German attempts to use the port at Danzig and to divert German forces from other fronts. It was not expected that the Submarine Flotilla could rely on replenishment at Gdynia or other Polish ports, so plans were discussed with the submarine commanders to attempt to break out to Britain through the Danish Straits or to take refuge in neutral Baltic ports, depending upon the circumstances.

OPERATIONAL DOCTRINE

Polish operational doctrine was of a conventional nature, and was heavily influenced by French teachings. However, it differed from French and other European doctrine in a number of respects due to the different historical experiences of the Polish Army, as well as to differences in its resources.

Polish operational doctrine stressed a war of maneuver, based on the experiences of the Polish Army in the fast-paced war of 1920 against the Soviet Union. However, it has to be kept in mind that the maneuver doctrine bears little resemblance to German doctrine of the period, since it was based on the use of infantry divisions supported by cavalry brigades. In this respect, it bears a closer resemblance to German doctrine adopted in the wake of the 1870 war with France.

Two other features unique in Polish doctrine at this time were the emphasis on night fighting and reliance on improvisation. Night fighting was stressed since it was felt that it could counterbalance Polish numerical weaknesses when fighting armies like the Red Army. Night attacks, if properly conducted, would have more shock value than daylight attacks and so would act as a force multiplier for the outnumbered Polish Army.

Improvisation was a characteristic of Polish planning and operational thinking that had been emphasized by Pilsudski. Because the Polish Army was likely to be influenced by events outside its own theater of operations, such as French intervention in a war being fought by Poland, and because circumstances could readily change, it was felt that long-term operational planning was neither necessary nor desirable. As a result, operational plans developed in conjunction with strategic plans like Plan Z often covered only the main objectives of armies and operational groups and provided detailed plans of operation only for the first phase of the war. Contingency plans were frequently absent or not prepared in a detailed fashion. The stress on the ability of commanders to make prompt tactical decisions was an admirable offshoot of this tendency, but it also led to an unfortunate attitude by which the army ignored farsighted investigations by army and divisional staffs of operational and tactical options available to units.

The most noticeable difference in Polish operational doctrine from that of the major European armies was the lack of attention paid to the threat of mechanized units, the relative prominence given to the employment of cavalry units, and the overextension of infantry and cavalry in operational planning.

The Polish evaluation of the threat of Soviet and German mechanized units was clouded by internecine controversies within the Polish Army. Until 1933, the small Polish armored force was larger than that of either Germany or the Soviet Union. However, in 1933 the Red Army embarked on a major program to build up mechanized units, and Germany likewise began a similar program. The effects of these efforts became manifest by 1936 when the Polish Army was considering its own modernization needs as part of the KSUS rebuilding program. Most branches of the army favored a mechanization of the cavalry as economic resources permitted, but this was resisted by many cavalry advocates. In defending their traditional role, the cavalry advocates denigrated the value of mechanized units and emphasized alleged weaknesses of armored units in combat. Because many cavalry advocates were unfamiliar with mechanized tactics, they offered peculiar arguments. For example, armored divisions were said to be especially vulnerable to night attack and their logistical tail was said to limit their effective operational range. Many of these self-serving arguments would have had less credibility if it had not been for Poland's own limited and uninspiring experiences with tank units. Most Polish tank units

The Polish armored force was based on light tankettes such as this TK tankette.

were not equipped with tanks at all, but with tiny tankettes and armored cars. The tankettes were slow, poorly armored, not very mobile in rough or muddy terrain, and armed only with a single machine gun. Operations above company size were restricted by the lack of suitable radios to coordinate larger formations. Summer maneuvers convinced the Poles that these vehicles were suitable for little more than scouting and infantry or cavalry machine gun support. It was not until the late 1930s that any substantial number of modern light tanks became available, and by this time, it was too late to substantially alter the outlook of many army commanders on this vital subject. Moreover, the use of tanks in Spain by the German Condor Legion and various Soviet units had not been notably successful. There were a number of studies warning of the threat posed by mechanized formations. However, many officers felt confident that tank units could be dealt with by the excellent new antitank weapons the Polish Army was acquiring under the 1936 KSUS plan.

The experiences in Spain and their own limited experiences with armor did not prepare the Poles to understand that the main threat of tanks came from neither their guns nor armor. The guns and armor on most German tanks of the period was not impressive by later standards. What was significant was the tanks' mobility. Undoubtedly, a tank unit foolish enough to make a frontal attack on a Polish infantry or cavalry unit was going to suffer extensive casualties. But the whole point of German mechanized doctrine was to avoid direct confrontation with well-prepared formations. Armored-car units, motorcycles, and motorized infantry would scout ahead of the tank units to seek out weakly defended positions. Because of the speed and mobility of the tank units, they could be passed through gaps much more quickly than infantry or even cavalry could be dispatched from the reserve to plug the holes in the defensive cordon. Moreover, these intrusions into and past defensive cordons would not be limited to platoons or companies, but could quickly become divisions or even armored corps. This doctrine was fundamentally different from the 1920 French doctrine, with which the Poles were so familiar, which envisioned the subordination of tank units to infantry formations to carry out limited tactical tasks. The Polish maneuver doctrine was undermined because its opponents were able to maneuver so much faster.

The second factor undermining the maneuver doctrine was the Polish Army's tendency to overextend its forces. Polish operational doctrine envisioned assigning an army to a front of 100–200 kilometers, depending upon the terrain. This army was expected to have five to six infantry divisions, two cavalry brigades, and a tank battalion. Armies along the main route of enemy attack would also have one of the new mechanized brigades. In contrast, Soviet operational doctrine held that one of its armies, which had far greater strength than a Polish army, would have a defensive front of only 80–100 kilometers. A Soviet army possessed twelve to fifteen infantry divisions, and one or two tank divisions. The reasons for this enormous discrepancy was the relatively small size of the Polish Army compared to the relatively large fronts it was expected to defend according to Polish strategic doctrine. The effect of the low density of Polish forces during defensive operations became all too clear in 1939. Though the army was supposed to wage a fighting retreat, it became impossible for the infantry divisions and cavalry brigades to break off action with German forces. The forces allotted to each army were not extensive enough to permit deployment even on the scale envisioned in Polish operational doctrine. The inevitable result was that army commanders stripped their reserve to bolster the primary line of defense. As the units in contact with the Germans tried to retreat, they could not fall back to lines held by other Polish units and break off the engagement: there were no reserves to form major secondary lines of defense. One way of breaking contact was to withdraw at night. However, this tactic could only be used for a few days, at best, since the units could hardly be expected to remain in constant daily combat with enemy forces, then spend the night retreating and reestablishing positions all night before the next day's engagement. Polish tactical doctrine indicated that an infantry division could hold a front of fifteen to twenty kilometers in open terrain, but in 1939 the paucity of forces available to enact Plan Z meant that divisional fronts regularly exceeded these prudent limits.

In practice, Polish armies were frequently broken down into two operational groups. The operational group commander was responsible for coordinating the actions of the divisions and brigades in his group as well as the small nondivisional units. In some cases, these operational groups were used independently as small armies for limited tasks. Polish operational groups roughly corresponded to German corps, though they did not possess the wealth of nondivisional support units fielded by German corps. In contrast to German armies, the Polish armies were not organized into army groups. This is a particularly curious oversight since the communication links between the armies and General Staff and GISZ in Warsaw were not especially good. The lack of an intermediate organization above army level left Marshal Rydz-Smigly directly commanding a bewildering number of armies, independent operational groups, and reserve forces far beyond the prudent limits which could be handled by his staff. This hampered the coordination of neighboring armies and reserve groups.

Polish operational doctrine envisioned the use of infantry divisions on a divisional front ranging in width from 12 to 50 kilometers. The upper end of the scale was represented by divisions with terrain advantages or a lesser enemy threat. Divisions that were expected to encounter serious enemy attack were expected to cover a defensive front no wider than 12 to 25 kilometers, depending upon the tactics adopted. The two commonplace tactical defense options were static defense and mobile defense. Static defense was viewed as being especially applicable where terrain conditions favored the defender and when the divisional front was narrow, that is, less than 12 kilometers. Defenses were conventional and linear, with the divisional cavalry in front as much as nine kilometers as a scouting force and screen. The main defensive belt would be held by two infantry regiments holding several defensive lines about two kilometers deep. Each of these regiments would have two of their battalions in the initial defensive belt, with the third kept in reserve at the secondary line of defense. The division's third regiment would be kept in reserve, though some of the tactical plans called for the third regiment to divest itself of one battalion which could be used in the main defensive belt. Divisional artillery would be located about three kilometers behind the initial defense lines, and a tankette company, if present, would usually be kept in divisional reserve.

The mobile defense option stemmed from Polish experiences in the 1920 war with the Red Army and was deemed to be especially suitable in the event an infantry division had to cover a front of 20 to 26 kilometers. There were a number of variants in this tactic. Under one scheme, a thin screen of three infantry battalions and divisional cavalry formed the initial defense line. Two infantry regiments totaling six battalions would be kept in a reserve. Once the direction of the main enemy attack became evident as it struck the initial defense screen, this main divisional strength could move forward and concentrate against it. The other variation was essentially similar, but in the case of a 26-kilometer front, five battalions would be used as the initial defensive belt, with four battalions retained as the main divisional strength for the counterattack.

Defensive cavalry brigade tactics also were seen as having static or mobile options. Cavalry regulations envisioned a brigade being assigned a brigade front of two to four kilometers. On a narrow front of two to three kilometers, two regiments would hold a defensive belt about a kilometer wide from dismounted positions with the third regiment held in mounted reserve for rapid reinforcement and held about 2.5 kilometers back from the initial defense positions. The main line of defense held by the two regiments would be about a kilometer deep in two lines, each line held by two squadrons. In the case of a wider brigade front, another option would

A Polish cavalry troop on patrol.

be to hold the front with three dismounted regiments, two of which would shed a squadron each, and they would form the reserve along with the brigade's armored troop. In this option, the defense belt would be as deep, but the second line of the belt would be covered by only a single squadron, rather than two as in the scheme. In the case of the cavalry brigades with four regiments, the regulations suggested using three dismounted regiments in the initial defensive belt, with the fourth regiment held in mounted reserve about two to three kilometers from the front lines, supported by the brigade armored troop. As will be noticed, Polish defensive cavalry tactics stressed the use of troopers in a dismounted role where the rifle would be the primary weapon. Mounted action was confined mainly to scouting, screening, and reinforcement, as machine guns had made mounted charges with sabres and rifles suicidal.

The mobile defense tactic was deemed suitable when a three-regiment cavalry brigade had to defend a front as wide as eight kilometers. In this case, one regiment would hold an intentionally weak front up to five kilometers wide, while another would hold a narrower three-kilometer front. The plan presumed that the enemy would attack the more weakly held line of the first regiment, and this would precipitate a counterattack by the main brigade force consisting of the third cavalry regiment, the brigade armored troop, and two horse artillery batteries. A similar scheme was suggested for a four-regiment cavalry brigade assigned to cover a twelve-kilometer front. In this case, three regiments would hold fronts ranging from two to six kilometers, with the main brigade force ready for a counterattack with the fourth cavalry regiment plus two squadrons detached from other regiments, the armored troop and two horse artillery batteries.

Polish operational doctrine did envision the use of cavalry brigades as army reserve forces to be retained for counterattacks. However, because of the commitments of Plan Z, nearly all were used to hold frontal defensive positions. Frequently the brigade frontages were far in excess of prewar tactical doctrine, though the same can be said for infantry divisions as well. The mechanized brigades and three independent tank battalions were all assigned to army reserves. The mechanized brigades were supposed to be used by armies to counter enemy tank divisions. Polish tactical doctrine suggested that a mechanized brigade should be held in reserve up to 150 kilometers from the front, and rapidly brought forward once a tank division threatened. The main brigade strength would be concentrated fifteen to twenty kilometers from the front, with lead armored elements and specialist troops holding advance positions 15 kilometers forward. The Polish tanks would cover suitable avenues of approach, especially roads,

The most potent antitank weapon in the Polish arsenal was the Bofors 37mm antitank gun, which was license-produced in Poland after 1936.

while the specialist troops such as engineers would destroy bridges, lay mines, or otherwise hamper the enemy advance. Tanks and motorized infantry would then wage a fighting retreat as the enemy armor attempted to advance. During the courses of these delaying actions, the army would have time to build up a suitable antitank screen of antitank guns, artillery, and other tanks, about twenty kilometers behind the main brigade positions. As the tank division approached, the remainder of the brigade would gradually join into delaying operations, eventually falling behind and reinforcing the antitank screen erected forty kilometers behind the initial front line.

In view of the importance of tanks in the 1939 campaign, it is perhaps worthwhile to take an especially detailed look at Polish antitank doctrine. Although the Polish Army may not have fully appreciated the operational and strategic threat posed by panzer divisions, its tactical antitank policy was sensible and vigorously pursued. The details here are taken from the 1937 "Directive on Combat between Cavalry and Armored Units" since there has been so much rubbish published about Polish cavalry charges against tanks. Infantry antitank tactics were essentially similar. The directive began by stating, "In view of the massive development of armored forces, the cavalry will continually face them and must learn to deal with them if they are to fulfill their assignments." The directive then discussed the use of terrain in defeating tanks, that is, in a passive sense, setting up combat positions in terrain where tanks do not have easy access, and in an active sense, looking for terrain features like roads and forest openings where tanks were likely to pass and that were suitable for ambushes. The directive also stressed that cavalry units were likely to be forced to fight tank units over the course of several hours, and not just randomly encounter small units. The directive listed seven means for destroying tanks: antitank ammunition for rifles and machine guns, hand grenades, 37mm antitank guns, horse artillery, brigade armored troops, bomber aircraft, and engineer equipment. In fact, this list was neither complete nor particularly helpful. Polish 7.62mm antitank ammunition used in rifles and machine guns were not really adequate to deal with German tanks of the period. Hand grenades were useless, and no antitank grenade had been developed. The directive did not mention the new UR antitank rifle because it was so secret, but there was no particular problem presented by the secrecy as it worked like any bolt-action rifle. Without a doubt, the most effective weapons possessed by Polish units were the 37mm Bofors antitank guns and regimental guns, both of which could destroy any contemporary German tank at ranges of 500 to 1000 meters. The suggestion that bomber aircraft could be used to combat tanks was a pipe dream, not only because of the small numbers of Karas and Los bombers available, but also because of the lack of antitank bombs and the difficulty of hitting so small a target as a tank from an aircraft. Engineer equipment for defeating tanks consisted primarily of mines. The directive stressed that brigade commanders should make certain that not only the front lines be covered by antitank guns, but that an antitank gun reserve should be retained to deal with any breakthroughs.

As mentioned earlier, each army was allotted its own air units. Most of the armies each received two fighter squadrons of P.7 or P.12 aircraft for air defense and strafing, numbering twenty to twenty-two aircraft; one reconnaissance squadron, numbering eight to ten P.23 Karas aircraft; two observation squadrons, numbering fourteen Czapla or R-XIII aircraft; and one or two liaison platoons with three to six RWD-8 aircraft. The P.23 Karas was a unique type of aircraft stemming from Polish experiences in 1920. It combined the functions of a light bomber and observation aircraft but was not particularly well suited to ground attack because of its small payload and vulnerability to German fighters. Nevertheless, it was widely employed as a bomber during the fighting, and was also employed in the scouting role, as the Czapla and R-XIII were "meat-on-the-table" for German fighters. Many of the fighter and Karas squadrons did not remain under army commands very long and were withdrawn into central Poland and put at the disposal of the High Command or dispositional air force.

3. Organization of the Polish Armed Forces

The Polish national forces consisted of only the Army and the Navy: there was no separate air force. Though, by contemporary standards, there were substantial air units, they were part of Army and Navy formations. In addition to the active army, there was a Frontier Defense Corps (KOP), which functioned primarily to defend the Russian and Czech frontiers. To those forces should be added the National Guard cadre, amounting to about one tenth of the wartime armed forces strength, and reserve forces, comprising another one and half million men in the twenty-four to forty-two age group. These reserves, about 80 percent of the potential Polish military force of 2.5 million men, were the backbone of the armed forces—and the source of Poland's reputation as a leading military power.

The active forces in 1939 consisted of six armies (there was one reserve army), made up of thirty infantry divisions, eleven cavalry brigades, one mechanized brigade, two engineer brigades, eleven artillery regiments, and an air command having four bomber squadrons, eleven light bomber squadrons, fifteen fighter squadrons, eleven reconnaissance/observation squadrons, thirteen liaison platoons, and one each attack, torpedo, training, and transport squadrons. These units were deployed in peacetime in ten corps areas. Altogether, they included 500,000 men in August 1939.

The powers of the commander-in-chief of the Polish armed forces fell upon Marshal Edward Rydz-Smigly, who bore the title of Inspector-General of the Armed Forces (GISZ, Glowny Inspektorat Sil Zbrojnych). Before the war he prepared mobilization plans, supervised training, controlled tactical and administrative areas of the armed forces, and made recommendations on matters of defense. Until the onset of war, he shared power with the Minister of War, who represented the services—especially the Navy—in the President's cabinet. On 23 March 1939 Rydz-Smigly assigned the various wartime missions and commanders for the Polish defense and allocated resources among them. By 1 September, six first-line armies had been established, each having two to five infantry divisions, one or two cavalry brigades, three to five artillery groups, two to four tank companies, two to five air squadrons, various National Guard brigades, and other separate battalions. (Table 3–1 lists the order of battle resulting from these dispositions. The map on page 111 shows the geographical distribution of the units.) In the months before full mobilization, between March and August 1939, the active army grew from 300,000 to 500,000. After the invasion, three additional armies were formed on an ad-hoc basis, Army Warsaw, Army Lublin, Army Malopolska.

TABLE 3–1
POLISH ARMY, ORDER OF BATTLE, 1 SEPTEMBER 1939, 0400 HOURS

COMMANDER IN CHIEF: Marshal E. Rydz-Smigly
Coordinated with Minister for Military Affairs, the Reserve Army, including school units and national defense, and KOR Secretariat. He commanded:

HIGH COMMAND

Chief of Staff: Brig. Gen. M. Stachiewicz
Chief Quartermaster Gp
Propaganda Chief
Operations Chief of Staff

Air Force and Antiaircraft High Command: Brig. Gen. J. Zajac
Fighter Brigade: 111st, 112nd, 113rd, 114rd, and 123rd Sqdns
Bomber Brigade: 21st, 22nd, 56th, 64th, 65th, 211th, 212th, 216th, and 217th Sqdns
National AA units

Chief of Artillery: Brig. Gen. S. Miller
Chief of Engineers and Fortifications: Brig. Gen. M. Dabkowski
Chief of Armored Troops: Col. J. Kapciuk
Chief of Civilian Commission: Col. Kostek Biernacki
Delegate of Field Bishop

ARMY KARPATY Cmdr: Div. Gen. K. Fabrycy

	Army Support Units	*Air Command*
2nd Mtn Br.	1st Mtz. Arty Regt	31st Attack Sqdn
3rd Mtn Br.	9th Hvy Arty Det.	56th Recon. Sqdn
Detachment "Hungary"	12 AA sections	
2nd ("Podole") KOP Regt		
Karpaty National Guard Br.		
Group No. 2 "Kaw"		
Warsaw Mech. Br.		
46th Lt. Arty Det.		
47th Lt. Arty Det.		
*Group Tarnow		
*22nd Inf. Div.		
*38th Inf. Div.		

ARMY KRAKOW   Cmdr: Brig. Gen. A. Szylling

Group Slask: Cmdr. Brig. Gen. J.
    Jagmin-Sadowski
  23nd Inf. Div.
  55th Inf. Div.
  Katow Fortress Br. Gp
  95th Hvy Arty Det.
  1 AA section
Group Bielsko: Cmdr: Brig. Gen. M.
    Boruta-Spiechowicz
  1st Mtn Br.
  21st Mtn Inf. Div.
  Group Col. Misianga
6th Inf. Div.
7th Inf. Div.
10th Mech. Br.
Krakowska Cav. Br.
*11th Inf. Div.
*45th Inf. Div.
*5th Hvy Arty Regt

Army Support Units
64th Lt Arty Det.
65th Mtz Engr Bn
Armd Train 51
Armd Train 52
Armd Train 54
1st Mtz AA Bn
Krakow Local Def. Regt
12 AA sections

Air Command
121st Fighter Sqdn
122nd Fighter
    Sqdn
24th Attack Sqdn
23rd Recon. Sqdn
26th Recon. Sqdn

ARMY LODZ   Cmdr: Div. Gen. J. K. Rommel

Group Piotrkow: Cmdr: Brig. Gen.
    W. Thommee
  30th Inf. Div.
  Wolynska Cav. Br.
  2nd Bn, 4th Hvy Arty Regt.
  7th Hvy Machine Gun Bn
2nd Inf. Div.
10th Inf. Div.
(22nd Mtn Div.)
28th Inf. Div.
Kresowa Cav. Br.

Army Support Units
6th Hvy Arty Regt
4th Hvy Arty Regt (-)
2nd Tk Bn, Hq
50th Mtz Engr Bn
3rd Hvy Machine Gun Bn
Armd Train 53
4 AA sections

Air Command
161st Fighter Sqdn
162nd Fighter Sqdn
32nd Attack Sqdn
63rd Recon. Sqdn
66th Recon. Sqdn

ARMY MODLIN   Cmdr: Brig. Gen. E. Krukowicz-Przedrzymirski

8th Inf. Div.
20th Inf. Div.
Nowogrodzka Cav. Br.
Mazowiecka Cav. Br.

Army Support Units
Modlin Regt (improvised)
Kazan Regt (improvised)
Plock Local Defense Unit
Pultusk Local Defense Unit
Zegrze Local Defense Unit
60th Mtz. Engr Bn
Armd Train 13
Armd Train 14
Armd Train 15
*1st Hvy Arty Regt
*98th Hvy Arty Det.

Air Command
152nd Fighter Sqdn
41st Attack Sqdn
53rd Recon. Sqdn

ARMY POMORZE   Cmdr: Div. Gen. W. Bortkowski

Group East: Cmdr: Brig. Gen.
   M. Boltuc
  4th Inf. Div.
  16th Inf. Div.
  Jablomowo Local Defense
   Regt
Group Czersk: Cmdr: Brig.
  Gen. Grzmot-Skotnicki
  Pomorska Cav. Br.
  Chojnice Local Defense Regt
  Koscierzyna Local Defense
   Bn
9th Inf. Div.
15th Inf. Div.
27th Inf. Div.

Army Support Units
46h Mtz. Engr Bn
Vistula Local Defense Regt
Torun Local Defense Regt
Chelmno National Guard Regt (-)
River Flotilla (7 vessels)

Air Command
141st Fighter Sqdn
142nd Fighter Sqdn
42nd Attack Sqdn
43rd Recon. Sqdn
46th Recon. Sqdn

ARMY POZNAN   Cmdr: Div. Gen. T. Kutrzeba

14th Inf. Div.
17th Inf. Div.
25th Inf. Div.
26th Inf. Div.
Wielkopolska Cav. Br.
Podolska Cav. Br.
*Pomorze National Guard Bn

Army Support Units
7th Hvy Arty Regt
5th Hvy Machine Gun Bn
47th Mtz. Engr Bn
Armd Train 11
Armd Train 12

Air Command
131st Fighter Sqdn
132nd Fighter Sqdn
33rd Recon. Sqdn
34th Attack Sqdn

ARMY PRUSY   Cmdr: Div. Gen. S. Dab-Biernacki

Group Brig. Gen. J. Kruszewki
Group Kaw No. 1: Cmdr: Brig. Gen. R. Dreszer
  19th Inf. Div.
  Wilenska Cav. Br.
Group Brig. Gen. S. Skwarczynski
  3rd Inf. Div.
  12th Inf. Div.
  36th Inf. Div.
13th Inf. Div.
29th Inf. Div.
*39th Inf. Div.
*44th Inf. Div.

Army Support Units
1st Hvy Arty Regt
3rd Hvy Arty Regt
50th Hvy Arty Det.
1st Lt Tk Bn.
81st Mtz. Engr Bn
1st Co., 2nd Engr Bn
Armd Train 55
9 AA sections

GROUP GRODNO   Cmdr: Brig. Gen. J. Olsyna-Wilczynski

Grodno Local Defense Regt
Wilno Local Defense Regt Hq
Baronowicze KOP Regt
Kleck Lt Arty Bn
9 AA sections

GROUP KUTNO   (Never mobilized as a group)

5th Inf. Div.
24th Inf. Div.
9th Hvy Arty Regt
71st Lt Arty Det.

GROUP NAREW   Cmdr. Brig. Gen. C. Mlot-Fijalkowski

18th Inf. Div.	*Support Units*	*Air Command*
33rd Inf. Div.	Osowiec Local Defense Unit	13th Recon. Sqdn
Podlaska Cav. Br.	Wizna Local Defense Unit	5th Attack Sqdn
Suwalska Cav. Br.	53rd Mtz. Engr Bn	151st Fighter Sqdn
	34th Fortress Gp	
	*81st Lt Arty Det.	

GROUP WYSZKOW   Cmdr: Brig. Gen. S. Kowalski

1st Inf. Div.
41st Inf. Div.
Armd Train 55
*35th Inf. Div.
*2nd Hvy Arty Regt

COASTAL DEFENSE   Cmdr: Adm. J. Unrug

Coastal Land Defense	*Coastal Sea Defense*
Morska (Naval) National Guard Br.	Hel Fortified Region
1st Naval Rifle Regt	Destroyers: *Wicher, Burza, Grom, Blyskawica*
2nd Naval Rifle Regt	Minelayer: *Gryf*
4th National Guard Bn	Minesweepers: *Czajka, Czapla* (unfinished), *Jaskolka, Mewa, Rybitwa, Zuraw* (unfinished)
Naval Lt Arty Det.	Sloops: *Haller, Pilsudski*
Krakus Det.	Naval AA Det. 1 & 2
83rd Fortress Gp:	Coastal Air Defense
Naval Mtz. Engr Bn	Support Ships
Hvy Machine Gun Bn	Military Port Commands and Hel
	Naval Air Support Command:
	1st Torpedo Sqdn
	1st Training Sqdn
	Submarine Command: *Orzel, Rys, Sep, Wilk, Zbik*

*Originally assigned, but unable to fight with this command.

After the German mobilization in August 1939, the Polish Army found itself outnumbered in almost every way. Even an extremely efficient full mobilization would have left it at a 50 percent disadvantage in manpower at the time of the invasion. And, unfortunately, as the result of the inept counsel of Poland's allies, mobilization was delayed. Less than half of the Polish armed forces had been mobilized by 1 September, and only one quarter (600,000) were fully equipped and in position when hostilities commenced. In short, the Germans had twice the ground troops, more than four times the aircraft and about forty times the motorized vehicles of Poland. Their naval forces were at least ten times stronger.

As an overview of the different combat formations to be discussed below, Tables 3–2 and 3–3 show the components and strengths of the principal combat formations—divisions, brigades, and regiments. It is important to note that Table 3–3 shows organizational strengths that were not, in fact, achieved in practice. The "reported" strength typically fell below what was required, and the "field" strength lower still, because it excluded personnel en route, in training, in hospital, and so on. The TOE provided a point of reference against which weaknesses could be measured. For example, at the outbreak of hostilities, most of the infantry divisions stood somewhere between their peacetime and wartime footing, so that the Germans sometimes considered a Polish division the equivalent of a regimental or brigade-size battlegroup. Especially after the first few days of the campaign, the organizational allotments became increasingly meaningless, and unit improvisation became more common.

TABLE 3–2
COMPONENT UNITS OF POLISH DIVISIONS AND BRIGADES

	Infantry Division	Cavalry Brigade	National Guard Brigade
TOE Personnel	16,492	6,143[1]	5,000[2]
Headquarters	Div. HQ	Br. HQ	Br. HQ
Bicycles	Co.	Co.	Co.
Cavalry	Sqdn	3 Regts	—
Infantry	3 Regts	—[3]	—[4]
Artillery	Lt Regt & Hvy Det[5]	Horse Arty Regt	Plat.
Antiaircraft	Bty	Bty	—
Engineers	Bn	Sqdn	—
Other	Hvy MG Co.[6]	Armd Trp	—

[1]Nowogrodzka, Pomorska, Suwalska, and Wolynska Brigades had four regiments each, for a total strength of 7,184. [2]Estimated. [3]The majority of brigades had a battalion of infantry. [4]About eight battalions, mostly of Type IV. [5]Two battalions. [6]Some divisions had a tankette company.

TABLE 3–3
POLISH UNITS VS. GERMAN INFANTRY DIVISION

	Officers	NCOs & Pvts	Lt MGs	Hvy MGs	46mm Mortars	81mm Mortars	AT Rifles	37mm Guns	40mm AA	75mm Arty	100mm Arty	105mm Arty	155mm Arty	Horses	Bicycles	Horsedrawn Vehicles	Cars & Trucks	Tankettes
Polish Inf. Div.	515	15,977	320	132	81	20	92	27	4	30	12	12	3	6,939	76			
German Inf. Div.		*17,200*	*378*	*138*	*93*	*54*	*90*	*75*	*12*	*20*	*36*	*18*		*4,842*		*919*	*527*	*1,012*
Cav. Br. (3 Regt)	232	5,911	9	81	9	2	66	14	2	12				5,194	345		66	21
(4 Regt)	273	6,911	10	95	9	2	78	18	2	16				6,291	386		66	21
Cav. Regt.	30	812		12			13	4						850	41		3	
Mech. Br.			4	43	4		27	4	4									32
Inf. Regt	91	3,212	90	36	27	6	27	9		2				664	60	165	4	

A Polish infantry platoon stands to attention. The second rifleman in the first row is armed with the "rkm" squad automatic rifle derived from the Browning bar.

INFANTRY UNITS

Infantry was the backbone of the Polish Army, both numerically and organizationally. Numerically, the infantry, in 1939, ranged from 55 percent (in June) to 62 percent of the active army. By comparison, the armies of Russia and Germany averaged 43 percent infantry. Organizationally, most of the units mobilized in 1939 were infantry because it was easier and more practical for an impoverished country to deploy riflemen.

Altogether, there were about 2.1 million trained infantrymen in Poland in 1939, but the vast majority of them were Category A reservists, who, because of material limitations (weapons, communications, uniforms), were not included in plans for an initial mobilization. This figure, of course, represented the upper limit on infantry mobilization in a short war; actual plans called for the commitment of 700,000 infantrymen during the first month of warfare. By comparison, using the known strength of the active army in March 1939 (283,000 men), it has been calculated that the infantry amounted to 160,000, including almost 11,000 officers and over 25,000 noncommissioned officers. In the event, the number of infantrymen actually concentrated by 1 September was only 430,000. The explanation for this low figure is the delay in the final mobilization order, which was issued for the active army only on 29 August.

In terms of effectiveness, the infantry's value was determined by its training. The thirty active divisions trained their new personnel during the summer months, and then their strength dropped substantially as an officer and NCO training cycle took place. Thus most of the active army infantry consisted of recruits completing an eighteen-month training cycle, which started each March. This meant that even in the active army only about two thirds of the soldiers would be fully trained. The other one third would have completed only six months' training. And, as a consequence of the training cycle, if war came in the summer, the division would already be concentrated, but more mobilization time would be required if war came in the fall. Those divisions not mobilized before 1 September, for example, could not hope to complete their concentration on the first day of battle. For this reason some of the active divisions were not combat-ready until days after the Germans had invaded.

In peacetime the division, the largest combat unit, was considered to be operationally independent and was assigned to administrative areas within Poland. In wartime the division came directly under the control of an army, without provision for a corps command. In the place of corps there typically existed an "operation group" under a local commander or a division headquarters; such an operational group might include three tactical commands (usually equivalent to a task force). In actuality, this Polish army was the size of a Western corps.

In addition to the thirty active infantry divisions, there were nine reserve divisions. Their fighting capability was lower because most were weaker in equipment, such as artillery, antitank guns, and reconnaissance vehicles. In this group, the four divisions based on KOP units—the 33rd, 35th, 36th, and 38th—could be considered superior in quality. The 55th Division was based on National Guard troops. The other four reserve divisions came from older age classes and were considered of lower quality.

Since it was in such formations that Polish soldiers fought, it is important to distinguish their composition. At the divisional level, our concern is with combined arms rather than with the infantry arm alone. The components of a typical infantry division on a wartime footing are shown in Table 3–4. The components and strengths of special detachments—antiaircraft battery, bicycle company, cavalry squadron, and heavy machine gun company—are shown in Tables 3–5, 3–6, 3–7, and 3–8.

Table 3–9 lists the various infantry divisions and their component units. It reveals the weakness especially of the nine reserve divisions, which lacked heavy artillery, antiaircraft units, and even cavalry squadrons. Even at the authorized organizational level, the reserve divisions lacked artillery pieces, antitank guns, and reconnaissance vehicles.

TABLE 3–4
POLISH INFANTRY DIVISION COMPONENTS

Division staff & headquarters
Infantry regiments (3)
Artillery:
  Light regiment
  Heavy detachment
Special Detachments:
  Antiaircraft battery (3 types)
  Bicycle company (2 types)
  Cavalry squadron
  Heavy machine gun company

Engineer battalion
Services:
  Telephone company & radio platoon
  Field court & police platoon
  Medical company, field hospital, dentists
  Disinfection/bathing column
  Bacteriological/chemical unit
  Armament & veterinary parks
  Supply columns (3)
  Supply platoon & repair depot

TABLE 3–5
DIVISION ANTIAIRCRAFT BATTERY
(Three Types)

Officers	5	6	5
NCOs & privates	135	192	185
Heavy machine guns	9	12	16
81mm mortars	2	2	—
Horses	109	132	124
Horsedrawn vehicles	45	55	52

TABLE 3–6
DIVISION BICYCLE COMPANY
(Two Types)

Officers	4	5
NCOs & privates	211	210
Light machine guns	9	9
Antitank rifles	0	3
Horses	18	18
Bicycles	196	196
Horsedrawn vehicles	7	5
Cars & trucks	1	3

TABLE 3–7
DIVISION CAVALRY SQUADRON

Officers	5
NCOs & privates	210
Rifles	213
Horses*	213
Horsedrawn vehicles*	1

*Estimated.

TABLE 3–8
DIVISION HEAVY MACHINE GUN COMPANY

Officers	6
NCOs & privates	166
Heavy machine guns	12
81mm mortars	2
Horses	48
Horsedrawn vehicles	30

TABLE 3–9

POLISH INFANTRY DIVISIONS, COMPONENT UNITS

		Artillery			Special Troops					
Div.	Regiments	Lt Regt	Hvy Det.	Bcyl	Cav.	AA	Hvy MG	Engr Bn	Armor	Other
1L	1L, 5L, 6L	1L	1	Co.	1		Co.	1		
2L	2L, 3L, 4L	2	2	Co.	2					
3L	7L, 8L, 9L	3	3	Co.	3	Bty	Co.	3		
4	14, 63, (67NG)	4	4	Co.	4	Bty	Co.	4	81 TKS	
5	19, 26, 40	5	5	Co.	5	Bty	Co.	5		
6	12, 16, 20	6	6	Co.	6		Bn 4	6		
7	25, 27, 74	7	7	Co.	7	Bty	Co.	7		NG Bn
8	13, 21, 32	8	8	Co.	8	Bty	Co.	8	63 TKS	
9	22, 34, 35	9 + 56 Bn	9		9	Bty	Co.	9		NG Bn
10	28, 30, 31, NG	10	10	Co.	10	Bty	Co.	10	32 TKS & 92 TK	
11	48, 49, 53	11	11	Co.	11	Bty	Co.	11		
12	51, 52, 54	12	12	Co.	12	Bty	Co.	12		At Co.
13	43, 44, 45	13	13	Co.	13	Bty	Co.	13		
14	55, 57, 58, NG, NG	14	14	Co.	14	Bty	Co.	14	71 TKS	
15	59, 61, 62, NG	15	15	Co.	15	Bty	Bn 6	15	82 TKS	AT Co.
16	64, 65, 66, NG	16	16	Co.	16	Bty	Co.	16		Assault Bn
17	68, 69, 70	17	17	Co.	17	Bty	Co.	17	72 TK	
18	33, 42, 71	18	18	Co.	18	Bty	2 Cos.	18		
19	77, 85, 86	19	19	Co.	19	Bty	Co.	19		AT Co.
20	78, 79, 80	20	20	Co.	20	Bty	Co.	20	62 TK	
21 Mtn	3, 4, 202	21	21	Co.	21	Bty	Co.	21		
22 Mtn	2, 5, 6	22	22	Co.	22	Bty	Co.	22		
23	11, 73, 75	23	23 & 95	2 Cos.	23	Bty	Co.	23		
24	17, 38, 39	24	24	Co.	24	Bty	Co.	24		
25	29, 56, 60, NG	25	25	Co.	25	Bty	Co.	25	31 TKS	
26	10, 18, 37, NG	26 +	26	Co.	26	Bty			51 Armd Tn	
27	23, 24, 50	27	27	Co.	27	Bty	Co.	27		
28	15, 36, 72	28	28	Co.	28	Bty	Co.	28	91 TK	
29	41, 76, 81	29	29	Co.	29	Bty	Co.	29		
30	82, 83, 84	30	30	Co.	30	Bty	Co.	30	41 TK, 52 Armd Tn	
33 Res	133, 134, 135	32			33			43		
35 Res	205, 206, 207	32			35			35		
36 Res	163, 164, 165	40			36			46		
45 Res	154, 155, 156	55		Co.	45		2 Cos.	55		Not Completed
50 Res	178, 179, 180, 181									Not Completed
55 Res	201, 203, 204	65 + Bn		Co.			Co.			Not Completed
60 Res	182, 183, 184									Not Completed
1 Mtn	1 KOP, 2 KOP, NG	Bn +								
2 Mtn	1R, NG, NG/KOP	Bn								Not Completed
3 Mtn	KOP, NG, NG									Not Completed

To illustrate the weakness of the normal division structure, it is useful to compare the Polish infantry division to its German counterpart, which was only three percent larger in personnel. (See Table 3–3.) The Polish unit relied on horse-drawn transportation almost entirely; the German unit was also largely horse-drawn, but had three fourths the number of horses (5,375) *and* 942 motor vehicles, as well as 452 motorcycles. The Poles had 48 artillery pieces in total; the Germans had 74, of which 54 were 105mm or larger. The Poles had 101 mortars, the Germans 147. There were 27 Polish 37mm antitank guns against 20 German 75mm guns in an AT/AA battalion. The Polish signal unit was half the size of the German signal battalion, which, significantly, was as motorized (103 vehicles and 32 motorcycles) as an entire Polish division! On the basis of firepower, mobility, and communications, the Polish division, it can be argued, had only half the *combat* power of the German division.

The Polish division contained three regiments, which comprised 60 percent of the divisional personnel. Such regiments consisted of a headquarters staff, three infantry battalions, and support troops. (See Table 3–10.) German regiments had similar personnel strength, but over three times the indirect firepower, as well as 73 vehicles. The advantage in combat power here was also about two to one. The regiments are listed by name and mobilization region in Table 3–11.

TABLE 3–10
POLISH INFANTRY REGIMENT, PERSONNEL AND EQUIPMENT

	Officers	NCOs & Pvts	Lt MGs	Hvy MGs	46mm Mortars	81mm Mortars	AT Rifles	37mm Guns	75mm Guns	Horses	Bicycles	Horsedrawn Vehicles	Motor Vehicles
HG & HG co.													
Reconnaissance co.	3	105	4				2			53			
Antitank co.	4	120						9		39			
Special det.													
Pioneer plat.	1	60								19			
Arty plat.	2	50							2	46			
Antigas plat.	1	46											
Communications plat.													
Rifle bn (×3)													
Rifle co. (×3)	4	226	9		3		3			13			
Hvy MG co.	5	166		12		2				48			
Services													
TOTAL	91	3,212	90	36	27	6	27	9	2	664	60	165	4

TABLE 3–11
ROSTER OF POLISH INFANTRY REGIMENTS

Regt	Name or Designation	Home Station
1L	Pilsudski's Legion Inf.	Wilno*
1	Podhale Rifles	Nowy Sacz, with co. at Zakopane
2L	Legion Inf.	Sandomierz, with 1st Bn at Staszow
2	Podhale Rifles	Sanoz
3L	Legion Inf.	Jaroslaw
3	Bodhale Rifles	Bielsko, with 3rd Bn at Bogumin
4L	Legion Inf.	Kielce*
4	Podhale Rifles	Cieszyn
5L	Pilsudski's Zuchowaty Legion Inf.	Wilno*
5	Podhale Rifles	Przemysl*
6L	Pilsudski's Legion Inf.	Wilno*
6	Podhale Rifles	Sambor, with 2nd Bn at Drohobycz
7L	Legion Inf.	Chelm Lubelski
8L	Legion Inf.	Lublin
9L	Legion Inf.	Zamosc, with 3rd Bn at Tomaszow
10	(1775–1806–1918–1930)† Inf.	Lowicz, with 3rd Bn at Skierniewice
11	Infantry	Tarnowskie Gory, with 3rd Bn at Szczakowa
12	(Marching Soldier) Inf.	Wadowice, with 3rd Bn at Krakow
13	Infantry	Pultusk
14	Ziemia Kujawska Inf.	Wloclawek
15	Wilkow Inf.	Deblin
16	(Dawidow-Krasne-Murowa) Inf.	Tarnow
17	Infantry	Rzeszow
18	(Five Eagles) Inf.	Skierniewice*
19	"Saviours of Lwow" Inf.	Lwow*
20	Ziemia Krakowska Inf.	Krakow*
21	Warszawski Inf.	Warsaw
22	Infantry	Siedlice*
23	Leopold Lis-Kula Inf.	Wlodzimierz
24	(1918) Inf.	Luck
25	(1913) Inf.	Piotrkow
26	Infantry	Grodek Jagiellonski, with 3rd Bn at Lwow
27	Infantry	Czestochowa*
28	Kaniowski Rifles	Lodz*
29	Kaniowski Rifles	Kalisz,* with 2nd Bn at Szczypiorno
30	Kaniowski Rifles	Warsaw
31	Kaniowski Rifles	Lodz,* with 2nd and 3rd Bns at Sieradz
32	Infantry	Modlin,* with 3rd Bn at Dzialdowo
33	Infantry	Lomza*
34	Infantry	Biala Podlaska
35	Infantry	Brzesc
36	Academy Legion Inf.	Praga, Warsaw*
37	Prince Josef Poniatowski's Leczyce	Kutno
38	Lwow Rifles	Przemysl
39	Lwow Rifles	Jaroslaw,* with 1st Bn at Lubaczow
40	Children of Lwow Inf.	Lwow*

Regt	Name or Designation	Home Station
41	Marshal Josef Pilsudski's Suwalski Inf.	Suwalki
42	Gen. J. H. Dabrowski Inf.	Bialystok
43	Bayonne Legion Rifles	Dubno, with 2nd Bn at Brody
44	American Legion Rifles	Rowne*
45	Kresowy Rifles Inf.	Rowne*
48	Kresowy Rifles Inf.	Stanislawow*
49	Huculski Rifles	Kolomyja
50	Francesco Nullo Inf.	Kowel,* with 3rd Bn at Sarny
51	Kresowy Rifles Inf.	Brzezany
52	Kresowy Rifles Inf.	Zloczow
53	Kresowy Rifles Inf.	Stryj
54	Kresowy Rifles Inf.	Tarnapol*
55	Poznan Inf.	Leszno, with 3rd Bn at Rawicz
56	Wielkopolski Inf.	Krotoszyn
57	King Karol II of Romania Inf.	Poznan*
58	(King Boleslaw Chrobry) Inf.	Poznan*
59	Wielkopolski Inf.	Inowroclaw
60	Wielkopolski Inf.	Ostrow
61	(Golden Helmet) Inf.	Bydgoszcz*
62	Infantry	Bydgoszcz*
63	Torun Inf.	Torun*
64	(Pomorski) Murmansk Rifles	Grudziadz*
65	Starogard Inf.	Grudziadz, with 2nd Bn at Gniew
66	Marshal Josef Pilsudski's Kaszubski	Chelmno, with 1st and 3rd at Grudziadz
67	Infantry	Brodnica, with 2nd Bn at Torun
68	Infantry	Wrzesnia, with 2nd Bn at Jarocin
69	(11 XI 1918) Inf.	Gniezno*
70	12th Wielkopolski Rifles	Pleszew
71	Infantry	Zambrow
72	Col. D. Czachowski Inf.	Radom
73	(5 VI–6 VII 1920) Inf.	Katowice,* with 2nd Bn at Oswiecim
74	Gornoslask Inf.	Lublinice
75	Infantry	Krolewska Huta, with 1st Bn at Rybnik, 3rd Bn at W. Hajduki
76	Ludwig Narbutt's (Lidzki) Inf.	Grodno
77	(12 XII 1918) Inf.	Molodeczno, with 3rd Bn at Krasne U
78	(10 VI 1920) Inf.	Baranowicze*
79	Infantry	Slonim
80	Infantry	Slonim
81	King Stefan Batory's Grodzienski Inf.	Grodno*
82	Thadeus Kosciuszko's Syberyjkki Rifles	Brzesc
83	Romuald Traugutt's Poleski Rifles	Kobryn*
84	Poleski Rifles	Pinsk, with 3rd Bn at Luniniec
85	Wilenski Rifles	Nowowilejka
86	(17 XII 1918) Inf.	Moledeczno,* with 3rd Bn at Krasne

Regt	Name or Designation	Home Station
93 94 95		Rembertow
96 97 98	KOP	Luminiec
114 115 116		Ostrow
133 134 135	KOP	Grodno*
144 145 146		Lowicz
154 155 156		Krakow*
163 164 165	KOP	Czortkow*
176 179 180 181		Brzoza*
182 183 184		Kobryn*
201 202‡ 203 204	NG	Bedzin*
205 206 207	KOP	Wilno*

*Division headquarters was located near this unit.
†Parentheses indicate this emblem appeared on unit insignia.
‡Deployed with 21st Mountain Div.

Finally, the Polish infantry consisted of 471 infantry battalions. There were 273 active battalions, including eighteen Highland battalions, and three mountain rifle battalions. There were 82 National Guard battalions and 105 reserve battalions. Of the latter, 34 were controlled by the Frontier Defense Corps. And there were seven KOP regiments on the eastern frontier.

The Polish infantry division could not expect the same level of support that was found in other armies. There were only four artillery pieces supporting a battalion, compared to over eight in the French and Soviet armies. There was less than one antiaircraft gun to a battalion, compared to four times as many in the German Army, and twelve times as many in the Soviet Army. There was only about one tank to a battalion, compared to a ratio of seven to one in the French Army, and nine to one in the Soviet Army. There was less than one aircraft to each battalion, compared to twelve in the French Army and sixteen in the German Army. In practice, there were few antitank guns and antiaircraft cannons.

All in all, Polish infantry could scarcely avoid being outgunned and outmaneuvered. The infantry division—the only type of Polish division in 1939—had men and weapons adequate to defend a front of ten to twelve kilometers. Unfortunately, the Polish-German border stretched for about fifteen hundred kilometers. So even if *all* the Polish divisions could have been mobilized and in position on the frontier (an absurd cordon defense

A captain of a highland rifle regiment. The troops of the 21st and 22nd Highland Divisions wore the Podhale mountaineer's cap in lieu of the square top "rogatywka" fatigue cap worn elsewhere in the Army. The 11th Highland Division wore a huculski cap derived from the mountaineer's cap of the eastern Carpathian mountain range.

that was never even considered), they would still have been stretched more than three times beyond their capability. Thus there was never a realistic chance that the army could conduct more than a delaying action, given existing limitations on manpower and equipment. Polish organizational effectiveness can only be evaluated if this fact is taken into account.

NATIONAL GUARD

A large territorial force also existed, known as the Obrona Narodowa, or National Guard (literally, Guard of the Nation). There were 82 such battalions. Eleven of these would quickly be absorbed or combined with active units. This force consisted of about 1,600 officers and 50,000 men, organized into eleven brigades of infantry—one for each mobilization area—and a naval brigade on the northern coast.

When the force was first created in December 1936, it was intended as an organization of Polish volunteers that had been declared loyal and suitable for paramilitary duties. By March 1937, the National Guard was taken over by the infantry branch of the armed forces and became integrated with the national training system. The Guard consisted of fully trained men without mobilization assignments and partially trained men, including those surplus to the draft quotas, and volunteers not yet subject to the draft.

National Guard troops tended to be equipped with older French helmets and older weapons like this Hotchkiss heavy machine gun.

By conducting limited training and providing an organizational structure, the National Guard units acted to decrease overall training time and to expand the peacetime force structure. Table 3–12 notes the structure of the two most common types (IV and I) of National Guard battalions and reveals their inherent weakness in artillery and automatic weapons. Type I was considered suitable primarily for guard duties. Types II and III were both substantially weaker than active infantry units. Type IV had manpower comparable to an active unit, but was equipped with French weapons and had fewer mortars and machine guns. Type S was a reduced-strength heavy machine gun battalion.

With the exception of the Morska (Naval) Brigade and the Gornoslaska Brigade, which was equipped with Polish weapons and converted into two regiments of the 55th Infantry Division, even the meager strengths shown in the table were seldom attained when the units went into combat. Therefore, although a typical National Guard brigade included two regiments of four battalions each, with 2,500 to 4,000 men in all, it was seldom as strong in combat as a single active infantry regiment.

Members of the National Guard typically kept their equipment at home and, with some minor uniform variations (French helmets were common), went to war as regular infantry. Despite shortages and inferior French equipment, the troops usually fought as well as the regular army when properly led. This is explained by the higher percentage of volunteers and the fact that the units were typically employed in familiar areas near their homes. Table 3–13 provides the regional affiliation of the various National Guard battalions and also shows their relative strength by indicating organizational types (I–IV, S).

TABLE 3–12
NATIONAL GUARD BATTALIONS, PERSONNEL AND EQUIPMENT

	Type IV	Type I
Officers	19	16
NCOs & privates	683	404
Light machine guns	9	9
Heavy machine guns	6	2
46mm mortars	1	1
Antitank rifles	3	—
Horses	70	34
Bicycles	50	—
Horsedrawn vehicles	32	15
Motorcycles	4	4
Cars & trucks	1	—

NOTE: There are also six Type II battalions, each having 545 men, all in the Torun region; and nine Type II battalions, each having 608 men, all in the Slask region. Two Type S (heavy machine gun) battalions, each having 526 men, had 18 heavy machine guns and 2 mortars each.

TABLE 3–13
POLISH NATIONAL GUARD UNITS

Mobilization Region		Deployment
Region I, Warsaw		
Warszawski Brigade (Warsaw)		
1st Warszawski Bn	Type IV	21st Mtn Div.
2nd Warszawski Bn	Type IV	21st Mtn Div.
3rd Warszawski Bn	Type IV	36th
1st Mazurski Bn	Type IV	3/32nd
2nd Mazurski Bn	Type IV	32nd
Kurpiowski Bn	Type IV	5th Lancers
Region II, Lublin		
Wolynska Half Brigade (Lublin)		
Chelminski Bn	Type I	7th
Kowelski Bn	Type I	50th and 23rd
Lucki Bn	Type I	24th and 43rd
Region III (KOP)		
Dzisnienska Half Brigade (Postawy)		
Braslawski Bn	Type I	KOP Slobodka Bn
Postawski Bn	Type I	23rd Lancers
Region IV, Lodz		
Sieradzka Brigade (Lodz)		
Klobucki Bn	Type IV	27th Inf. Div.
Lublinecki Bn	Type IV	74th
1st Wielunski Bn	Type IV	31st
2nd Wielunski Bn	Type IV	31st
Region V, Krakow		
Gornoslaska Brigade (Katowice)		
Chorzowski Bn	Type S	75th
Katowicki Bn	Type III	73rd Regt.
Oswiecimski Bn	Type III	73rd Cadre Regt.
Rybnicki Bn	Type III	75th
Sosnowiecki Bn	Type III	73rd Regt.
Tarnogorski Bn	Type III	11th Regt.
Zawiercianski Bn	Type III	11th Regt.
Dabrowska Half Brigade (Dabrowa Gornicza)		
Chrzanowski Bn	Type IV	204th Regt., 55th Div.
Dabrowski Bn	Type IV	204th Regt., 55th Div.
Olkuski Bn	Type IV	204th Regt., 55th Div.
Slaska-Cieszynska Half Brigade (Bielsko)		
Bielski Bn	Type III	3rd
1st Cieszynski Bn	Type III	4th
2nd Cieszynski Bn	Type III	4th
Podhalanska Brigade (Krakow)		
Gorlicki Bn	Type IV	16th
Jasielski Bn	Type IV	16th
Limanowski Bn	Type IV	1st
Sadecki Bn	Type IV	1st
Zakopianski Bn	Type IV	12th
Zywiecki Bn	Type IV	12th

Mobilization Region		Deployment
Region VI, Lwow		
Lwowska Brigade (Lwow)		
Brzezanski Bn	Type I	51st
1st Lwowski Bn	Type I	26th
2nd Lwowski Bn	Type I	40th
Sokalski Bn	Type I	19th
Tarnopolski Bn	Type I	54th
Karpacka Half Brigade (Stanislawow)		
1st Huculski Bn	Type I	49th
2nd Huculski Bn	Type I	49th
Stanislawowski Bn	Type I	48th
Stryski Bn	Type I	53rd
Region VII, Poznan		
Kaliska Brigade (Kalisz)		
Kepinski Bn	Type IV	
Kozminski Bn	Type IV	
Krotoszynski Bn	Type IV	
Ostrowski Bn	Type IV	
Ostrzeszowski Bn	Type IV	
Poznanska Brigade (Posnan)		
Obornicki Bn	Type IV	
Opalenicki Bn	Type IV	
1st Poznanski Bn	Type IV	
2nd Poznanski Bn	Type IV	
Rawicki Bn	Type IV	
Szamatulski Bn	Type IV	
Region VIII, Torun		
Chelminska Brigade (Torun)		
Brodnicki Bn	Type IV	67th
Bydgoski Bn	Type IV	61st
Jablonowski Bn	Type IV	63rd
Kcynski Bn	Type II	62nd
Nakielski Bn	Type II	61st
Wagrowiecki Bn	Type IV	62nd
Zninski Bn	Type IV	62nd
Pomorska Brigade (Swiecie)		
Czerski Bn	Type II	1st
Koronowski Bn	Type S	61st
Koscierski Bn	Type II	2nd
Starogardzki Bn	Type II	2/65th
Swiecki Bn	Type IV	66th
Tucholski Bn	Type II	1st Naval Brig.
Region IX, Brzesc-Litovsk		
None		
Region X, Przemysl		
Podkarpacka Brigade (Przemysl)		
Brzozowski Bn	Type IV	2nd
Jaroslawski Bn	Type I	39th
Krosnienski Bn	Type IV	2nd
Przemyski Bn	Type I	38th
Rzeszowski Bn	Type I	17th
Samborski Bn	Type I	6th

Mobilization Region		Deployment
Sanocki Bn	Type I	2nd
Turczanski Bn	Type I	6th
Coastal Region, Gdynia		
Morska (Naval) Brigade (Gdynia)		
1st Gdynski Bn	Type IV	2nd Naval Brig.
2nd Gdynski Bn	Type IV	2nd Naval Brig.
3rd Gdynski Bn	Type IV	2nd Naval Brig.
5th Kaszubski Bn	Type IV	1st Naval Brig.
Krakus Group	na	

THE FRONTIER DEFENSE CORPS

The Frontier Defense Corps (KOP) was organized in 1924, after the border wars with the Soviet Union and the demobilization of the emergency army units. Personnel were specially selected, and usually underwent training and assignment to line units being permanently assigned to KOP. For most of the prewar period the KOP units typically maintained a high state of readiness, because the threat from the east surpassed the risk from Germany. The units, consisting primarily of ethnic Polish troops, often engaged in skirmishes against border incursions or in pacification campaigns against the Ukrainians. In 1939, after the German occupation of Czechoslovakia, the KOP also assumed control of the Slovak frontier.

When war came, the KOP could quickly mobilize four division headquarters (the 33rd, 35th, 36th, and 38th) and three mountain brigade headquarters (1st, 2nd, and 3rd), twelve regimental headquarters, thirty-four infantry battalions, twelve cavalry squadrons, two light artillery battalions, and four engineer companies. These units incorporated reserve and National Guard components prior to deployment.

After mobilization, the remaining KOP cadres and battalions deployed as seven understrength "regiments," primarily under Brigade Polesie (Baronowicze, Glebokie, Podole, Rowne, Sarny, Wilejka, and Wilno), to screen the eastern frontier. They were grouped east of Grodno (the Wilno and Baronowicze units) and along the eastern frontier (the other units); after often courageous resistance, they were overwhelmed by the Soviet invasion.

Of the twelve squadrons of cavalry, three operated under Group Grodno, and six as Cavalry Regiment West in Army Lodz. After 17 September a Cavalry Regiment East was formed with three squadrons to fight against the Soviets. These units, as was typical of other KOP formations, operated in small screening detachments until tactical circumstances forced them to consolidate on their parent headquarters.

CAVALRY

By western standards, the Polish cavalry, though the second most important branch of the armed forces, was an anachronism. It amounted to 10 percent of the active army, totaling 70,000 men; this was five times the percentage of the German Army and one and a half times that of the French or Soviet army. Moreover, the cavalry was not mechanized; one brigade had been mechanized in 1937, and another began forming in 1939.

The major cavalry unit was the brigade, which had a maneuver mission and could operate independently. Additional cavalry operated as divisional detachments and consisted of traditional cavalry guided by a doctrine based on providing flank security, reconnaissance, and support functions.

The eleven independent brigades consisted of thirty-eight regiments of lancers (Ulans), light horse (Szwolezerow), hussars, and mounted rifles. Four brigades had four regiments; and the remainder had three. Because the training year ended in early September, these units were particularly up to strength at the outbreak of war. Furthermore, because the training cycle lasted twenty-two months, the units had time to develop combat skills. Their mobility also gave the Polish High Command some flexibility, so that, late in the campaign, an attempt was made to improvise cavalry into operational groups of divisional size. (There was a written doctrine for cavalry divisions—prepared in the 1920s—but training had been limited.)

Unfortunately, the cavalry brigade lacked firepower: there were no heavy artillery and few mortars (see Tables 3–14 and 3–15). The cavalry units were well suited neither to defense nor to offense. In given battles, except for a few unique situations, the Polish cavalry accomplished little more than the equivalent infantry formations. They did not live up to the exaggerated expectations of prewar cavalry advocates, but they were exceptionally valuable because of their mobility and durability: when an infantry unit lost a battle, it was usually overrun and destroyed, but the cavalry escaped to fight again and again.

TABLE 3–15
POLISH CAVALRY REGIMENT, TABLE OF ORGANIZATION AND EQUIPMENT, 1939

	Men	Sabres	Rifles	BAR	MG	AT Rifle	AT Gun	Horses	Jeep	Truck	Bikes	Radios
HQ, admin. spt	25	20	16					25	1			
Line sqdns (4)	456	356	420	16		12		456				
MG sqdn	168	4	76		12			190				
AT plat.	36	1	20				4	44				
Signals plat.	52	1	51					47				2
Bicycle plat.	42		36	2		1		1			41	
Support sqdn	33	7	26					26				
Quartermaster	37	12	23					52		2		
TOTALS	842	401	648	18	12	13	4	850	1	2	41	2

TABLE 3–14

POLISH CAVALRY BRIGADE, TABLE OF ORGANIZATION AND EQUIPMENT, 1939

	Men	Sabres	Rifles	BAR	MG	Mortars	AT Rifle	AT Gun	AA Gun	75mm Gun	Horses	Bike	Radio	Vehicles	AFV
HQ & br. spt															
Cavalry regt[1] (3/4)	2526/3368	1320/1800	5200/6350	54/72	36/48		39/52	12/16			2550/3400	123/164	6/8	9/12	
Rifle bn[2]	1066		900	24	12	11	9	2			220	20	1		
Signals sqd	151										124	6		8	
AA bty									2						
Bicycle sqd	216		195	9			3–6				18	196			
Engineer sqd	62		60								18			5	
MG plat.	31		19		3						13				
Artillery bty[3]	765/988	78/104	282/376	2						12/16	276/368		4	25	
Armored trp	96				19										21
AT plat.	36		20					4			44				
TOTALS	6143/7184	1320/1800	4675/5850	89/104	81/95	11	66/78	18/22	2	12/16	5194/6291	345/386	16/18	65/66	21

[1]Polish cavalry brigades in 1939 did not have a homogeneous organization. Standard brigades had three cavalry regiments; reinforced brigades had four. Strength figures for the latter are shown here after the slash. [2]Not all Polish cavalry brigades had an attached rifle battalion in 1939. [3]The strength of the horse artillery batteries varied from 12 to 16 guns.

TABLE 3–16

POLISH CAVALRY BRIGADES, COMPONENT UNITS

Brigade	Regiments	Horse Arty	Armd Gp	AA Bn	Bicycle Sqdn	Engr Sqdn	Sig. Sqdn	Supply	Rifle Bn
Krakowska	3L, 8L, 5R	5th	51st	85th	Yes	Yes	Yes	Yes	4th
Kresowa	20L, 22L, 6R	13th	42nd 61st	33rd	Yes	Yes	Yes	Yes	3rd
Mazowiecka	7L, 11L, 1H	1st	11th	na	Yes	2nd	Yes	Yes	5th
Nowogrodzka	25L, 26L, 27L, 4R	9th	91st	na	Yes	9th	Yes	Yes	None
Podlaska	5L, 10L, 9R	14th	32nd	94th	Yes	1st	Yes	Yes	7th
Podolska	6L, 9L, 14L	6th	62nd	86th	Yes	Yes (+)	Yes	Yes	2nd
Pomorska	16L, 18L, 8R	11th	81st	91st	Yes	Yes	Yes	Yes	none
Suwalska	1L, 2L, 3R, 3H	4th	31st	84th	Yes	11th	11th	Yes	none
Wielkopolska	15L, 17L, 7R	7th	71st	87th	Yes	Yes	Yes	Yes	10th
Wilenska	4L, 13L, 23L	3rd	33rd	83rd	Yes	Yes	Yes	Yes	11th*
Wolynska	12L, 19L, 21L, 2R	2nd	21st	82nd	Yes	Yes	Yes	8th	None
10th Mech.	24L, 10R	16th	101st 102nd	71st	121st Tk Co.	Yes	Yes	Yes	None
Warsaw Mech.	1R, 2H	2nd	11th 12th	7th	12th Tk Co.	Yes	Yes	Yes	None
Wolkowysk	101L, 102L, 110L, 113H				Formation never completed				

*Reinforced by bn. 84th Inf. Regt.

TABLE 3–17
ROSTER OF POLISH CAVALRY REGIMENTS

Regt	Name & Home Station
1H	J. Pilsudski's Light Horse, Warsaw
1L	Col. B. Moscicki's Krechowiecki Lancers, Augustow
1R	Mounted Rifles, Brody
1	Cavalry KOP (3 squadrons on eastern border, 6 on western)
2H	Rokitnianski Light Horse, Warsaw
2L	Gen. J. Dwernicki's Grochowski Lancers, Suwalki
2R	Mounted Rifles, Hrubieszow
3L	Slaski Lancers, Tarnowskie Gory
3R	Hetman S. Czarnecki's Mounted Rifles, Wolkowysk
3H	Col. Kozietulski's Mazowiecki Light Horse, Suwalki
4L	Zaniemenski Lancers, Wilno
4R	Leczycka Region Mounted Rifles, Plock
5L	Zaslawski Lancers, Ostroleka
5R	Mounted Rifles, Debica
6L	Kaniowski Lancers, Stanislawow
6R	Hetman S. Zolkiewski's Mounted Rifles, Zolkiew
7L	Gen. K. Sosnkowski's Lubelski Lancers, Minsk Mazowiecki
7R	Wielkopolski Mounted Rifles, Poznan
8L	Prince J. Poniatowski's Lancers, Krakow
8R	Mounted Rifles, Chelmno
9L	Malopolski Lancers, Tremblocwa
9R	Gen. K. Pulaski Mounted Rifles, Gryjewo
10L	Litewski Lancers, Bialystok
10R	Motorized Mounted Rifles
11L	E. Smigly-Rydz Legionary Lancers, Ciechanow
12L	Podolski Lancers, Krzemieniec
13L	Wilenski Lancers, Nowa Wilejka
14L	Jazlowiecki Lancers, Lwow
15L	Poznanski Lancers, Poznan
16L	Gen. G. Orlicz-Dreszer's Wielkopolski Lancers, Bydgoszcz
17L	King Boleslaw Chrobry's Gnieznienski Lancers, Lezno
18L	Pomorski Lancers, Grudziadz
19L	Gen. E. Rozycki's Wolynski Lancers, Ostrog
20L	King Jan III Sobieski's Lancers, Rzeszow
21L	Nadwislanskich Lancers, Rowne
22L	Podkarpacki Lancers, Brody
23L	Grodzienski Lancers, Postawy
24L	Motorized Lancers
25L	Wielkopolski Lancers, Pruzana
26L	Hetman K. Chodkiewicz's Wielkopolski Lancers, Baranowicze
27L	King Stefan Batory's Lancers, Nieswicz
101L	Lancers, *Not completed*
102L	Lancers, Wilno
110L	Lancers, Grodno
113H	Light Horse, *Not completed*

A lancer troop on patrol before the war. The lance was not commonly used in 1939.

The Polish cavalry regiments, though carrying different designations—lancer, or mounted rifle, and so on—were much the same. The distinction among the regiments was almost entirely traditional and was indicated largely by uniform. (Most cavalry wore old French helmets.) Table 3–16 lists the brigades and their commanders and indicates their component regiments. The brigades carried the name of the region of the country in which they were stationed or bore the name of some historical personage. Regimental units are given in Table 3–17.

ARMOR

Although an armored branch had been established in September 1930, its growth was limited by financial and technical factors, especially the availability of vehicles. Many Polish military leaders, imitating the faulty British and French doctrine, also did not grasp the strategic implications of armor and continued to consider it an infantry and cavalry support force. In fact, the two mechanized brigades (10th, Warsaw) were part of a planned conversion of four cavalry brigades and consisted largely of motorized cavalry and infantry forces. With the exception of a few light tank battalions in high command reserve, the tank units were attached to infantry or cavalry units. The type of independent role evident in German planning was therefore beyond the reach of the Poles for both doctrinal and economic reasons.

Polish cavalry and infantry had attached armor based on tankettes.

Table 4–4, on page 91 , itemizes the specific tank types and their dispositions. There were eighteen scout tank (or tankette) companies assigned to the infantry divisions (see Table 3–18), some of which were later subordinated to army or group command. Each company had four officers and 87 men in two platoons, and was equipped with thirteen tankettes, four trucks with four fuel trailers, seven motorcycles, a radio car, a staff car, and a field kitchen.

Each cavalry brigade included an armored group of two "squadrons." This troop had a headquarters company with four officers and 92 soldiers, two tankettes, an armored car, nine motorcycles, nineteen heavy trucks with three fuel trailers, two staff cars, one radio car, and a field kitchen; an armored car squadron with three officers and 42 men in two platoons equipped with seven armored cars, five motorcycles, three heavy trucks with one fuel trailer, a radio car, and a field kitchen; and a tankette squadron with three officers and 42 men in two platoons and equipped with 11 tankettes, five motorcycles, two heavy trucks with one fuel trailer, one staff car, a radio car, and a field kitchen. These infantry and cavalry component units comprised much of the conventional Polish armored force.

The two mechanized brigades each had two tank reconnaissance "squadrons," consisting of a light truck company, and two motorized rifle

TABLE 3–18
POLISH ARMORED FORCE DISPOSITION, 1 SEPTEMBER 1939

Armored Unit & Commander	Equipment	Peacetime Disposition	Wartime Disposition	
			Army Group	Division, Brigade or Operation Group
11 Armd Gp, Maj. S. Majewski	TKS	Cent. Armd Tng Sch.	Modlin	Mazovian Cav. Br.
21 Armd Gp, Maj. S. Glinski	TKS	12th Armd Bn	Lodz	Wolynian Cav. Br.
31st Armd Gp, Capt. B. Bledzki	TKS	7th Armd Bn	Narew	Suwalska Cav. Br.
32nd Armd Gp, Maj. S. Szostak	TKS	7th Armd Bn	Narew	Podlaski Cav. Br.
33rd Armd Gp, Capt. W. Lubienski	TKS	7th Armd Bn	High Cmd	Wilenski Cav. Br.
51st Armd Gp, Maj. H. Swietlicki	TK	5th Armd Bn	Krakow	Krakowski Cav. Br.
61st Armd Gp, Capt. A. Wojcinski	TKS	6th Armd Bn	Lodz	Kresow Cav. Br.
62nd Armd Gp, Capt. Z. Brodowski	TKS	6th Armd Bn	Poznan	Podolski Cav. Br.
71st Armd Gp, Maj. K. Zolkiewicz	TKS*	1st Armd Bn	Poznan	Wielkopolski Cav. Br.
81st Armd Gp, Maj. F. Szystowski	TK*	8th Armd Bn	Pomorze	Pomorska Cav. Br.
91st Armd Gp, Maj. A. Sliwinski	TK	4th Armd Bn	Modlin	Nowogrodzki Cav. Br.
11th Ind. Sct Tk Co., Lt. J. Pieniazek	TKS*	Cent. Armd Tng Sch.	Lublin	Warsaw Mech. Br.
12th Ind. Sct Tk Co., Capt. S. Letowski	TKS*	Cent. Armd Tng Sch.	Lublin	Warsaw Mech. Br.
31st Ind. Sct Tk Co., Capt. M. Szalek	TKS	7th Armd Bn	Poznan	25th Inf. Div.
32nd Ind. Sct Tk Co., Capt. F. Kazimierczak	TKS	7th Armd Bn	Poznan	10th Inf. Div.
41st Ind. Sct Tk Co., Capt. I. Witanowski	TK	10th Armd Bn	Lodz	30th Inf. Div.
42nd Ind. Sct Tk Co., Capt. M. Grabowski	TK	10th Armd Bn	Lodz	Kresowa Cav. Br.
51st Ind. Sct Tk Co., Capt. K. Poletyllo	TK	5th Armd Bn	Krakow	Opn Gp Bielsko
52nd Ind. Sct Tk Co., Capt. P. Dubicki	TKS	6th Armd Bn	Krakow	Opn Gp Slask
61st Ind. Sct Tk Co., Capt. W. Czaplinski	TKS	6th Armd Bn	Krakow	Opn Gp Slask
62nd Ind. Sct Tk Co., Capt. S. Szapkowski	TKS	6th Armd Bn	Modlin	20th Inf. Div.
63rd Ind. Sct Tk Co., Lt. M. Kosiewicz	TKS	6th Armd Bn	Modlin	8th Inf. Div.
71st Ind. Sct Tk Co., Lt. S. Skibniewski	TKS	1st Armd Bn	Poznan	14th Inf. Div.
72nd Ind. Sct Tk Co., Capt. L. Szczepankowski	TKS	1st Armd Bn	Poznan	17th Inf. Div.
81st Ind. Sct Tk Co., Capt. F. Polkowski	TK	8th Armd Bn	Pomorze	4th Inf. Div.
82nd Ind. Sct Tk Co., Capt. J. Wlodkowski	TKS	8th Armd Bn	Pomorze	15th Inf. Div.
91st Ind. Sct Tk Co., Capt. S. Krainski	TK	4th Armd Bn	Lodz	28th Inf. Div.
92nd Ind. Sct Tk Co., Capt. W. Iwanowski	TK	4th Armd Bn	Lodz	10th Inf. Div.
101st Ind. Sct Tk Co., Lt. Z. Ziemski	TKF*	2nd Armd Bn	Krakow	10th Mech. Br.
121st Ind. Sct Tk Co., W. O. L. Pruszynski	TKS*	2nd Armd Bn	Krakow	10th Mech. Br.
1st Lt Tk Bn, Maj. A. Kubin	7TP jw	3rd Armd Bn	Prusy	High Cmd
2nd Lt Tk Bn, Maj. E. Karpow	7TP jw	2nd Armd Bn	Prusy	High Cmd
21st Lt Tk Bn, Maj. J. Lucki	R-35	12th Armd Bn	Lublin	High Cmd
111st Lt Tk Co., Capt. S. Wlodarski	M-17 FT	2nd Armd Bn	Reserve	
112th Lt Tk Co., Lt. W. Stoklas	M-17 FT	2nd Armd Bn	Reserve	
113th Lt Tk Co., Lt. J. Ostrowski	M-17 FT	2nd Armd Bn	Reserve	
12th Lt Tk Co., Capt. C. Blok	Vickers	Cent. Armd Tng Sch.	Lublin	Warsaw Mech. Br.
121st Lt Tk Co., Lt. Raczkowski	Vickers	2nd Armd Bn	Krakow	10th Mech. Br.

*Tankette unit partially equipped with upgunned 20mm heavy machine gun command tanks.

regiments, with supporting artillery. There were also two battalions and a company of light tanks (7TP), an uncommitted R-35 tank battalion and three companies of light obsolete tanks (M-17 FT) in reserve. The failure to mass the various tank formations, their over-all quality, and their predominantly subsidiary role relegated the armored branch to a subordinate role in the September campaign.

The description of Polish armor must include mention of armored trains. In terms of manpower these usually equaled the number of personnel in the tankette and armored car units. Often the armored train was the only "armor" in a division or brigade, especially after the High Command began improvising mobile reserves. They were of particular importance in areas that depended primarily on rail transportation, instead of developed road networks. The characteristics of these trains are described in the section of this book on weapons; their locations are shown in Table 3-1, except for two later improvised for the defense of Warsaw and one ("Kashub Dragon") for the seacoast command. The Polish armored train disposition is summarized in Table 3–19.

ARTILLERY

Since Napoleonic times, artillery has been the king of battle and, along with mortars, caused most of the casualties in World War II. Polish organic artillery included 93 platoons of infantry guns (one per regiment); 39 light artillery regiments, each having twenty-four 75mm guns and twelve 100mm guns; 30 heavy artillery sections, each having three 105mm guns, and three 155mm howitzers; eleven horse artillery detachments each having three or four batteries (five in the 1st Bn); and a motorized battery in each of the two mechanized brigades.

Antitank guns were allocated at the rate of one company per rifle regiment, one platoon per cavalry regiment; one 37mm antitank gun section with two squadrons per mechanized brigade; one platoon in each reconnaissance section and independent rifle or machine-gun battalion.

Antiaircraft artillery was allocated at the rate of one 40mm battery to each infantry division and cavalry brigade. The infantry divisions and the 10th Mechanized Brigade had a Type A battery with four guns; the cavalry brigades had a Type B battery with two guns. The Warsaw Mechanized Brigade had no organic battery. Most of the Polish artillery was found as components to the field units.

The remaining independent artillery, outside of the units, had fewer pieces, but substantial firepower. There were eight regiments of heavy artillery, each with a section of 105mm guns and 155mm howitzers; three sections of 120mm guns (one motorized); four sections of 155mm howit-

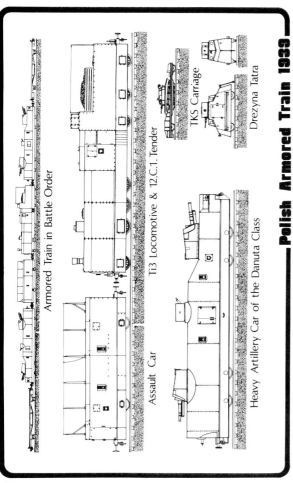

Armored Train in Battle Order

Ti3 Locomotive & 12.C.1. Tender

Assault Car

Heavy Artillery Car of the Danuta Class

TKS Carriage

Drezyna Tatra

Polish Armored Train 1939

TABLE 3-19
POLISH ARMORED TRAIN DISPOSITION, 1 SEPTEMBER 1939

Armored Train & Commander	Peacetime Disposition	Army Group	Division, Brigade, Etc.
			Wartime Disposition
11 Danuta, Capt. B. Korobowicz	1st Armd Tn Gp	Poznan	26th Inf. Div.
12 Poznanczyk, Capt. K. Majewski	1st Armd Tn Gp	Poznan	Wielkopolski Cav. Br.
13 Gen. Sosnkowski, Capt. S. Mlodzianowski	1st Armd Tn Gp	Modlin	High Cmd
14 Paderewski, Capt. J. Zelechowski	1st Armd Tn Gp	Modlin	High Cmd
15 Smierc, Capt. Kubaszewski	1st Armd Tn Gp	Modlin	High Cmd
51 Marszalek, Capt. L. Cymborski	2nd Armd Tn Gp	Krakow	Army Gp Cmd
52 Pilsudczyk, Capt. M. Gonczar	2nd Armd Tn Gp	Krakow	30th Inf. Div.
53 Smialy, Capt. M. Malinowski	2nd Armd Tn Gp	Lodz	Wolynski Cav. Br.
54 Grozny, Capt. J. Rybczynski	2nd Armd Tn Gp	Krakow	Opn Gp Slask
55 Bartosz Glowacki, Capt. J. Podgorski	2nd Armd Tn Gp	Prusy	Opn Gp Wyszkow

The most common artillery piece in the Polish Army in 1939 was the venerable French "soixante-quinze" 75mm field gun of World War I fame.

zers; three superheavy sections of motorized 220mm mortars with two guns per battery; three batteries of 75mm fortress guns; one KOP 75mm battery ("Kleck"); three mountain batteries; and twenty platoons of foreign or obsolescent pieces. There were only three independent antitank units. A great number of semifixed and nonunit antiaircraft artillery units existed, including 82 platoons of 40mm guns and 42 batteries of 75mm guns. None of the 75mm AA guns were within line units, and all were mainly used to protect important installations (factories, airfields, headquarters).

One seventh of the Polish Army consisted of artillery troops. This was comparable to the Soviet Army but less than in Western armies, such as those of Germany and France (with one fifth of their troops in the artillery). In general, the Polish organic units had a third less indirect firepower than comparable German units and usually were also outranged by German weapons. Inferior communications and less efficient ammunition resupply compounded the inferiority. The Germans typically had more modern weapons with superior fire control systems and a more reliable supply of ammunition. The artillery training cycle was similar to that of the infantry and presented like difficulties in mobilization.

ENGINEERS

The engineer branch (sappers and pioneers, not construction troops) constituted 3 percent of the Polish Army. It was an important branch that had been much neglected and reduced since 1920. It was rebuilding slowly after 1936. Financial and technical reasons precluded modernization. At the outbreak of the war the branch was therefore inferior to the Germans in numbers and equipment, although a twenty-four-month training cycle did facilitate higher readiness than in other branches.

When the war broke out, each infantry regiment and motorized regiment had an engineer platoon, whereas cavalry regiments had a squad. Essentially, each active division had an engineer battalion, and each cavalry brigade had a squadron. Outside of the units there were 7 partly motorized army-level battalions, 54 reserve companies, 24 pontoon columns (four heavy), 36 bridging companies (30 for rail bridges), 26 platoons (22 vehicle parks), and 14 electrotechnical platoons. These units could not provide the full range of defensive and rearguard needs of the September campaign, and they were commonly deployed as infantry units.

Most Polish units relied on horse transport because sufficient motor vehicles were lacking and roads in much of rural Poland were not adequate.

COMMUNICATIONS

The signal branch, one of the most outdated branches of the Polish armed forces, included almost 3 percent of the total force. It began serious development in 1931, but it was only in 1935 that adequate organic radios were available to establish communications among major tactical units. Telephone and telegraph provided most of the communication among units, and heavy use was made of liaison planes to provide messenger service.

The decision was also made to increase army communications in both width and depth from the extremely low 1936 level. For example, the Polish infantry division had only nineteen radios, less than a quarter of what was available to French or Russian divisions and a seventh of what was available to a German division. The number of radios was to be tripled (to fifty-six) according to the new plan. Unfortunately, when war broke out, only 30 percent of the plan had been achieved.

Only the essential tactical units had radios or telegraphs. This included most battalions and regiments. Artillery units had the greatest allocation of radios, as well as telephones. A division headquarters had only a telephone company and a signal platoon. The army or group headquarters had a telephone company, a fixed company, a telephone installation company,

A horse-drawn field radio station in operation.

a motorized radio company, a signal park, and a carrier pigeon team. (The Germans had a signal regiment at this level.)

The High Command had a signal company, a long-range radio (W1) platoon, two independent radio platoons, four telephone cable companies, three telephone installation companies, twenty-four independent telephone installation platoons, and four carrier pigeon teams. To compensate for these weak assets, civilian telephone systems were used when possible. For example, the antiaircraft alarm system was based on the postal telephone system and alarm sirens at police stations. An extensive messenger service, including liaison aircraft, was an essential part of the communication system.

Polish signal equipment was often of good quality. The troops also had a twenty-four-month training cycle and a higher state of readiness. Unfortunately, the acute shortage of radios and telephones precluded adequate command and control of tactical units. German reaction time and fire control were therefore much more effective. Polish communications, since they included civilian systems, were particularly vulnerable to interdiction. It was common for tactical units, even armies, to receive messages too late for appropriate action.

AIR FORCE AND ANTIAIRCRAFT

The Polish air force constituted about 2.5 percent of the army and was intended to be employed primarily in a general support role. The modernization plan of 1936–42 was halted by the war. The air force included four Los bomber squadrons (211, 212, 216, 217); eleven Karas scout/bomber squadrons (21, 22, 24, 31, 32, 41, 42, 51, 56, 64, 65); a RWD-14 light bomber squadron (34), and a naval torpedo squadron; twelve squadrons of observation planes, either Czapla (13, 23, 53, 63); or R-XIII (16, 26, 33, 43, 46, 56, 66, and 1st Naval Training); and fifteen P.7 or P.11 fighter squadrons (111–114, 121–123, 131–132, 141–142, 151–152, 161–162). The first-line strength was 388 aircraft versus a planned strength of 688. There were also twelve liaison platoons (1–10, 13, Naval), each with three RWD-8 aircraft, and one transport squadron of nine F-VIIs. The bomber strength was only one fifth of the total planned, and observation aircraft were two thirds of the plan. Both fighter and scout/bomber strengths were close to plan but of obsolescent quality. There were also 950 other aircraft in repair, training units, reserve, or in a liaison role. Organizationally, the Polish air force was unprepared for an offensive role, but could partly accomplish a defensive mission in support of the army. Even if the High Command had intended most of their aircraft for one mission, offensive or ground support, the air force would probably not have been adequate.

The principal fighter in the Polish Air Force in 1939 was the P.11. One of the finest fighters in the world in its day, by 1939 it was obsolete compared to German or Soviet fighters.

As it was, most of the fighters and reconnaissance units were allocated to the field armies, but the High Command retained control of one bomber (eight squadrons) and one fighter brigade (five squadrons) as shown in Table 3-1. This decision dissipated the air force strength among the ground support and offensive and air defense missions, making it impossible to fulfill any of them properly. The air force personnel were particularly well trained, and many escaped to Britain to seek revenge on the Germans. The record of the Polish squadrons in the Royal Air Force, for example, is a distinguished one by any measure, including eighty thousand sorties and the destruction of one thousand German aircraft.

Although included in the artillery branch, a large portion of the antiaircraft guns constituted part of the Polish air defense system in conjunction with the air force. (German doctrine included AA units as part of the air force.) Because of scarce resources, only the most vital installations could be defended, and the units were deployed primarily in western Poland. Warsaw and the coastal area had the strongest defenses, with concentrations at Krakow, Deblin, and Lodz. Cities like Lublin, Lwow, Poznan, Torun, and Wilno were lightly defended. The national air defense consisted of some two hundred guns and the High Command fighter brigade. After 2 September, Germans gained air superiority and operated wherever they chose to deploy bomber units. The lack of Polish planes and guns, coupled with inefficient communication, precluded an efficient air defense.

SUPPLY AND SERVICES

Supply units existed at company level and above. In wartime, civilian assets would be mobilized to augment the military. Thus the supply units came in all shapes and sizes. Light one-horse carts and two-horse wagons were common.

In contrast to modern weaponry at the front, such supply columns would stretch along the roads, impeding maneuvers and slowing combat. The Poles had much less motorization than the Germans, and had barely improved beyond World War I standards. Transport columns were particularly vulnerable to air attack because more time was spent in movement. This typically forced commanders to leave their supply trains well in the rear and to rely on improvised local depots or specially chosen vehicles. This problem naturally compounded for the Polish, because the Germans had air supremacy for most of the campaign.

The Polish Army was also supported by medical and veterinary services. Various maintenance, ordnance, and quartermaster units provided necessary support functions. Together with the supply troops these services constituted almost 7 percent of the total army.

MILITARY POLICE

The Zandarmia (gendarmes) consisted of special police units formed to maintain order and traffic control. They were found in divisions and larger units under a special staff officer. Civilian police units also maintained a paramilitary organization and could be activated for active military duty.

NAVY

The naval units included both ships and units of the coastal defense in the vicinity of Gdynia and Hel, as well as river flotillas. The ships were organized into three divisions—viz., four destroyers, five submarines, and six minesweepers and one minelayer. This third group came under the Naval Coastal Defenses; the other two came under fleet command. Since the capability for naval war was limited, the land forces would be more significant to the September campaign.

The Navy had a KOP battalion "Hel" and two infantry companies with a heavy machine gun platoon, plus artillery and antiaircraft detachments. There were also two naval brigades, antiaircraft, naval artillery and two improvised armored trains. They had the difficult mission of holding the area around Gdynia and between East Prussia and Germany proper.

The Polish Destroyer Flotilla on exercise in the Baltic before the war.

ASPECTS OF ORGANIZATIONAL EFFECTIVENESS

Perhaps the Polish infantry and cavalry hoped to compensate in courage for what the army lacked in equipment. Polish history goes back to the tenth century, and the lineage of most of the regiments goes back to the Polish Army in the Napoleonic wars and to earlier significant battles (especially against Germany). When Columbus was discovering America, the Polish national borders included most of European Russia; and the Poles even controlled Moscow for a time. Poland's location in central Europe involved the country in many wars until its partitions in 1772 and 1795. Polish units and legions fought within Napoleon's army in hopes of reestablishing their country. The French defeat crushed this bid for Polish independence. It was not until after World War I, largely thanks to American pressure and Russian collapse, that the country again appears on the maps of Europe.

Efforts were made to preserve the long military tradition. Special regimental badges were awarded to soldiers who had proven themselves by service or in combat, sometimes in a special ceremony on the regimental day. The names of the Polish regiments, shown in Table 3–11, were sometimes derived from this rich historical heritage. More often, they were based on the historical regional affiliation of the units. Several regiments carried the title "Legion" from the volunteer Polish Legion led by Pilsudski in World War I. The 44th, for example, traced its heritage to a World War I rifle legion of Polish-American volunteers. The 15th Regiment was known as the Wolves' Regiment from its emblem. The name of the 19th Regiment commemorated a battle in the Russo-Polish war. The 36th commemorated the four large colleges in Warsaw. From the Napoleonic period to the end of World War I Poland did not exist on the map of Europe, but Polish units distinguished themselves in other armies. The 42nd, 50th, 51st, 52nd, and 81st included the colors of the House of Savoy in North Italy, and Francesco Nullo was an Italian who fought in the 1863 revolution. The 42nd, 43rd, 49th, and 52nd were once affiliated with France. The 32nd and 86th had a heritage from the Polesie (Byelorussia) region. The 76th and 77th Regiments could claim roots in the historic alliance between Poland and Lithuania. Silesian eagles are a part of the badges of the 73rd and 75th Regiments. Other regiments commemorated the names of famous Polish leaders.

The designation "rifles" was also used to symbolically differentiate units. Table 3–11 also shows some coat-of-arms descriptions of the units (in parentheses since these did not serve as official names).

The cavalry units were similarly distinguished by regional names or by the names of places, national heroes, or Polish kings. The 3rd Light Horse regiment, for example, traced its roots to the Mazovian region and to the colonel who led the equivalent French (Polish) Imperial Guard unit in 1807. The 8th Lancers (and 37th Infantry) commemorated Prince Joseph Poniatowski, a marshal of the French Empire, and commander of the army of the Grand Duchy of Warsaw. It should also be mentioned that the Polish

Polish light horse regiments wore a round garrison gap in place of the square rogatywka worn in other army units.

cavalry "regiments" are really of a battalion size (similar to British units). The heritage of the units was most prominent in the uniform and accoutrements of the lancers, light horse, or mounted rifles (dragoons). These units went into battle fully equipped with sabres.

The honorary significance of unit identification added character to the regimental ciphers and could inspire an added spark of patriotism at critical times. Unfortunately for the Polish, World War II casualty statistics indicate that most combat losses (60 percent) result from artillery and mortar shells, not from an infantryman's or cavalryman's individual courage. The bravery of flesh and blood could not make up for a lack of weapons and equipment.

The steel in a soldier's soul would not shield him from exploding shell and shrapnel. The Polish allies betrayed their trust and condemned Poland to hope and sacrifice for a lost cause; an old (and new) story. The words of the Polish national anthem echo the stoic resignation of the brave soldiers who fought in 1939. Heroism is measured by the hopelessness of the situation. Any soldier can fight when adequately prepared and equipped with the newest technology. Struggling against overwhelming numbers and resources requires true courage.

RESURRECTION: THE POLISH ARMY AFTER THE SEPTEMBER CAMPAIGN

How many men served in the Polish armed forces in the September campaign? From the chaos of war, it has never been possible to establish firm figures, but if we total the known dead, the German and Russian claims of captured Poles, and if, to those figures, we add those who escaped to fight again, we can say that perhaps 1.1 million Polish men were mobilized in September 1939 to fight in defense of their homeland.

The defeat in Poland itself was not the end of the story. Polish formations were created in France as early as 9 September 1939. And by June 1940 those soldiers who had escaped to Hungary and Romania raised the total of Poles fighting abroad to 84,500. An army was mobilized under General Sikorski in Syria, Britain, and France, and by 1945 it had grown to over 220,000 men. The Russians, too, began mobilizing Polish units in 1943, and by August 1944 had raised an army of 108,000. With the incorporation of Polish territory and former underground units, this army grew to over 300,000.

In all, Poland lost 320,000 soldiers in World War II, if we include all these formations. At least half of these men died in the September campaign. To see those losses in perspective, we should recall that the United States Army lost only 300,000 men in the European and Pacific theaters combined.

4. Equipment of the Polish Armed Forces

SMALL ARMS

During the Russo-Polish War, the Polish Army was equipped with a hodgepodge of weapons, including even Mexican and Japanese rifles. After the war, efforts were made to standardize small arms by selling off some of the more obscure types. By 1925, fourteen infantry divisions were equipped with French rifles (mainly the Lebel Model 86/93 rifle, Berthier Model 07/15-16 rifle and Berthier Model 92/16 carbine); fourteen infantry divisions used German rifles (mainly the Mauser Model 98 rifle and carbines); and two divisions used Austrian rifles (mainly the Mannlicher Model 88 and Model 95 rifles and the Model 95 carbine). The Russian Moisin Models 91/98 carbine was in use with the cavalry, and in 1925 it was rechambered to fire Mauser ammunition, becoming the wz.25 (for *wzor,* model).

Although the army had hoped to standardize on a single rifle, economic difficulties forced this program to drag on for nearly two decades. The Mauser Model 98 was selected not only because of its modernity, but because the Poles had received the Danzig Mauser factory in war reparations. The machine tools were transferred to the Warsaw Rifle Factory, and production of the wz.98 rifle began in 1922. Experience indicated that the shorter wz.98 carbine was preferable, leading to selection of this weapon as the standard Polish rifle. Production in Warsaw began in 1924, completely supplanting the wz.98 rifle by 1926. There was some dissatisfaction with the wz.98 carbine, partially caused by the use of the new Type S high-velocity round. As a result, an improved version, the wz.29 carbine was developed. Production of this weapon began in 1930 at the National Weapons Factory in Radom (PFB) and some of the older wz.98 were modernized to wz.29 standards by Arsenal Nr. 2 in Warsaw. Radom manufactured 264,000 wz.29 carbines by the time of the war's outbreak, of which about 7900 were exported. The Sepewe organization exported over

140,000 older rifles during this period as well. At the time of the 1939 war, the Polish Army possessed 1.2 million rifles of which 31 percent were the various long rifles, and 69 percent were the carbines. First-line infantry divisions and the cavalry were equipped predominently with the Mauser rifles and carbines, the older French and Russian rifles being used primarily by National Guard infantry, border guards, rear service elements, and certain reserve formations.

The principal pistol of the Polish Army was the 9mm wz.35 ViS, which was heavily based on the American Colt .45. Production was undertaken at Radom, and about 18,000 were produced by 1939. They were used by officers and professional NCOs. There were a variety of other foreign pistols in service in 1939, the most common of which was the Nagant Model 93 revolver, of which 7166 had been produced at PFB from 1931 to 1935 prior to the introduction of the ViS.

At war's outbreak, there were two automatic weapons under development for the Polish Army. An automatic rifle had been developed by J. Maroszek, designated the kb sp M (wz.38), and several hundred had been built in Radom by 1939. In 1936 the KOP received small numbers of Thompson submachine guns, and the 1st Gendarme Detachment purchased small numbers of Finnish Suomi submachine guns. In 1939 the Warsaw Rifle Factory began limited production of the wz.39 Mors submachine gun, which resembled the Suomi. About fifty of the completed guns were used by the 3rd Infantry Regiment in the Warsaw fighting and by the 39th Infantry Division elsewhere.

One of the most secret weapons developed in Poland was the 7.92mm Kb ppanc wz.35 "Ur" antitank rifle. This rifle was remarkable both for its light weight and for its excellent antitank performance. It was capable of penetrating 33mm of armor at one hundred meters, enabling it to penetrate most German tanks of the period. This was made possible by a revolutionary tungsten-carbide-core SC round which was later successfully copied by the Germans for tank rounds. A total of about 3500 were produced before the war, with 92 per infantry division and 66 to 78 per cavalry brigade. The rifles were kept sealed until mobilization, with stamps indicating "Rifles for Uruguay" on the boxes, hence the Ur name. They were not issued until the war's outbreak, but this did not hamper their use, since they worked like any standard bolt-action rifle. They proved very effective in 1939.

The Polish Army used the French Model 15 Chauchat as its squad automatic weapon in 1920. These were modified to fire 7.92mm ammunition after the war and were used by some reserve units in 1939. The standard squad automatic weapon was the rkm wz.28, a licensed version of the

Browning automatic rifle (BAR) Model 1918 in 7.92mm. By the outbreak of war, over ten thousand had been manufactured, primarily by PFK, and 1445 exported. They were used by both the cavalry and the infantry, an infantry division having 326 and a cavalry brigade (three regiments) having 80. There were some older Austrian Model 08/15 and Bergman Model 15 light machine guns in use in 1939, primarily by artillery units for local defense.

The three main types of machine guns in Polish service in 1920 were the Maxim Model 08, the Hotchkiss Model 14, and the Schwarzlose 07/12. The Maxims included a variety of models and there were a number of attempts to standardize them and provide them with more modern bases. For example, the Russian Model 05S was modified in 1928–29 to fire 7.92mm ammunition as the Model 10/28. In 1939, the Model 08 was used as the standard heavy machine gun of reserve infantry regiments, reserve cavalry regiments (on wheeled taczankas), in antiaircraft heavy machine-gun companies, in independent heavy machine-gun companies, and in National Guard battalions. Similarly, the Hotchkiss Model 14 was used by some

The standard machine gun of the Polish Army in 1939 was the ckm wz.30, an unlicensed copy of the American Browning water-cooled machine gun.

reserve and National Guard battalions, but most were in poor technical shape by 1939. Some of the Model 25 and Model 30 guns were obtained and used by light artillery batteries, horse artillery batteries, KOP battalions and as armored vehicle weapons. About twenty-four Model 30s were used by the Navy's 1st AA Artillery Regiment for air defense. The relegation of these weapons to reserve formations had been made possible by the production of an unlicensed copy of the Browning water-cooled machine gun, designed to fire standard Polish 7.92mm ammunition. This entered production at PFK in Warsaw in 1930 as the ckm wz.30. It was mounted mainly on the wz.30 tripod, but a small number of cavalry units received it on the wz.34 tripod, which permitted its use in the antiaircraft role as well. By 1939, it equipped all the active infantry divisions, some reserve infantry regiments and many cavalry regiments. Infantry division heavy machine-gun companies had twelve, nine with horse-drawn carriages for carrying additional ammunition and three on taczankas.

Taczankas were small carriages towed by three horses with the machine gun firing over the rear. They were developed primarily for cavalry use. Each infantry division had 132 wz. 30 machine guns, and the four-regiment cavalry brigade had 95. In contrast to the infantry, most cavalry machine guns were on taczankas. There were two types of taczankas. The older wz.28 was designed for the heavy Maxim Model 08 fitted with a Schwarzlose sledge mount. These were gradually replaced by the wz.37, which was hinged in the center to provide better turning and was designed for the wz.30 machine gun. The wz.30 did not entirely replace the older Maxim in

In the cavalry, machine guns were carried on taczankas. These carts, first employed in the 1920 war, provided a mobile firing platform.
This particular taczanka is one of the earlier wz.30 types.

the cavalry by 1939. A motorized taczanka was developed for mechanized units, and this consisted of a wz.30 on a special antiaircraft mount fitted in the rearbed of a modified Polski-Fiat 508/518 Lazik jeep known as the 320T. About 86 of these were ordered in 1938 and served with the 10th Mechanized and Warsaw Mechanized Brigades.

The Polish Army had a large stockpile of various types of grenades, but gradually disposed of them in favor of the wz.31 defensive and offensive grenades. These were similar in appearance to American concussion and "pineapple" fragmentation grenades.

Fire support in both cavalry and infantry units was provided by the wz.30 and wz.36 platoon mortars. These were small 46mm mortars of

Fire support for infantry was provided by these peculiar 46mm mortars, the initial wz.30 shown in the foreground, and the more common wz.36 (minus its baseplate) in the background.

TABLE 4–1
SMALL ARMS

Name	ViS	Mors	Mauser	Ur	rkm	ckm	granatnik	Stokes
Model	wz. 35	wz. 38	wz. 98	wz. 35	wz. 28	wz. 30	wz. 36	wz. 31
Type	Pistol	Sub-MG	Carbine	AT rifle	Lt MG	Hvy MG	Mortar	Mortar
Caliber	9mm	9mm	7.92mm	7.92mm	7.92mm	7.92mm	46mm	81mm
Weight (kg)	1.0	4.2	4.0	9.1	9.5	14.5	8.0	53.5
Length (mm)	200	930	1090	1760	1215	1200	640	
Rate of fire (min)	30	400	12	6	60	450	15	20
Range (m)	50	100	300	500	1100	4500	800	3200
Magazine (rounds)	8	25	5	1	20	350	1	1
Projectile wt. (g)	11.7	11.7	23.9	12.8	23.9	23.9	760	3400
Muzzle vel. (m/s)	345	400	840	1275	853	845	95	210

Polish design which fired a 0.76 kg round. The wz.30 had a range of 700 meters and the wz.36 had a range of 800 meters. About 3850 were produced up to 1939 and there were 81 per infantry division, with three per infantry company. During the 1920 war, the Polish Army had used various German and French mortars, but these were phased out after the war in favor of Stokes 81mm Model 18 mortars acquired in France beginning in 1923 and totaling about seven hundred by 1926. The Poles began unlicensed production of the ammunition. In 1930, the Poles began production of a locally developed mortar, the Avia wz.28, and seven hundred were built in 1930–31. Further production was halted in 1932 as the French Brandt firm had learned that the Poles were producing 81mm ammunition to which Brandt had the patents and were not paying royalties. Due to French pressure, the Poles settled the claim by buying rights to the wz.31 Stokes-Brandt mortar and ammunition. About 1050 were purchased from 1935 to 1938 by ZSMPzA in Pruszkow. In 1939, the Polish Army had about 1200 81mm mortars, mostly the wz.31. Distribution of the mortars was uneven due to uncompleted plans to equip each infantry battalion with four mortars. Independent heavy machine gun companies had six to nine mortars, KOP battalion had two mortars, and cavalry regiments had two mortars.

The Polish cavalry used a wide variety of foreign cavalry sabres of various French, German, and Russian types. The newer wz.21/22 sabres in officer and trooper patterns were produced by the G. Borowski, W. Gorzkowski, and A. Mann firms. In 1935, the Ludwikow Mill began production of the modified wz.34 sabre. Sabres were also permitted for officers in other branches of the service, though they were often not carried in combat. As of 1936, the Polish Army still had 9907 French cavalry lances and 1323 German cavalry lances in inventory. They were still commonly used for cavalry training, although in 1934 they had been officially dropped as a cavalry weapon. In 1939 a few cavalry regiments still carried some in the baggage trains, but their only common use was to carry regimental pennons, not as weapons.

ARTILLERY

Besides the Ur antitank rifles, Polish units were equipped with the wz.36 37mm antitank gun. This gun was a licensed version of the Swedish Bofors 37mm antitank gun. An initial order was placed with Bofors in 1937 for three hundred guns which were manufactured in Sweden and assembled in Poland. Subsequent production was undertaken by SMPzA in Pruszkow; by 1939 the Polish Army had about twelve hundred of these guns. The Polish version had a number of modifications from the Swedish original.

The Bofors was one of the finest light guns of the period, being lighter than the German 37mm PaK 36, and having 17 percent better armor penetration. The wz.36 could penetrate 40mm of armor at 30 degrees at a range of 100m, 33mm at 500m and 26mm at 1000m. Polish sources credit it with accounting for 120 to 150 German tanks and 100 armored cars in the 1939 fighting. Active infantry regiments had nine guns, as did the reserve regiments of the 33rd and 36th Reserve Infantry Divisions. The remaining reserve divisions each had a four-gun company. The KOP battalions had a three-gun platoon, and rifle battalions attached to cavalry brigades had a two-gun platoon. In the cavalry, first-line regiments had a four-gun platoon while second-line regiments had two-gun platoons. KOP cavalry regiments had six-gun platoons. The mechanized brigades had 27–28 Bofors guns, and during the defense of Warsaw, three motorized antitank companies numbered 11 to 13 were formed with 27 guns each. Nearly all of the wz.36 guns were horse-drawn, the exception being those of the mechanized brigades and motorized AT companies, which used PZInz 302T artillery tractors, a derivative of the Lazik jeep.

The horse artillery batteries (or dak, dywizjon artylerii konnej) of the cavalry were mainly equipped with the 75mm wz.02/26 field gun. This was a rechambered version of the Russian Putilov 3-inch divisional gun adapted to fire French 75mm ammunition. In 1939, the Polish Army had

The cavalry's horse artillery units were equipped with Russian Putilov Model 02 field guns that had been rechambered to fire French 75mm ammunition. These were used with surprisingly good effect against German tanks in 1939.

466 of these guns, twelve to sixteen per dak, and two in each infantry regiment artillery platoon. In spite of the antiquity of this gun, it proved surprisingly successful in 1939 against tanks, largely due to the quality of the horse artillery crews, who were considered by many to be the "cream of the cream" in the cavalry. Each infantry division was equipped with a light artillery regiment (or pal, pulk artylerii lekkiej) with twenty-four 75mm wz.97 field guns and twelve 100mm wz.14/19 howitzers. The 75mm guns were the famous French "soixante-quinze" of World War I fame, and there were 1374 of these in the Polish Army in 1939. The 100mm howitzer was the Model 14/18 P howitzer manufactured by Skoda in Plzen. A small number were purchased, along with production rights. There were several versions, including the modernized wz.4 and wz.38. There were about nine hundred in the Polish Army in 1939, and there were twelve in each infantry pal.

There were three main heavy artillery pieces in Polish use in 1939, the 105mm Schneider Model 13 and Model 29 gun, the 120mm Schneider Model 78/09/31 gun, and the 155mm Schneider Model 17 howitzer. A small number of the 105mm Model 13 guns had been obtained in 1920, and were followed by purchase of some Model 28 after the war. In 1934, production of the modernized Model 29/34 105mm gun was undertaken by two Polish factories, and in 1939 there were 254 guns of these models in service. The heavy artillery battalions (or dac, dywizjon artylerii ciezkiej) of the infantry divisions had a three-gun battery of these and a three-gun battery of 155mm howitzers. Heavy artillery regiments (or pac, pulk artylerii ciezkiej) had two battalions, one with nine 105mm guns in three batteries and another with nine 155mm howitzers. The 155mm Schneider Model 17 howitzer was used in the heavy artillery regiments and heavy artillery battalions as mentioned, as well as in the 60th, 88th, 95th, and 98th Independent Heavy Artillery Battalions, each with nine howitzers in three batteries. These had been obtained from France, and there were 340 in service in 1939. There were 43 of the old Schneider 120mm Model 78/09/31 guns in service in 1939. These had been modernized using Russian 6-inch gun tubes. They served in the 6th Motorized Heavy Artillery Battalion, and in the 46th and 47th Heavy Artillery Battalions, each with nine guns.

During the mid-1930s, the Polish Army began to modernize its artillery force by motorizing a number of units, using the new C4P half-track artillery tractor. Since all of the existing artillery pieces were designed for horse draft, they had to be modified for motor towing. This mainly involved the addition of new rubber-tired wheels, and improvements to the suspension. Several of the artillery pieces were modernized in this fashion, notably small numbers of 75mm Model 97 guns, 105mm Model 29 guns,

120mm Model 31 guns, and 155mm Model 17 howitzers. The Polish Army had two new artillery pieces in development in 1939 which did not enter service in any quantity due to the war's outbreak. The Starachowice Works had developed an excellent 155mm long-range gun, the wz.39. A 120mm breech-loading mortar had also been developed.

The only superheavy artillery of the Polish Army were twenty-seven 220mm Skoda Model 32 heavy mortars, which equipped the 1st Superheavy Artillery Regiment. These had an effective range of ten kilometers and fired a 128kg high-explosive projectile. They were towed in three parts—tube, trunnion, and base plate—by C7P tracked artillery tractors.

The Polish Army also had three batteries of old Model 06 65mm mountain guns. The 151st and 152nd Mountain Gun Batteries served with the 1st

The heaviest weapon in the Polish arsenal was the Skoda 220mm mortar, which is seen here being towed in its component form by C7P tracked artillery vehicles.

TABLE 4–2
FIELD GUNS

Caliber Model Type	75mm wz. 97 Field gun	75mm wz. 02/26 Field gun	100mm wz. 14/19 Howitzer	105mm wz. 29 Gun	120mm wz. 09/31 Gun	155mm wz. 17 Howitzer	220mm wz. 32 Mortar
Barrel L (caliber)	36	30	24	31	27	15	19
Firing wt. (tonnes)	1.2	1.1	1.5	2.8	3.5	3.3	13.7
Max. elev. (degrees)	18	11	48	43	42	42	75
Max. range (km)	11.2	10.7	10.0	15.2	12.4	11.2	15.0
Projectile wt. (kg)	7.9	7.9	16.0	15.7	20.3	43.4	128.0
Rate of fire (min)	12	10	8	6	3–4	3	1
1939 Inventory	1374	466	900	254	43	340	27

TABLE 4–3
ANTITANK AND AIR DEFENSE ARTILLERY

Caliber	37mm	40mm	75mm	75mm
Model	wz. 36	wz. 36	wz. 14	wz. 36
Type	AT gun	AA gun	AA gun	AA gun
Barrel L (caliber)	45	56.2	36	50
Firing wt. (tonnes)	0.4	1.7	7.0	3.7
Max. elev. (degrees)	25	90	70	85
Max. range (km)	7.1	3.9	6.5	14.5
Projectile wt. (kg)	1.4	0.9	7.3	6.5
Rate of fire (min)	10	120	20	25
1939 Inventory	1200	306	12 (110)	44

Mountain Brigade, and the 153rd with the 2nd Mountain Brigade. There were twenty-eight two-gun platoons of fortress artillery equipped with 75mm wz.02/26 guns scattered along the frontier. Some of the fortresses were also equipped with 37mm guns in embrasure mounts. The Seacoast Defense Force had two concentrations of artillery. There was a variety of towed artillery pieces with the naval infantry units around Oksywie. The naval base at Hel had the 31st Battery of the Coastal Artillery Battalion equipped with four emplaced Bofors 152mm Model 30 coastal guns, which were used with some success against the Kriegsmarine in 1939. The battalion also had conventional towed artillery.

Polish antiaircraft units used a variety of machine guns, and three main types of artillery, the 40mm wz.36 autocannon, the 75mm wz.14 self-propelled gun, and the 75mm wz.36 heavy gun. The 40mm wz.36 was a licensed version of the Swedish Bofors 40mm autocannon. A total of 68 were purchased in Sweden up to 1938 when production began in Poland. A total of 168 were exported to England, Romania, and Holland up to 1939. In 1939, the Polish Army had 306 guns of this type in 35 batteries and 93 platoons. In 1936, design and production began of the small C2P tractors, based on the TKS tankette, which were used to tow the 40mm antiaircraft guns. During the 1939 fighting, the 40mm guns were used not only for air defense, but for antitank defense as well. The 75mm wz.14 self-propelled antitank gun was a French weapon originally mounted on a Dion Bouton truck. In the 1930s, twelve of these were remounted on the more modern Polski-Fiat 621L truck. Besides the self-propelled version serving with the 1st Antiaircraft Artillery Regiment, there were three other versions of French 75mm antiaircraft guns in service in 1939. There were two of the mobile towed Model 17 guns, 82 examples of the Model 97 and 97/25 semimobile guns and 14 examples of the Model 22/24 static gun. In all, this amounted to forty-six 75mm batteries using the older French guns. The

The most numerous Polish antiaircraft gun was the Bofors 40mm
gun, license-produced in Poland.

*The wz.36 75mm antiaircraft gun was designed and manufactured in Poland.
There were too few available in 1939 to provide an adequate air defense of major
Polish installations.*

most modern antiaircraft gun in service in 1939 was the 75mm wz.36 semiautomatic AA gun. This was designed and built at the Starachowice Works, and 44 of a planned 460 were completed before the outbreak of the war. It had a rate of fire of 20–25 rounds per minute and a maximum range of 14.5 kilometers. A special towing vehicle, the PZInz 342 was developed for its units along with other specialized equipment including searchlights and sound-detection systems.

ARMORED VEHICLES

Although the Polish armored force could hardly compare to that of the Red Army or Wehrmacht, it was still larger, and in some respects more modern, than the tank units of the United States Army of the time. At war's outbreak, the Polish Army possessed about 887 tanks, 100 armored cars, and 10 armored trains. The most numerous type of tank was not a tank at all, but the TK and TKS tankettes. These were small, turretless armored scout vehicles having a two-man crew. Their sole armament was a 7.92mm Hotchkiss machine gun. A total of 300 TK tankettes (and minor deriva-

The most common armored vehicle in the Polish Army was the TKS tankette, seen here being carried on auto-transporters. These auto-transporters, an ingenious device powered by the tankette's engine, allowed the vehicle to be moved long distances without wear on the track. Short track life was a major weakness in 1930s tank design, and led to frequent mechanical breakdowns.

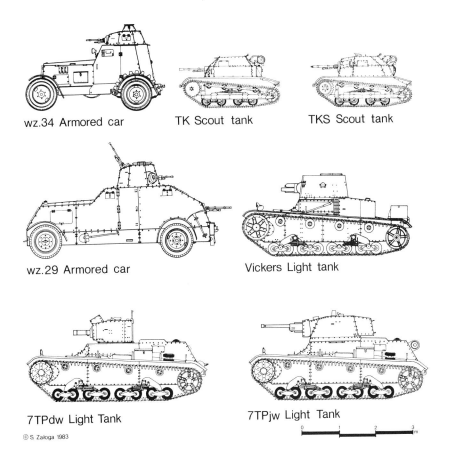

wz.34 Armored car   TK Scout tank   TKS Scout tank

wz.29 Armored car   Vickers Light tank

7TPdw Light Tank   7TPjw Light Tank

© S. Załoga 1983

tives) and 293 TKS tankettes had been built, of which about 574 were in service in 1939. Many of these, especially the older TKs, were in poor mechanical condition because of a lack of spare parts. They equipped independent scout companies attached to infantry divisions, and armored troops of cavalry brigades, with thirteen tankettes in each of these units. They were also used for rail scouting in armored train units. In 1939, some of the TKS began to be rearmed with 20mm NKM autocannons. Only about twenty-four were modified by September, with eight each going to the mechanized brigades and the remainder to the cavalry brigades. These were the only tankettes that were capable of dealing with German tanks. The other tankettes were not supposed to be used against enemy tanks due to the weakness of their firepower, and were intended mainly for scouting or attacking enemy infantry.

The mechanized cavalry brigades each had a company of these modified British Vickers tanks in service in 1939. The Polish 7TP tank was derived from the Vickers.

Poland's best tank in the 1939 campaign was the 7TP, seen here in the more common single-turret version.

In 1931, Poland purchased thirty-eight Vickers E light tanks. Of these, twenty-two were later equipped with a single turret and 47mm gun and the remainder had twin turrets armed with machine guns. Although neither of these guns was well suited to tank warfare, the Vickers served with great success in 1939 as the principal tank of the two mechanized brigades. In 1935, the Polish Army ordered a Polish version of the Vickers which had been improved through the addition of a new diesel engine, giving the tank better speed. The initial version, the 7TPdw, had two turrets, each with a wz. 30 7.92mm machine gun. About forty of these were in service in 1939. The later version, the 7TPjw, had a new single turret with a 37mm Bofors gun. This was the best tank in Polish service in 1939 and about ninety-five were in service. The Poles had also developed a cavalry tank with Christie suspension, the 10TP, but only prototypes had been completed by 1939. Also, plans were under way to replace the tankettes with the 4TP light tank, armed with a 20mm gun; only prototypes had been completed by September. Generally speaking, the TK and TKS tankettes were inferior to any tank in German service in 1939, while the 7TPjw was superior to any tank in German service with the exception of the PzKpfw III and PzKpfw IV medium tanks.

Besides the tanks of Polish design, the Polish Army had 102 obsolete FT-17s. These were French tanks of World War I vintage. About half were used by the armored train units for scouting, and the remainder were used by three independent companies which saw combat around Brzesc in the third week of the fighting. The Poles received a battalion of fifty Renault R-35 infantry tanks which equipped the 21st Tank Battalion. The battalion was only partly trained and was withdrawn into Romania without seeing any fighting. A small number of R-35s in an improvised unit did see some fighting, however. Poland received a few Hotchkiss H-38 tanks for trials, and at least one British Matilda infantry tank in August 1939.

TABLE 4–4
ARMORED VEHICLES

Designation	TK	TKS	Vickers	7TPdw	7TPjw	wz. 29 AC	wz. 34 AC
Length (cm)	258	258	487	488	488	549	375
Width (cm)	178	178	241	243	243	195	195
Height (cm)	132	160	208	219	230	248	222
Weight (tonnes)	2.4	2.6	7.4	9.4	9.9	4.8	2.4
Crew	2	2	3	3	3	4	2
Main armament	mg	mg	47mm gun	2 × mg	37mm gun	37mm gun	37mm gun
Engine (hp)	40	42	92	110	110	35	23
Max. speed (km/h)	46	40	35	32	37	35	55
Armor (mm)	3–8	3–10	5–13	5–17	5–17	4–10	6–8
1939 Inventory	250	300	38	40	95	8	80

The cavalry armored troops each had eight armored cars. All these units except the 11th Armored Troop were equipped with the wz.34 armored car, the 11th using the older wz.29 Ursus armored car. The wz.34 was a small, two-man armored car. About a third of the wz.34 were armed with a single 7.92mm machine gun, and the remainder with a 37mm SA.18 gun. The Ursus was a larger vehicle with mixed 37mm gun and machine gun armament. Both types of armored cars had poor cross-country performance and were not comparable to the more modern German armored cars.

The Polish Army fielded ten armored trains in 1939. These were used to provide mobile fire support for infantry and cavalry units. They had proved extremely useful in 1920, and although the Luftwaffe undercut their utility in 1939, they enjoyed modest success in 1939 if only because of the tenacity and imagination of their crews. The combat portion of the train consisted of an armored locomotive, an assault car carrying an infantry unit and machine guns, and two artillery cars with machine guns and turreted artillery pieces. The class of the train was determined by the number and caliber of guns in the artillery cars. Additional flatcars were

The standard armored car of Polish cavalry armored troops was the wz.34 Ursus, this particular version being armed with the 37mm gun.

Armored train 53 Smialy on patrol before the war. The Smialy was used with considerable success in support of the Wolynski Cavalry Brigade against the German 4th Panzer Division at the battle of Mokra on 1 September 1939.

attached at either end to carry supplies, tankettes, and equipment, and the armored train was accompanied by a supply train having sleeping quarters for the crew. Of the trains in 1939, five were of Polish construction, three of Russian construction, and two of Austrian construction. The captured Russian and Austrian trains had been rebuilt by the Poles after 1920, however, and modernized in various ways. Armored trains had their own tank detachments, which rode on special self-propelled rail trailers. The FT tank or tankette rail transporters rode along the tracks ahead of the train to scout, and could be used to attack enemy infantry away from the train. The light armored trains (PP 15, 55) were equipped with only a single gun on each artillery car. The medium armored trains (PP 13, 51, and 54) each had two 75mm guns (although PP 54 had a 100mm howitzer in place of one 75mm gun). The remaining heavy armored trains (PP 11, 12, 14, 52, and 53) had various armament, which usually included a gun in the 75mm range and a 100mm howitzer on each of their two artillery cars. A number of improvised armored trains were built during the 1939 fighting in Warsaw and in Gdynia on the coast. The Germans used a number of armored trains in Poland, including some captured Czech trains. There were no confrontations between these trains, though there were a few battles between Polish armored trains and German tanks, with the tanks inevitably being blasted by the much heavier firepower of the trains. Most of the trains were lost when they were trapped in various pockets or when key rail bridges were taken. Four were knocked out by air attacks.

VEHICLES

The Polish Army used a variety of motorcycles, primarily those manufactured by the PZInz Factory in Warsaw under the Sokol label. The most important types include the Sokol 1000 (3400 built), with a 1000cc engine, the Sokol 600 (1800 built), with a 575cc engine, and the Sokol 200 (800 built). Although the entire production runs were not bought by the army, many were drafted into army use in 1939. Likewise, the army subsidized vehicle purchase by Polish industries, and in time of war, the trucks or cars, generally of the same pattern as army vehicles, were absorbed into the army.

Probably the car most typical of the Polish Army was the Poski-Fiat 508/518 series. These were popularly called Lazik (jeeps) and were based on an Italian sedan with body modifications more suitable for army use, such as a pedestal mount for a light machine gun. Total production was about 1500 Laziks and 400 of the PZInz 302T gun tractor version. Over 7300 Polski-Fiat 508s of all types were built, many of which were taken over by the army in 1939. A total of 1200 of the improved Polski-Fiat 518 Mazurs were built; they were more powerful and had a strengthened chassis. The Laziks were used as staff cars, for scouting, and for towing light guns, engineering equipment, or communications gear.

The standard truck of the Polish Army was the Polski-Fiat 621 series, of which 13,000 were built from 1933–39 by PZInz for both military and civilian clients. Most ended up in army service. Of these 9,300 were the

The standard staff car of the Polish Army was the Polski-Fiat 508 Lazik, a derivative of an Italian sedan.

The standard truck of the Polish Army was the Polski-Fiat 621L, seen here carrying a field kitchen.

621L heavy truck version, 2,870 were the 621R bus, 330 were the army field hospital or workshop types, and 400 were the half-track type C4P artillery tractor or half-track ambulance. There were also several hundred of the old Ursus A trucks in service in 1939. The Polski-Fiat 618 truck was built in small numbers, about 600, and had a carrying capacity of 1500 kg. There were also a number of imported trucks in Polish Army service as well as small numbers of experimental types. These included the PZInz 342 heavy truck used to tow the 75mm wz.36 AA gun, the PZInz 312 artillery tractor, the PZInz 202 and 222 half-tracks used by mechanized cavalry squadrons, and the PZInz 303 all-terrain light truck. However, when Poland went to war in 1939, its units, except for a handful of mechanized and armored units, were primarily horse-drawn, with very small numbers of trucks and jeeps in the infantry, artillery or cavalry units.

Besides the wheeled transport vehicles, the Polish Army fielded two fully tracked transport vehicles, the C2P and C7P, based on armored vehicles. The C2P was a small artillery tractor based on the TKS tankette and used primarily to tow 40mm antiaircraft guns. A total of 196 of the first series were completed, but it is uncertain how many of the second series of 117 vehicles was completed in 1939. The C7P was a heavy artillery tractor based on the 7TP tank chassis. A total of 76 were built. These were used by the 1st Superheavy Artillery Regiment for towing Skoda mortars, and each Vickers and 7TP light tank company had two C7P for recovery work.

AIRCRAFT

The principal fighter aircraft of the Polish Air Force were the P.7 and its improved derivative, the P.11c. They were parasol gullwing aircraft with fixed undercarriages. The P.7 was armed only with two 7.7mm machine guns, while the P.11 had 2–4 machine guns. The P.7 had a maximum speed of 327 km/h; the P.11 was a bit faster at 343 km/h. Neither aircraft had the speed or firepower of the German Bf-109, but the P.11 was more maneuverable and in skilled hands could deal with the Bf-109. Strangely, Polish pilots feared the Bf-110 more than the Bf-109, presumably because of its tremendous firepower in frontal attack. In 1939, there were 185 P.11 and 115 P.7. However, only thirty P.7 were with combat units and many of the remainder were undergoing repair or were stationed with training units.

Numerically, the most important Polish aircraft was the P.23 Karas, appropriately named after the ungainly freshwater carp. The P.23 was a three-seat, single-engine monoplane, similar in conception and design to the American O-46. It was intended for scouting and light bombing and was heavily patterned after the 1920 experiences. It had a mediocre bomb load of only 400 kg when operating off grass strips. Its main attribute was

Some of the older P.7 fighters were still in use in 1939. These are from the 142nd Squadron of the 4th Air Regiment.

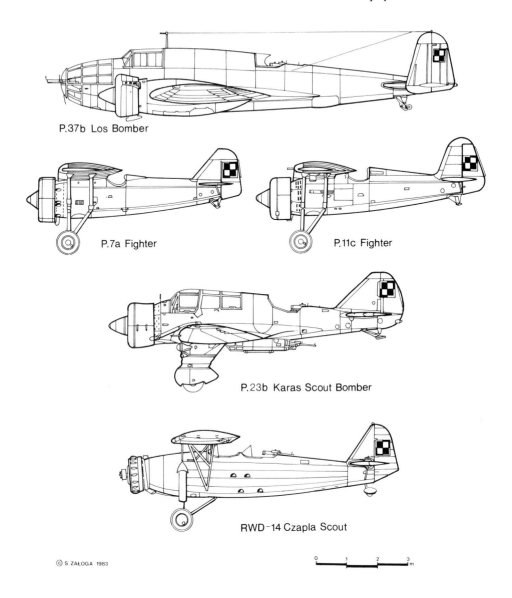

P.37b Los Bomber

P.7a Fighter

P.11c Fighter

P.23b Karas Scout Bomber

RWD-14 Czapla Scout

© S ZAŁOGA 1983

its ability to absorb considerable damage. It was not an effective scout aircraft, lacking panoramic cameras, and it had insufficient forward firing armament for strafing. The Karas was a compromise between a true reconnaissance aircraft and a true ground attack aircraft, proving less than adequate in either role but for the heroic determination of its crews. There were about 240 in service in 1939, of which 120 were assigned to combat squadrons and the remainder in repair, reserve, or with training units.

The PZL P.37 Los (Elk) bomber was the finest medium bomber of its day, but they were too few in number. These aircraft were from the 210th Bomber Wing, photographed at Okencie airport outside Warsaw in March 1939.

The RWD-8 trainer was pressed into service in 1939 as a liaison aircraft.

The P.37 Los bomber was a brilliant medium bomber design, carrying a greater effective bomb load than the basic weight of the aircraft. It could carry 3000 kg of bombs at 445 km/h. Only 75 were available in 1939, with 36 in combat units and the remainder in training units or being prepared for issuance to the air force. Many were squandered in low-altitude ground attacks for which they were not designed. There were also about fifteen of the LWS 4 Zubr bombers, as failed a bomber design as the P.37 was successful.

There were a variety of other light aircraft in service, mainly for scouting and liaison. There were 225 old Lublin R-XIII observation planes, of which only 49 were actually stationed with combat units. The Lublins were being replaced by the more modern RWD-14 Czapla, which was the Polish equivalent of the German Hs126. During mobilization, 60 of the 280 RWD-8 trainers were turned over to the armies as liaison aircraft.

Besides these major types, there was a host of minor auxiliary and obsolete types on air force inventory that were occasionally pressed into service for communications and liaison roles. There were also a handful of prototype aircraft that saw some combat use. For example, the P.24, a more advanced version of the P.11c, shot down two German aircraft over Deblin on 14–15 September. The replacement for the P.23, the P.46 Sum, was used to carry messages into Warsaw through the end of the siege.

TABLE 4–5
AIRCRAFT

Designation	P.7	P.11c	P.23B	P.37B	RWD-8	RWD-14
Name			Karas Scout/	Los		Czapla
Type	Fighter	Fighter	Bomber	Bomber	Liaison	Scout
Wingspan (m)	10.3	10.7	13.9	17.9	11.0	11.9
Length (m)	7.1	7.5	9.7	12.9	8.0	9.0
Weight (kg)	1362	1590	3520	8560	748	1700
Engine (hp)	527	645	680	2×918	110	420
No. of MGs	2	4	3	3	—	1
Bomb load (kg)	—	50	400–700	3000	—	—
Max. speed (km/h)	327	343	304	445	170	247

WARSHIPS

The major warships of the Polish Navy were a pair of *Simoun* class destroyers, ORP *Wicher* and *Burza*, ordered from France and delivered by 1932; three minelaying submarines, ORP *Rys, Wilk*, and *Zbik*, delivered from France in 1931–32; two Polish-designed destroyers, ORP *Grom* and *Blyskawica*, built in Britain and delivered in 1937; the minelayer ORP *Gryf*, delivered from France in 1938; and a pair of ocean-going submarines, ORP *Orzel* and *Sep,* built in the Netherlands and delivered in 1939. Although the Polish Navy was relatively modern, its total displacement and firepower was exceeded by that of a single German cruiser. Poland's shipyards were

TABLE 4–6
WARSHIPS

Class	*Simoun*	*Grom*	*Gryf*	*Rys*	*Orzel*	*Jaskolka*
Type	Destroyer	Destroyer	Minelayer	Submarine	Submarine	Minesweeper
Displacement (t)	1920	2144	2250	980/1250	1100/1650	183
Length (m)	107	114	103	78	84	45
Beam (m)	3.1	3.3	3.6	4.2	4.2	1.7
Main guns	4–130mm	7–120mm	6–120mm	1–100mm	1–105mm	1–75mm
AA guns	2–40mm	4–40mm	4–40mm		2–40mm	
AA machine guns	4–13mm	2–13mm	8–13mm	2–13mm	1–13mm	13mm, 7.62mm
550mm torpedo tube	2-triple	2-triple		6	12	
Mines	60 wz. 08		600 wz. 08	40 SM-5		20 wz. 08
Max. speed (knots)	33	39	20	14/9	19/9	18
Crew	155	190	205	54	62	30
Builder	France	UK	France	France	Holland	Poland
						Jaskolka
						Mewa
						Rybitwa
				Rys		*Czajka*
	Wicher	*Grom*		*Wilk*	*Orzel*	*Zuraw*
Ships in class	*Burza*	*Blyskawica*	*Gryf*	*Zbik*	*Sep*	*Czapla*

The pride of the Polish fleet was the ORP Blyskawica, *which in 1939 escaped to Britain and served alongside the Royal Navy for the remainder of the war.*

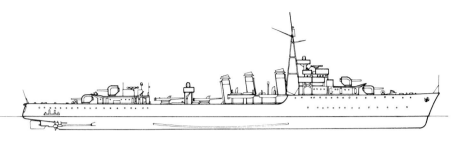

O.R.P. Wicher

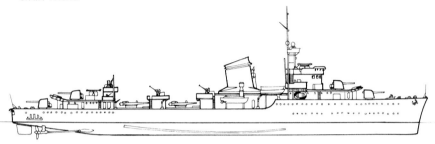

O.R.P. Grom

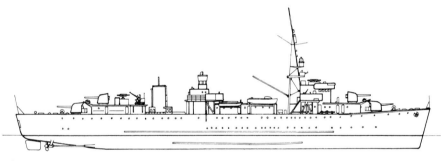

O.R.P. Gryf

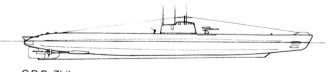

O.R.P. Zbik

O.R.P. Orzel

© S ZAŁOGA 1983

0	10	20	30
			m

The ORP Rys *was one of three French-built submarines in service in 1939.*

on the verge of being capable of producing major warships, and the keels of two *Grom* class destroyers had been laid in Gdynia before the war. They were not completed, and during the fighting were broken up to make armored trains. Besides the major combat ship, the Polish navy had six *Jaskolka* class minesweepers, two old Tsarist gunboats and a number of other minor auxiliaries. The Polish armed forces also included the River Flotilla, operating in eastern Poland. It had three assault groups, each with two gun monitors, a gunboat, and armed launches. Characteristics of these ships are given in Table 4–6.

5. The September Campaign

OPENING MOVES

Although many English and German accounts of the Polish campaign claim that the Wehrmacht succeeded in gaining tactical surprise in the invasion of Poland in 1939, this was clearly not the case. This mistaken belief stems from the confused state of affairs in Poland following the repeated delays in initiation of general mobilization, as well as general ignorance about details of Polish military affairs in this period.

By the end of the summer of 1939, the strength of the Polish Army had doubled through secret mobilization during the course of normal summer maneuvers. By the end of August, about 700,000 troops were mobilized. Hitler had planned to launch the invasion of Poland on 26 August 1939, and in fact orders were dispatched to the Wehrmacht on 25 August 1939 to execute Case White, the German invasion plan. However, negotiations with Mussolini over Italy's entry into the war were not going smoothly, and the announcement of a new Anglo-Polish mutual aid pact on 25 August left Hitler "considerably shaken," according to Gen. Franz Halder. As a result, Hitler ordered a postponement of the invasion. However, because the cancellation did not reach all German units, there were a number of local attacks of a fairly minor nature. One of the most serious incidents occurred in the Jablonka Pass area, where a Brandenburg unit attempted to seize a key rail station and tunnel. This was hardly the only sign of the likelihood of war. There was a marked increase in border raids by Abwehr units, and sabotage actions by German guerrilla units in Western Poland. The Germans also increased the number of overflights of Polish territory by high-altitude reconnaissance aircraft. The Poles were not capable of intercepting these intruders, but did take note of their activities. As a result of these and other signs, Marshal Rydz-Smigly decided to put the country on a war footing on 30 August, two days before the Germans actually planned to strike. On 30 August, the Navy was instructed to

The old German battleship Schleswig-Holstein *entered Danzig (Gdansk) several days before the outbreak of the war, and fired the first shot of World War 2 at the Polish Westerplatte garrison.*

activate Operation Pekin and dispatch the Destroyer Flotilla to Britain so that it had time to clear the Danish Straits before the war broke. All Polish units were placed on alert status, and this was repeated the following day.

The Poles had delayed general mobilization until the last minute in order to assuage French and British fears that public announcement of mobilization would provide the Germans with suitable provocation to begin a war. This fear stemmed from vivid memories of the unwanted outbreak of war in 1914, which was precipitated by provocative mobilizations. Unfortunately, in 1939 the situation was completely different, as the Wehrmacht was already fully mobilized and concentrated and planning to go to war on 1 September no matter what the Poles did. As a result of this, when Marshal Rydz-Smigly did finally announce mobilization on 30 August, the French embassy pressured him into revoking the announcement three hours later. The Poles could not ignore French concerns because they were dependent on the French should war break out. However, by the following day, the situation on the frontiers was looking so ominous that the Poles again announced general mobilization, in spite of French and British protests. However, the delays in general mobilization and the confusion surrounding it, caused by the earlier cancellation, had deleterious effects on the readiness of the Polish Army to confront the Wehrmacht. On 31 August, air force units were ordered to disperse their aircraft to secret wartime bases. The Wehrmacht forces deployed for Case White were divided into Army Group North with the Third and Fourth Armies, and the much larger Army Group South, with the Eighth, Tenth, and Fourteenth Armies. (See Appendix 1, "German Army Order of Battle.") The aim of these forces was to encircle and destroy the Polish armed forces in a precipitous fashion in order to permit the bulk of Wehrmacht strength to be shifted against France if the French attempted any major operation against the Westwall. The attack on Poland was to be accomplished through the use of all of the Wehrmacht's panzer divisions, light and motorized divisions, and the majority of its active infantry divisions, the equivalent of seventy divisional formations. While over thirty divisions remained in the west, these were all infantry, and only twelve were active infantry divisions, the remainder being second or third-line divisions. This, of course, was a

A Polish infantry company prepares for action.

tremendous gamble, since the forces in western Germany would be vastly outnumbered by the French. But Hitler correctly anticipated the feeble French and British response to the onset of war. The aim of Army Group North was to sever the Polish Corridor, thereby connecting East Prussia with the rest of Germany, and cutting off the Polish seaport of Gdynia from the rest of Poland. With the corridor open, the XIX Panzer Corps with its one panzer and two motorized divisions could transit further east to begin a southward pincer toward Warsaw and Brzesc, along with the Third Army. The heaviest concentration of forces was with the Tenth and Fourteenth Armies in Army Group South. They possessed four of Germany's six panzer divisions and all four of the light divisions. The aim of Tenth Army was to overwhelm Polish formations in the border area and press toward Warsaw. Fourteenth Army would protect its southern flank from the attention of the Polish Army Krakow, and send its mobile formations deep into Poland to meet elements from Army Group North on a Deblin-Lublin-Chelm axis.

Since Poland would become landlocked once the Pomeranian Corridor was severed, the German fleet was largely irrelevent to the conduct of the Polish campaign. The small Polish surface fleet was in any case an easy target for German air units, and the menace of the few Polish submarines could be averted by restricting German merchant marine traffic to East Prussia for the duration of the fighting. A comparison of Polish and German aircraft strengths reveals even greater disparities than between the land units. The Luftwaffe deployed a total of 2085 aircraft against Poland, of which 648 were medium bombers, 219 were Stuka dive bombers, and 426 were fighters. This made a total of 1323 first-line combat aircraft, with the remainder being transport, reconnaissance, and support aircraft. In contrast, the Polish air force could deploy only 313 combat aircraft, of which 36 were medium bombers, 118 were light bombers, and 159 were fighters. Counting auxiliary types, liaison aircraft, and transports, the Poles had only 433 military aircraft, most of them obsolete.

A clearer picture of the disparities in strength between the Polish and German armies can be seen in the Table 5–1. However, it should be kept in mind that these figures do not take into account that because of the delay in mobilization, many of the Polish units listed were not actually concentrated or prepared and that therefore the German advantage was even greater than it seems.

HOSTILITIES COMMENCE

On 31 August 1939, Hitler signed the orders for initiation of the Case White plans for the invasion of Poland, to commence the following day. To provide a pretext for the invasion, SD chief Reinhard Heydrich was assigned to Operation Himmler. The plan called for SS troops dressed in Polish uniforms to attack the radio station in Gleiwitz and broadcast inflammatory statements summoning the Polish minority in eastern Germany to take up arms against Hitler. To add further realism, the bodies of several concentration camp inmates outfitted in Polish uniforms were left behind as proof to display to foreign correspondents.

The war was scheduled to start at 0445, though in fact the first action came at about 0430 when Stuka dive bombers of the 3/1st Stuka Geschwader prematurely bombed the key Tczew bridge in the Pomeranian Corridor in hopes of damaging Polish demolition charges. The attempt was unsuccessful. This action was followed by air attacks throughout Poland, directed initially at Polish airfields and rail centers.

THE FIGHTING IN POMERANIA ON 1 SEPTEMBER

The start of the war in Pomerania was signaled by a salvo from the old battleship *Schleswig-Holstein* against the Polish Westerplatte base in the Free City of Danzig. The Germans began air attacks against Polish coastal gun batteries, sank several small auxiliary ships, and wiped out the small

TABLE 5–1
STRENGTH COMPARISON OF GERMAN AND POLISH ARMIES, 1 SEPTEMBER 1939

Region of the front	Branch of Service	Polish Army	German Army	Force Ratio	Density per km (Polish/German)
Polish theatre	Infantry battalions	376	559	1:1.5	0.2/0.3
	Field artillery	2065	5805	1:2.8	1.01/2.08
	Antitank guns	774	4019	1:5.2	0.3/2.0
	Tanks	475	2511	1:5.3	0.2/1.2
Northern front (East Prussia)	Infantry battalions	85	77	1:0.9	0.2/0.2
	Field artillery	494	758	1:1.5	1.5/2.5
	Antitank guns	212	506	1:2.4	0.7/1.6
	Tanks	91	243	1:2.7	0.3/0.8
Northwest front (Pomerania)	Infantry battalions	132	159	1:1.4	0.16/0.2
	Field artillery	735	1322	1:1.8	0.9/1.8
	Antitank guns	233	1058	1:4.5	0.3/1.4
	Tanks	143	324	1:2.3	0.17/0.4
Western front (Silesia)	Infantry battalions	80	199	1:2.5	0.26/0.5
	Field artillery	444	2366	1:5.3	1.4/6.2
	Antitank guns	185	1543	1:8.3	0.6/4.0
	Tanks	130	1215	1:9.3	0.4/3.2
Southwest front (Carpathians)	Infantry battalions	79	124	1:1.6	0.17/0.26
	Field artillery	392	1359	1:3.4	0.8/2.8
	Antitank guns	145	912	1:6.7	0.3/1.9
	Tanks	111	729	1:6.6	0.2/1.5

German troops demolish a Polish customs station on the border during the initial attacks of 1 September.

naval air squadron at Puck. The Submarine Flotilla left bases at Oksywie and Hel and took up combat stations off the Hel Peninsula. The Coastal Defense Flotilla revolving around the minelayer ORP *Gryf* and the sole remaining destroyer, ORP *Wicher,* left Gdynia for Hel and began minelaying operations. These ships came under air attack, were able to fight off the German aircraft without loss. The Germans did begin small-scale land actions against the Coastal Defense Force to cover the left flank of the Fourth Army during its lunge through the Pomeranian Corridor.

In Danzig itself, the SS "Heimwehr Danzig," supported by a Marinesturmkompanie and some paramilitary units, began attacks on the Polish Westerplatte base and overwhelmed the Polish Post Office, where the workers had armed themselves and resisted. Following their surrender, most of the Polish postal workers were shot. The principal land operations in the Pomeranian Corridor took place further south in the attacks of the Fourth Army against Army Pomorze.

The area was smothered in a dense morning ground fog which prevented substantial Luftwaffe close air support of the attacking Wehrmacht units. The aim of the Fourth Army was to isolate the Polish coastal forces from the rest of the country while at the same time securing vital rail links across the corridor to facilitate the transit of units into East Prussia, whence they could join Third Army in an attack on Warsaw from the north. The aim of Army Pomorze once war began was to impede German attacks across the corridor and to cover the northern flank of neighboring Army Poznan from German drives southward.

The Germans attempted to capture the main stations and facilities on the key Chojnice-Tczew rail line at dawn using armored trains. Polish troops and railwaymen at Chojnice successfully repulsed the attack. At Tczew, the Germans attempted a ruse by placing several armored assault cars at the end of a normal civilian transit train. Polish railwaymen in Szymankowo warned the Polish troops at the Tczew bridge. The bridge had been prepared for detonation, and the early morning Stuka attack had failed to damage the charges. The transit train pulled onto the bridge disgorging German troops, who were repulsed by machine gun fire. As the train began to withdraw, the Polish engineer troops blew up the bridge. In retaliation, the Germans later murdered nineteen Polish customs officials and railwaymen, an atrocity that would prove all too characteristic of German behavior in the Polish campaign.

The main attack took place south of the rail line. The Germans attacked through the Tuchola Forest with three infantry divisions to the south, the

German SS troops crouch behind an ADGZ armored car during the attack on the Polish Post Office in Danzig (Gdansk) on 1 September.

3rd Panzer Division in the center, and two motorized infantry divisions in the north. The Poles had not expected the Germans to try to push mechanized units through the forested region. The forest was being covered by the 9th Infantry Division while the Pomorska Cavalry Brigade in Brusy and the 27th Infantry Division in Ocypel withdrew southward. These units had been the northernmost elements of Army Pomorze and were to be the trigger forces if the Germans attempted a limited operation to seize the corridor. With a full-scale war taking place, their political role came to an end, and they began moving southward to take up more tenable defensive positions. The fighting was extremely intense, but the 9th Infantry Division was overextended and vastly outnumbered. The 3rd Panzer Division found a gap in the Polish defenses on the Brda River, which was protected by a lone bicycle infantry company. They made an unopposed crossing beginning in the afternoon. The Poles were unaware that the Brda had been crossed. In the early evening, an incident occurred which has shaped the popular image of the September campaign more than any other. The 18th Lancer Regiment and a company of tankettes of the 81st Armored Troop were holding the northernmost Polish positions near Chojnice while the remainder of the Pomorska Cavalry Brigade withdrew southward from Brusy. Day-long fighting with the German 20th Motorized Infantry Division had caused severe losses, but attempts by the regimental commander to obtain permission to withdraw to more favorable defensive positions across the Brda were denied. In the late afternoon, the regimental commander, Colonel Kazimierz Mastelarz, decided to mount half his force, amounting to two depleted line squadrons, and attempt to swing around the German infantry positions and hit them from the rear. None of the tankettes were taken as they were in poor mechanical shape. Around 1900, the two squadrons located a German infantry battalion in a forest clearing. Having the advantage of surprise, Mastelarz decided on a mounted sabre charge. Galloping out of the forest, the squadrons wiped out the German formation, but in the meantime, several armored cars happened on the scene and began opening fire on the mounted troops with automatic cannon fire. About twenty troopers, including the regimental commander, were killed before the squadrons could withdraw behind a nearby hillock. Italian war correspondents who visited the scene the following day, were told that the troopers had been killed while charging tanks. The story, more embellished with every telling, became a continual source of German propaganda.

Tales of Polish cavalry charges against tanks are still believed today, even by military historians. In fact, Polish cavalry troops were quite familiar with tanks and armored cars, since each cavalry brigade had an ar-

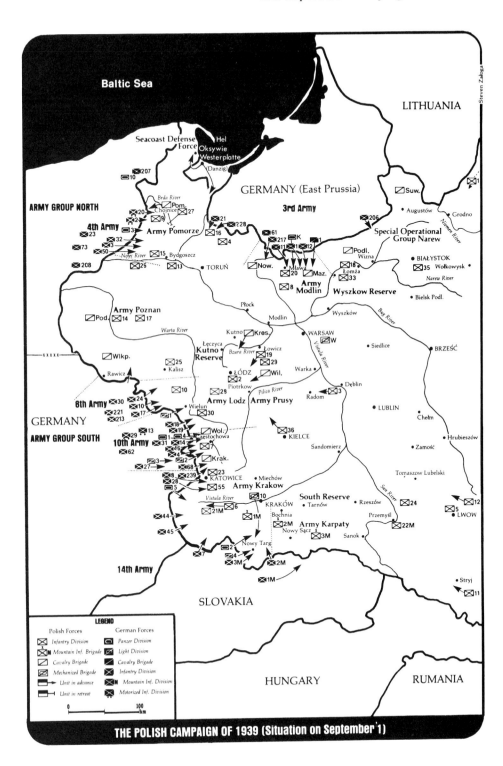

THE POLISH CAMPAIGN OF 1939 (Situation on September 1)

A Polish cavalry regiment on maneuvers shortly before the outbreak of the war.

mored troop attached to it. The occasional encounters between mounted troops and German armored vehicles usually resulted in the Poles trying to escape such a hopeless skirmish in order to deal with them by using anti-tank rifles from dismounted positions. Although the mythical cavalry charge is widely remembered, it has long since been forgotten that, on the evening of 1 September 1939, one German motorized infantry division was on the verge of retreating "before intense cavalry pressure." This intense pressure was applied by the 18th Lancers, which had already lost 40 percent of its strength in the day's fighting, and was only a tenth the size of the opponent. Although by the end of the day the 9th Infantry Division and the 18th Lancers had suffered serious losses, they had held the German infantry, and in some cases pushed it back. However, the threat posed by the 3rd Panzer Division's unopposed crossing of the Brda was not fully appreciated by Army Pomorze.

COMBAT ON THE PRUSSIAN FRONTIER

While awaiting reinforcements from the Fourth Army, which was fighting its way across the corridor, the German Third Army in East Prussia began offensive actions on its own to break through the Polish defenses north of Warsaw. The German ground attacks, beginning at about 0500, consisted of a two-pronged attack by the First Army Corps and the Wodrig Corps on its left flank. The German 11th and 61st Infantry Divisions, supported by tanks of the Kempf Panzer Division, began attacks on the Mlawa strong-hold, which was held by the Polish 20th Infantry Division. Mlawa was one of the few locations where the Poles had any significant fortifications, and headlong attacks against these pillboxes cost the Germans a number of tanks and armored cars. The Kempf Panzer Division was broken up into a number of smaller components to support the infantry advances, but its lack of success against the Mlawa fortifications led to the bulk of its forces being transferred the next day to the Wodrig Corps in hopes that it might skirt the troublesome defensive positions. On 1 September, the Wodrig Corps attacked the right wing of the Polish 20th Infantry Division with the 1st Infantry Division while the 12th Infantry Division and 1st Cavalry Brigade ganged up on the Mazowiecka Cavalry Brigade's positions along the Ulatkowka River. Combat between the German 1st Cavalry Brigade and the Polish Mazowiecka Cavalry Brigade was one of the rare examples of cavalry vs. cavalry engagements during World War II. While most of the encounters between these units were dismounted, there were a number of sabre clashes when mounted patrols encountered each other in the forested areas on the Prussian frontier. The Mazowiecka Cavalry Brigade was

A Polish infantry unit under fire.

forced to withdraw because of the intensity of the German infantry attacks on its overextended positions. However, by the end of the day, the Germans had failed to make any substantial inroads elsewhere in the Polish positions. To the east, the Polish Special Operational Group Narew (SGO Narew), lacking any strong contact with German forces, concentrated on border patrols.

THE BATTLE IN THE SOUTHWEST

The heaviest fighting on 1 September took place in the southwestern area defended by Army Lodz and its southern partner, Army Krakow. In contrast, Army Poznan, covering the central region, saw virtually no serious fighting during the first day of the war.

The German Eighth and Tenth Armies opposite Army Lodz launched a series of infantry attacks on a broad front through the forested frontier areas. While none of these attacks met the main Polish line of defense, which was fifteen to twenty kilometers from the border, there were numerous battles on a regimental scale between Polish and German infantry. The most intense battle took place at the hamlet of Mokra, north of Czestochowa, on the line dividing Army Lodz and Army Krakow. Mokra had been selected as an ideal defensive position by the Wolynska Cavalry Brigade, as forests covered nearly the entire length of this portion of the front, and from a rail line looking out over the fields toward the frontier the Armored Train 53 ("Smialy") could provide covering fire. The brigade, fully dismounted and entrenched, was attacked repeatedly by the 4th Panzer Division. Though badly outnumbered and outgunned, the cavalry pushed back every German attack that day. The German attacks showed poor coordination between infantry and armor, and the Germans lost more than fifty armored vehicles to the cavalry's 37mm antitank guns and antitank rifles. The Polish cavalry also suffered heavy losses in the fighting, and a large number of horses and supply wagons were destroyed by Stuka attacks on the rear areas.

Although Army Krakow was the largest of the Polish armies in 1939, it faced one of the most challenging and difficult tasks. Geographically, it had to defend such varied terrain as the industrial regions of Upper Silesia and the mountainous region of the Carpathians. Facing it were not only the largest concentration of German troops, but also the majority of its armored units, including four panzer divisions and all four light divisions. While fighting was going on at Mokra, the 1st Panzer Division was able to wedge itself between the Wolynska Cavalry Brigade and its southern neighbor, the 7th Infantry Division without any significant opposition. The 7th Infantry Division's 74th Infantry Regiment became heavily entangled

A Pz.Kpfw.II of the 4th Panzer Division, knocked out by a direct hit by an antitank gun. The 4th Panzer Division lost 81 tanks during the campaign.

with elements of the German 46th Infantry Division near the frontier. To the south, the 2nd Light Division tied down the Krakowska Cavalry Brigade, but was able to inject an armored column between the Polish cavalry and the 7th Infantry Division. These actions served to sandwich the 7th between two strong armored formations with three German infantry divisions ready for a direct frontal assault if needed. To the south of VII Corps, the VIII Corp's 8th and 239th Infantry Divisions began the thankless task of assaulting the Polish fortified zone that defended the industrial center of Katowice. The heaviest fighting in Upper Silesia involved a combined attack by the 28th Infantry Division with some support from the 5th Panzer Division against the Polish 55th (Reserve) Infantry Division around Mikolow. The remainder of the 5th Panzer Division overran border positions of the 1/75th Infantry Regiment and began to tangle with the 6th Infantry Division around Pszczyna later in the day where heavy fighting broke out. To the south, the 44th and 45th Infantry Divisions began a slow advance against minor Polish border positions near Karwina and Cieszyn. The most deliberate attacks in the region occurred further south when the 7th Infantry Division began a cautious attack through the Jablonkow Pass. However, most of these attacks did not make serious inroads into Polish positions.

In contrast, the XXII Panzer Corps, consisting of the 2nd Panzer Division, 4th Light Division, and 3rd Mountain Division, made a very determined onslaught on the mountain positions held by the 1st KOP Regiment at Jordanow and on National Guard Zakopane Battalion along the lower Dunajec below Nowy Targ. The 2nd Panzer Division suceeded in outflanking the Polish Dunajec line, which forced Army Krakow to commit the 10th Mechanized Brigade and elements of the 6th Infantry Division later in the day to stem the attack, which they succeeded in doing.

One of the most distasteful tasks of Army Krakow was dealing with sizable numbers of German guerrilla units in the industrial areas of Upper Silesia. The area had a large German minority, decidedly pro-Nazi, that had been secretly armed and organized by the Abwehr before the war's outbreak. There were numerous outbreaks of fighting between small German bands and Polish units, and many instances of sabotage.

BATTLE IN THE CARPATHIANS

In Poland's mountainous south the Germans began probing attacks to the east of Army Krakow's sector with the 1st and 2nd Mountain Divisions, supported in some cases by Slovak troops. The mountains on the Slovak border are extremely steep, and in many places barren of forest cover. This made German attacks on the small Polish garrisons of Army Karpaty extremely difficult, and no serious gains were made on 1 September.

COMBAT IN THE AIR

Contrary to a widely held belief, the Polish air force was not destroyed on 1 September on its airfields. On 31 August, the air units were dispersed to secret airstrips. Early morning attacks on the prewar runways were frustrated by a morning mist over many fields. The only airfield to be strongly attacked was at Rakowice near Krakow, where twenty-eight unserviceable aircraft that had not been dispersed were destroyed. There were air engagements between fighter squadrons attached to the armies and German units, but the Luftwaffe ruled the skys over most of Poland, if only because there were so few Polish fighter aircraft. The exception was Warsaw, where the Pursuit Brigade intercepted a number of bomber attacks through the day, scoring 16 confirmed kills with a loss of 10 Polish fighters and 24 damaged. German air attacks concentrated mainly on rail lines, airfields and various troops concentrations, though the Luftwaffe seemed to pay special attention to the roads near the frontier battles which were crowded with refugees. The Luftwaffe attacks successfully disrupted the mobilization of Polish army units, which were dependent on rail transport in many cases.

WITHDRAWAL FROM THE NORTH

By the morning of 2 September, the Polish forces of Operational Group Czersk had largely withdrawn from the northern extremities of the Pomeranian Corridor, thereby severing its last ties with the Seacoast Defense Forces. Into this gap the Germans began pushing their forces, mainly the 2nd Motorized Infantry Division, while the 20th Motorized Infantry Division continued its attacks on the Polish 9th Infantry Division and the Pomorska Cavalry Brigade. The fighting in the Tuchola Forest between these units continued all day. The 3rd Panzer Division had forced its way into the forest on the southern flanks of the 9th and 27th Infantry Divisions, and sharp engagements broke out near Tuszyny. Nevertheless, while the Polish infantry was kept tied down by three-sided attacks from north, west, and south, the 3rd Panzer Division managed to push its lead elements almost all the way to Poledno, across the main branch of the Brda River, nearly behind the main Polish defensive positions. To the south, the German 3rd and 50th Infantry Divisions made little headway against the Koronowo National Guard Battalion and the 22nd Infantry Regiment, but the 32nd Infantry Division squeezed through a gap in the Polish lines, pushing eastward as far as the Pruszcz rail station, and thereby covering the southern flank of the 3rd Panzer Division advance. On Army Pomorze's eastern flank, the German 21st and 228th Infantry Divisions continued their attacks against the Polish 16th and 4th Infantry Divisions, but the Poles gave little ground. Nevertheless, by the evening of 2 September, the position of Operational Group Czersk was critical. During the forest fighting, many units had become separated, and the advance of the German 3rd Panzer and 32nd Infantry Divisions threatened to encircle the northern elements of the Polish forces. Attempts were made to counterattack on the northern flanks of the German advance and to strengthen ties with neighboring units to the south. Although most of the 27th Infantry Division was successfully withdrawn southward to the outskirts of Bydgoszcz, by 3 September, most of the Pomorska Cavalry Brigade and all of the 9th Infantry Division had been trapped. For the rest of the day, these units fought a costly battle in an effort to break out of the trap. Remnants of the Pomorska Cavalry finally reached the defensive positions of the 27th Infantry Division north of Bydgoszcz late on 3 September and into the next day. The fighting on 3 September crushed the main Polish defenses in the Pomeranian Corridor and caused the Poles severe losses. At 1600, the surviving units were ordered to begin a retreat to the "main defense line" behind the Vistula. This retreat was prompted not only by the heavy losses in the corridor fighting, but by German successes against Army Modlin immediately north of Warsaw. The rout of

Polish forces around Mlawa left German mechanized forces only about sixty kilometers north of Warsaw and the main defense line, whereas Army Pomorze was more than twice as far away. Elsewhere in the Army Pomorze sector, the 4th Infantry Division had launched morning assaults on German forces attacking from East Prussia, but with little success. The two infantry divisions under General Mikolaj Boltuc, the 4th and the 16th, were ordered to retreat with the rest of Army Pomorze around 1900. In the southern sector, the 15th Infantry Division was ordered to withdraw past Bydgoszcz around 1600. In anticipation of an imminent capture of the city by German forces, guerrilla forces had begun an armed uprising at around 1000 on 3 September. They had badly miscalculated, and the rising was crushed by local militia with some army help. The German guerrilla forces lost about 160 of the 200 men involved, both in combat and in subsequent court martials of captured guerrillas. The German security forces later used the suppression of the uprising as a pretext for massacres of Polish civilians after the city was taken by the Wehrmacht on 5 September.

The fighting in Pomerania cost the Polish Army about ten thousand casualties, mainly in Operational Group Czersk. The Germans succeeded in breaching the corridor, although the mop-up of trapped Polish troops continued for the next two days. The Germans began shifting forces into East Prussia in anticipation of the main drive toward Warsaw, with the newly formed 10th Panzer Division being the first major unit sent across.

Polish infantry moving into action. Motor transport was seldom available in 1939.

THE EAST PRUSSIAN FRONTIER

To the north of Warsaw, on 2 September, the German 1st and 11th Infantry Divisions continued the attempt to overcome the 20th Infantry Division and the Mlawa fortifications. While they were not successful, the Wodrig Corps did make inroads to the east on the overextended Mazowiecka Cavalry Brigade. As a result, the Third Army shifted the Kempf Panzer Division in this direction; the aim was to swing around the right flank of the Mlawa defenses and either surround the 20th Infantry Division or force it back. The 8th Infantry Division was committed to the fighting around Przasnysz, but was routed as the Kempf Panzer Division probed forward. As a gap between the two infantry divisions and the Mazowiecka Cavalry Brigade expanded, the divisions began to withdraw toward Ciechanow. By the late afternoon, the whole of Army Modlin was ordered to begin its retreat to the main defense line on the Vistula. The last Polish troops around Mlawa withdrew at about 0700 on 4 September. Army Modlin had succeeded in slowing the advance of the Third Army on Warsaw, but at great cost. By the morning of 4 September its forces had suffered very heavy casualties. After three days and nights of fighting, the exhausted and badly outnumbered troops of the 20th Infantry Division and the Mazowiecka Cavalry Brigade were in no condition to form an adequate defensive barrier against the German reinforcements that were pouring through the corridor.

During the night of 2–3 September, a curious attack was launched by units of the Podlaska Cavalry Brigade of Special Operational Group Narew. In contrast to the heavy fighting around Mlawa, the eastern front had been calm, and so the brigade launched a small raid into East Prussia. The attacks encountered and overwhelmed some Landwehr territorial reserves. These attacks, the first and only Polish operations on German soil, had more propaganda value than military utility, and the cavalry units soon withdrew into Poland.

Army Poznan's sector was also relatively tranquil. The 26th Infantry Division had repulsed German attempts to cross the Notec River, but otherwise contact was very limited. On 3 September, communications with High Command in Warsaw were finally secured, and General Kutrzeba proposed that southern elements of Army Pomorze be used to attack the northern flank of the German Eighth Army, which was attacking Army Lodz to the south. This plan was rejected by Smigly-Rydz, since he feared it would simply provide the Germans an opportunity to engage and crush these forces at an earlier date, even if it might offer temporary relief to the beleaguered Army Lodz. This option was also examined on 5 September but was eventually rejected on that day as well.

FIGHTING IN SILESIA

The main thrust of the German Army Group South remained concentrated with the Tenth Army at the juncture of Polish Army Lodz and Army Krakow. On 2 September, after having fought their way past minor border positions, the Germans encountered the main defensive positions of Army Lodz. The city of Wielun fell, but the Polish lines largely held after a hard day of fighting. Although the Wolynska Cavalry Brigade succeeded again in restraining the advance of the 4th Panzer Division, the situation to the south was worsening. The 7th Infantry Division was forced to retreat toward Czestochowa under pressure from the 1st Panzer Division and two infantry divisions. The retreat left one bridge over the Warta open to passage by the 1st Panzer Division. The Krakowska Cavalry Brigade held back elements of the German 4th Infantry Division at Koszecin, but was eventually pushed back over the Warta by repeated attacks of the 2nd Light Division around Wozniki. Attempts to coordinate the defensive actions of the Krakowska Cavalry Brigade and the 7th Infantry Division on 3 September were unsuccessful because the onslaught of the German mechanized and infantry formations was overwhelming. The 7th Infantry Division was finally crushed on 4 September: only two battalions and a field-gun troop escaped. The Krakowska Cavalry Brigade, already heavily engaged by the 2nd Light Division, was next hit by the fresh 3rd Light Division. The Brigade lost its 8th Lancer Regiment and was sent reeling back. The consequence of the losses suffered by the 7th Infantry Division and the Krakowska Cavalry Brigade would soon be felt. The Germans effectively smashed the right flank of Army Krakow by the unrelenting pressure of numerous mechanized units, and at the same time drove a wedge between Army Krakow and Army Lodz along the key Piotrkow-Warsaw axis. In the end this failure proved more costly to the Poles than the withdrawal of the northern armies.

The 23rd and 55th Infantry Divisions continued to hold back the advance of German infantry formations, but the 6th Infantry Division was mauled during renewed fighting with the 5th Panzer Division. The division lost three battalions and twenty artillery pieces in the fighting at Pszczyna, but in spite of its troubles it managed to keep the 5th Panzer Division from crossing the Vistula. There was little contact between the 21st Mountain Division and the German 44th, 45th, and 7th Infantry Divisions, but in the Jablonka area a day-long battle raged between KOP troops and the 10th Mechanized Brigade and the 2nd Panzer Division. The outnumbered Polish mechanized troops repelled repeated tank attacks around Wysoka, and KOP troops dealt successfully with the 4th Light Division. Nevertheless, it was evident that the Polish forces were engaging only a fraction of the

German Fourteenth Army's strength, so at 1400, Gen. A. Szylling asked permission from High Command to begin withdrawing the southern elements of Army Krakow toward Krakow. Marshal Rydz-Smigly at first agreed, then rescinded his permission, instructing Szylling to hold the Germans on the Dunajec-Nida river line. The elements in the center were ordered to begin falling back toward Krakow. This started a two-day withdrawal, but the units involved managed to retreat in good order and to reestablish positions on the outskirts of Krakow. The hardest task was left to the 10th Mechanized Brigade, supported by KOP troops and a regiment from the 6th Infantry Division. These troops managed to fight back heavy attacks from the German 2nd Panzer, 4th Light, and 3rd Mountain Divisions for two days while trying to keep the German forces from access to the Dunajec River through Tymbark. These actions prevented the Germans from enveloping Krakow from the south, and stymied attempts to form a wedge between Army Krakow and Army Karpaty to the east.

German air attacks on 2 September continued to concentrate on prewar airfields, destroying some training aircraft, but again failing to destroy any combat aircraft. Polish P.11 and P.7 fighters that day scored 21 confirmed kills, and the Karas squadrons began scouting and bombing operations,

A grim reminder of the heroic attempts by Polish P.23 Karas light bomber units to stop the German panzer attacks toward Warsaw. This Karas was brought down near Piaseczno.

particularly in the Army Krakow and Army Lodz sectors. If the Luftwaffe was ineffective against the small and highly scattered Polish air force, it was having far more success against ground targets. Polish rail stations in the frontier areas came under repeated attacks that substantially disrupted train traffic and hampered the Polish mobilization effort. After receiving repeated pleas for further air support, the Karas units made a string of valiant attacks against the tank column of the 1st and 4th Panzer Divisions north of Czestochowa, losing five P.23s to German antiaircraft fire and seven more to crashes on landing because of battle damage. In spite of these heavy casualties, the morale of the Karas squadrons was buoyed when a radio message from 4th Panzer Division indicated it had lost 28 percent of its armored equipment. Although the Karas squadrons attributed these losses to their attacks, the heavy casualties had in fact been inflicted during the two-day battle with the Wolynska Cavalry Brigade.

On 3 September, in keeping with their treaty obligations to Poland, France and Britain finally declared war on Germany. While this caused rejoicing in the streets of Warsaw, it offered little solace to the Polish armed forces. Both allies were slow in making any efforts to attack Germany, aside from token French border patrols and shelling during the first week of the war. The military situation on 3 September was very bleak. The rate of German advance was far faster than the Polish High Command had anticipated, and Polish mobilization was not keeping pace with the need for the reserve armies. The withdrawal from Pomerania and the East Prussian frontier came sooner than expected. In other areas, the Polish forces seemed to be holding, and reports from Army Krakow and Army Lodz seemed to indicate that the Wehrmacht was suffering massive tank losses. Some divisions were claiming as many as sixty tanks destroyed in their sectors. In fact, the heaviest German losses were not that severe. The 4th Panzer Division lost about 80 armored vehicles in its engagements with the Wolynska Cavalry Brigade, but some of these could be repaired. The 5th Panzer Division suffered the next highest casualties, having about thirty tanks disabled during the fighting around Psczyna with the 6th Infantry Division on 1 September. Nevertheless, German losses in troops and materiel did not come close to matching the heavy losses suffered by the Polish Army in Pomerania. Polish civilian losses were also alarming. The Luftwaffe engaged in indiscriminate strafing attacks on roads clogged with fleeing civilians, and frequently bombed targets having no military value.

THE BATTLE FOR PIOTRKOW

With Army Modlin and Army Pomorze withdrawing, there was little heavy fighting in northern Poland on 4–5 September. The main attention of the

Polish Supreme Command was focused on the Piotrkow sector between Army Lodz and Army Krakow. The worrisome advance of the German 1st and 4th Panzer Divisions would have to be countered by the main reserve, General Stefan Dab-Biernacki's Army Prusy, which was still mobilizing in the area south of Lodz. The original timetables had called for the reserve to be fully mobilized within two weeks of the war's outbreak but there was clearly no time for that. The main strength of Army Prusy consisted of the 19th, 13th, and 29th Infantry Divisions and the Wilenska Cavalry Brigade. General Dab-Biernacki suggested that a counterattack be launched, but this was delayed by the difficulties in concentrating the units in the area. An attack was scheduled for late on 5 September 1939, but in the meantime the Germans struck. The 1st Panzer Division marched directly on Piotrkow. Two battalions of the 19th Infantry Division covering the approaches to the city repulsed the first attacks around 1000. But in the early afternoon, German scout units found a gap in the Polish defenses, and the 1st Panzer Division succeeded in enveloping the Piotrkow defenses. It is interesting to note that during the morning fighting in the western outskirts of Piotrkow, the first major encounter of Polish and German tanks oc-

The 7TP light tanks of the Polish 1st Light Tank Battalion, being reviewed by Marshal Rydz-Smigly shortly before the outbreak of the war.

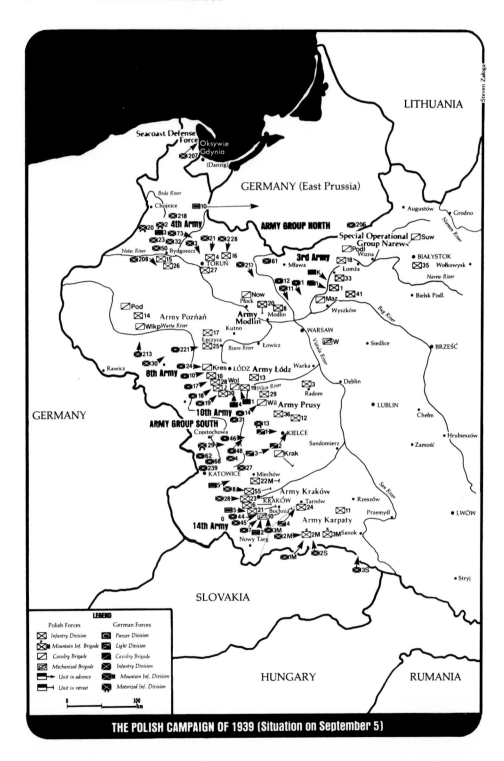

THE POLISH CAMPAIGN OF 1939 (Situation on September 5)

curred as elements of the Polish 2nd Light Tank Battalion knocked out seventeen tanks, two self-propelled guns, and fourteen armored cars of the 1st and 4th Panzer Divisions, taking a loss of only two of their own tanks. In spite of this minor success, the Polish command failed to use the armor accumulated in this sector in any coherent fashion, and so frittered away one of the few opportunities where the small Polish armored force might have had some tactical effect on the course of the September campaign.

With Piotrkow outflanked, the Polish defense of the key Piotrkow-Tomaszow Mazowiecki-Warsaw road was completely undermined. The successes of the 1st Panzer Division were bolstered by 4th Panzer Division attacks along its left flank to relieve the division of the threat of a Polish counterattack. A vicious battle was fought with the 2nd Infantry Regiment for Borowa Gora, with the Poles losing over half their men. Equally alarming was the success of the German 30th Infantry Division in pushing back the Kresowa Cavalry Brigade's defense of the northern flank of Army Lodz. By the evening of 5 September, Army Lodz had been separated from Army Prusy and Army Krakow by the advance on Piotrkow, and 30th Infantry Division inroads threatened to flank it in the north. Army Prusy was in little better shape, as German forces were already pressing against its partly formed southern elements while moving toward Kielce. Word of cancellation of the proposed counterattack of Army Prusy south of Piotrkow did not reach all elements of the 29th Infantry Division, which attacked the headquarters elements of the 1st Panzer Division before being repulsed. Although the Polish High Command was not in full contact with Army Krakow, it seemed evident that the situation in general had seriously degenerated and that the expectations that Army Prusy might blunt the main German drive were forlorn. As a result, on the evening of 5 September, Marshal Rydz-Smigly ordered Army Krakow, Army Prusy, Army Poznan, and Army Lodz to begin withdrawing to defensive positions east of the Vistula and behind the Dunajec River. On 6 September, the 13th Infantry Division attempted to hold back the 1st Panzer Division from Tomaszow Mazowiecki. Intense fighting raged all day long, but by 2200 the situation was hopeless, and the remnants of the division, four weak battalions, were ordered withdrawn.

Army Krakow's situation worsened considerably in the 5–6 September fighting. On 5 September, the 10th Mechanized Brigade attempted to rebuff German attacks on Dobczyce with a mechanized cavalry regiment, but two squadrons were cut off in the unequal struggle with the 2nd Panzer Division and elements of the 3rd Mountain Division. Elements of the 22nd Infantry Division finally began taking up positions, but by the end of the day, the German 4th Light Division had succeeded in taking Tymbark on the Dunajec. That evening, Army Krakow was ordered to begin withdrawing over the Dunajec. The northern elements, consisting of the Jagmin Operational Group, the Krakowska Cavalry Brigade, and the 22nd Infantry Division, were to withdraw behind the Nida River by 7 September. The southern elements, constituting Operational Group Boruta, were to be transferred to Army Karpaty (subsequently renamed Army Malopolska), which was coming under increasingly heavy attack through the mountains. During the fighting on 6 September, the German 4th Light Division succeeded in breaching the Polish defenses, wedging itself between the 2nd Mountain Brigade and the 24th Infantry Division, and thereby threatening the left flank of Army Krakow.

In the north, Army Modlin had retreated south to the garrison town of Modlin. The heaviest fighting in the sector took place at Rozan between the 41st (Reserve) Infantry Division and the Kempf Panzer Division on 5 September. The Germans eventually succeeded in routing the Polish forces there and crossing the Narew River. Attacks followed the next day on Pultusk with an aim toward securing another bridgehead over the Narew. Special Operational Group Narew was ordered to retake Rozan to prevent the threat of German attacks against the rear of Polish defensive

Col. Stanislaw Maczek and his aide, F. Skibinski (in the berets), talk with a motorcycle scout unit of the 10th Mechanized "Black" Brigade. This unit was one of the few Polish units to retain the WW I vintage Austrian and German helmets. It was known as the Black Brigade because of its black leather tanker's jackets.

positions on the lower Narew. These attacks were not successful, and the Germans eventually secured another crossing at Pultusk. With the Narew breached, Marshal Rydz-Smigly was obliged to order a withdrawal to the San River line.

The Germans were not unaware of Polish attempts to avoid a decisive battle on the west bank of the Vistula. Illustrative of this plan was the inactivity of Army Poznan, which was sandwiched between Army Group North and Army Group South, but which was not in fighting contact with major German forces. The German OKH wished to envelop and smash the Polish Army on the west bank of the Vistula if possible, and was reluctant to push its forces too deeply eastward for fear that French intervention would require a rapid shift of some of its forces in Poland back to the Westwall. Nevertheless, beginning on the evening of 5 September, OKH began changing its original plans and instructing its field commanders that it would be necessary to push their forces further east to envelop the Polish forces. This particular reorientation had been urged on the OKH by some of the field commanders, who were well aware of the retreat of Polish forces from in front of their own units.

CRISIS IN COMMAND

The German breakthrough on the Piotrkow-Warsaw axis posed the most serious threat to the Polish defensive plans. Although Army Poznan and Army Pomorze were in the process of retreating to the main Vistula defensive line, they were further away from this natural barrier than German forces attacking around Tomaszow Mazowiecki. Moreover, the German mechanized units were markedly faster than the Polish units. The threat posed to the Vistula line led Marshal Rydz-Smigly to order the formation of Army Lublin, which was to begin preparations for the defense of central Poland. Army Lublin began to scrape together the available reserve units, including the partially formed Warsaw Mechanized Brigade.

On the evening of 7 September, Marshal Rydz-Smigly decided that the High Command would be shifted from Warsaw to Brzesc, with a small staff remaining in the capital until the High Command was reestablished. The decision was apparently made on the assumption that the Germans were likely to surround and isolate Warsaw in the next week, cutting the High Command off from the rest of the Army. In fact, the move from Warsaw to Brzesc effectively accomplished the same thing. Communications with the field armies had already been marginal at best, due to the Luftwaffe's success in disrupting communications lines and the outdated Polish military communications network. Nevertheless, what communications remained were netted to Warsaw, and Brzesc was not prepared to assume control, nor was there a reasonable prospect that it could be prepared. As a result, the Polish Army effectively lost control of its units at the key stage when defense of the main line was being prepared. On occasions, field commanders received one set of instructions from Warsaw and another set from Brzesc. The High Command was frequently out of touch with the fighting and issued orders that were clearly at variance with actions that had already occurred. The decision to abandon Warsaw for Brzesc was a costly and unfortunate mistake.

In the wake of the disastrous breakthrough on the Piotrkow-Warsaw road, the breakthroughs in southern Poland and the relentless push of Army Group North toward Modlin and Warsaw, the fighting in the first part of the second week of the war took on the appearance of scattered, uncoordinated actions as the Polish Army tried to escape to the Vistula while the Wehrmacht attempted to disrupt this operation and crush as many units as possible before the Polish defensive perimeter could be reestablished.

Communication with the field armies was very poor. There was little contact between the High Command and either Army Prusy or Army Krakow, and communication with Army Karpaty was indirect and delayed. Communication with the other armies was most frequently assured by the use of Lazik staff cars or liaison aircraft. On 8 September, a new set of instructions was sent from High Command to the field armies. Special Operational Group Narew was to continue to hold the Narew River with the forces between the Narew and the Bug and to resist the attacks toward Siedlice. General Przedzymirski was to begin establishing defensive positions on the east bank of the Bug River with the 33rd and 41st Reserve Infantry Divisions, the Mazowiecka Cavalry Brigade, and the 1st Infantry Division. Gen. Juliusz Rommel, commander of Army Lodz, was to organize the defense of the Vistula from the Bug-Narew positions south to the Pilica River using what forces had crossed the river. Army Lublin's task of defending the Vistula line from the Pilica to Annopol remained the same. Army Krakow and Army Malopolska were to defend the Vistula from Annopol to the Dunajec River. Army Pomorze and Army Poznan were to attack toward Lodz and Radom to break through to the Vistula.

Some of these orders, particularly those affecting Army Krakow, were wishful thinking. Late on 7 September, motorized elements of the 5th Panzer Division had burst through an undefended gap south of the Holy Cross Mountains, and were already at the rear of Army Krakow. Moreover, the 4th Light Division and the 45th Infantry, aided by the premature withdrawal of the 24th Infantry Division from the Nida River line, had seized Tarnow on 7 September, and so were already behind the Vis-

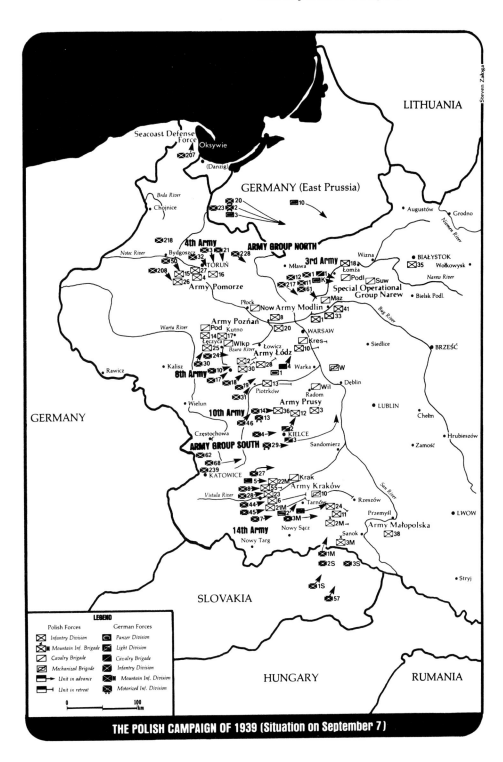

THE POLISH CAMPAIGN OF 1939 (Situation on September 7)

tula. The rear of the Polish positions was interrupted by an eight kilometer-long line of German tanks and motorized equipment moving on the Vistula bridge at Szczucin, which was blown up just as the column began crossing it. The Army Krakow commander, Gen. Antoni Szylling, remarked to his aides, "All this isn't too nice, but at least we have our first opportunity to launch an attack." The units under his command fought a day-long battle to break out eastward toward Baranow on the east bank of the Vistula. The Germans failed to grasp the predicament of Army Krakow, whose forces were able to fight past them.

Army Krakow's predicament had been made worse by the premature withdrawal of the forces of Gen. K. Fabrycy's Army Malopolska from the Nida-Dunajec line on the night of 6 September, contrary to High Command orders. This movement caused a complete rupture of Polish lines between Army Krakow and Army Malopolska, and the German 4th Light Division tried to exploit it. The German unit was repeatedly harried by the small but tenacious 10th Mechanized Brigade, which had already so distinguished itself in the earlier fighting in the Carpathians.

On 8 September, both Army Lodz and Army Prusy were in full retreat toward the Vistula. Nevertheless, there was very heavy fighting as rear-guard units attempted to slow the German assault. Army Lodz was pushed back from the city of Lodz, and elements of Army Prusy from the area around Radom. The problem was that the German motorized units were easily outpacing the horse-drawn Polish units, and numerous Polish units, once isolated, were destroyed piecemeal. Army Pomorze and Army Poznan were in a bad predicament as well. Army Pomorze was still only about sixty kilometers southeast of Torun, with German units pouring down toward Modlin in front of them and German infantry pursuing. Army Poznan had withdrawn in good order with little German contact, and Kutrzeba's plan to strike southward against the northern wing of Army Group South was receiving a more receptive hearing.

In the north, 8 September was the calm before the storm. Army Modlin continued to retreat on Warsaw, and Special Operational Group Narew continued its attempts both to form a defense line on the Bug and at the same time to restrain the advance of German forces over the Narew bridgeheads. In pursuit of these goals, on 9 September Army Modlin requested and High Command granted it permission to launch an attack with the 18th Infantry Division on Ostroleka and another with the Podlaska and Suwalska Cavalry Brigades toward Rozan. The attacks ran into determined resistance and were unsuccessful.

Special Operational Group Narew headquarters had failed to appreciate the heavy build-up of forces in East Prussia, particularly Heinz Guderian's mechanized units in the eastern sector. The OKW, after the intervention of several officers such as Guderian, decided to launch the new forces southeastward along the German-Soviet demarcation line instead of southward to converge on Warsaw as had been intended. This reflected a proper appraisal of Polish plans, which by this time were concentrating on defense of the east bank of the Vistula. The southeastward drive aimed at using the superior mobility of the German armored units, and the presence of negligible Polish forces in eastern Poland, to envelop and destroy the Polish Army between the Vistula and the Bug Rivers. This attack began on 9 September, with the German forces easily taking Wizna, and beginning their drive on Brzesc. At this point, the only substantial forces left in eastern Poland were scattered KOP units that were screening the Soviet frontier.

THE COUNTEROFFENSIVE ON THE BZURA

Gen. Tadeusz Kutrzeba, who had been suggesting a southward attack by Army Poznan for several days, was finally granted permission on 9 September. The operational aim of his most recent plan was to shield the retreat of Army Pomorze and permit it to escape into the Warsaw area, to join forces with the newly formed Army Warsaw. Although consideration was given to awaiting the arrival of Army Pomorze, this was rejected, since the bulk of its forces were three to four days' march from the battle area, and by this time, both armies might very well be surrounded and facing far stronger opposition. Rydz-Smigly's previous opposition to Kutrzeba's plans had been concern that they could eventually end in the encirclement and destruction of Army Poznan before the anticipated French offensive in the West, and Rydz-Smigly's desire to keep as large an army in the field for the most prolonged period possible. In view of the critical situation of 8–9 September, these viewpoints were irrelevant.

The main forces available for the counteroffensive were located in Gen. Edmund Knoll-Kownacki's operational group and consisted of the 25th, 17th, and 14th Infantry Divisions in the center and the Podolska and Wielkopolska Cavalry Brigades on either flank. The aims of the attack were to disrupt the German attacks toward Warsaw to the north of Army Lodz, and to retake Leczyca and Piatek from these forces. This would relieve pressure on Warsaw and on the harried Army Lodz. The Chief of Staff, Gen. Waclaw Stachiewicz, hoped also to coordinate the attack with Army Lodz and with forces in the Warsaw area, but the transferral of the High Command to Brzesc at this time frustrated these attempts. The Wehrmacht was certainly not unaware of the threat posed by Army Poznan, but mistakenly believed that most of its forces had been transported by rail to

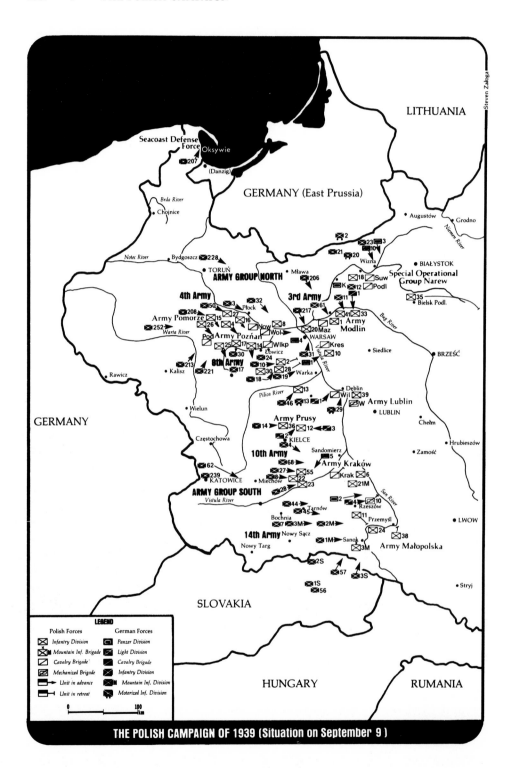

THE POLISH CAMPAIGN OF 1939 (Situation on September 9)

Warsaw. Gen. Gerd von Rundstedt had attempted to obtain some cavalry to screen his Eighth Army's northern flank, but was told none was available. He warned the Eighth Army commander, Gen. Johannes Blaskowitz to keep a careful eye on his northern flank, but his two northernmost units, the 30th and 24th Infantry Divisions were stretched out and inattentive to the threat.

The situation on the Bzura offered the Poles the rare opportunity of the September campaign where they actually had numerical superiority over neighboring German forces. In the Bzura sector, they had a threefold advantage in infantry, a twofold advantage in artillery, and sixty-five tankettes and armored cars without any German panzers present. However, it should not be forgotten that throughout the September campaign, Polish infantry divisions usually fought against similar or worse odds than those now faced by the Germans.

The initial attacks began on the evening of 9 September. The German divisions were quickly routed in very hard fighting. An especially difficult fight took place with elements of the German 26th Infantry Regiment in the streets of Leczyca. The strongest resistance was encountered at Piatek, and the initial attacks failed. Finally, reserves and some tankettes were thrown into the fray, and the German defenders withdrew in disorder. The German defenses finally broke down in total disorder on 10 September, with both divisions retreating. The Poles captured over fifteen hundred prisoners from the 30th Infantry Division alone.

The German response was immediate. The remainder of the Eighth Army was shifted to a northward orientation, and Blaskowitz requested reinforcements, especially armor, to stem the counteroffensive. The OKW was initially reluctant to shift major forces northward in view of the success of operations to this point and the potential rewards of a continued pursuit of the current aims. But in view of the strength of the Polish attack, some reorientation in German plans was necessary. The OKW decided to attempt to encircle the Polish forces rather than deal with them frontally. Reserve divisions of the Eighth Army, following up behind the routed 30th and 24th Infantry Divisions, would serve as western wings of the encirclement. The 3rd Light Division which was attacking toward Radom was reoriented back to support the attack from the west. The 1st and 4th Panzer Divisions, which were already in the outskirts of Warsaw, would be turned around and shifted back westward to attack the Polish eastern flank. The significant force of infantry divisions of the Third Army pursuing Army Pomorze would continue to close in from the north.

The Polish attacks continued for the next two days, but by 12 September had bogged down. By this time, they were facing the 17th, 10th, 18th, and

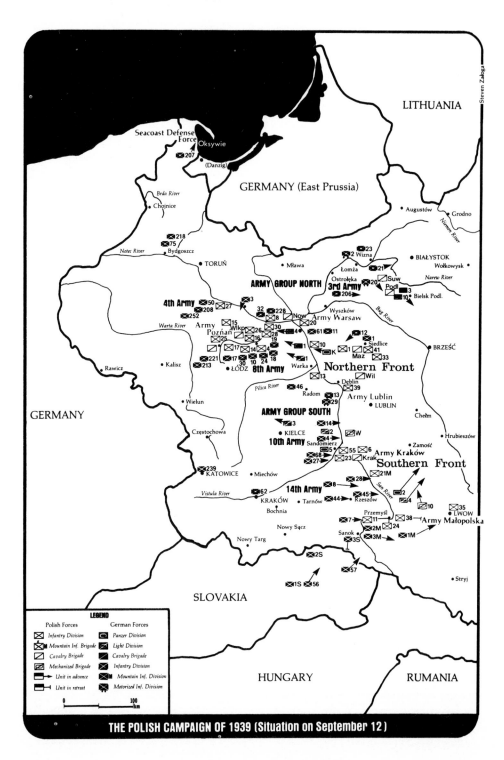

THE POLISH CAMPAIGN OF 1939 (Situation on September 12)

221st Infantry Divisions on their southern flank. Ironically, at this time, instructions from High Command ordered them to continue the attack toward Radom with an aim of breaking through to Krasnik and into the "Romanian bridgehead." This was sheer fantasy. By 12 September the Germans had been able to shift enough forces against Kutrzeba to restore numerical superiority. By the end of the day, the Germans outnumbered the Poles in the region by 1.3:1 in infantry, 2.4:1 in medium artillery and 4:1 in armor. There was no hope that the situation would improve, and every prospect that it would seriously worsen in view of the German strength concentrating on Warsaw. Kutrzeba decided to reorient the attacks from the south toward the east, and on the evening of 12 September began ordering a withdrawal behind the Bzura for the regrouping to begin. In addition, the strength of the German units in the area forced Kutrzeba to alter his plan from screening Army Pomorze's exit into Warsaw to requiring Army Pomorze to assist in breaking out to Warsaw via Sochaczew.

The regrouping of the Polish units took precious time and allowed the Germans to continue bringing up forces. While the 4th, 16th, and 26th Infantry Divisions kept the defensive cordon intact at Lowicz, General Knoll's operational group of the 14th, 17th, and 25th Infantry Divisions began moving eastward to attack Sochaczew. The attack was scheduled for 16 September, but that day, the XVI Panzer Corps attacked from the east, and the 1st Panzer Division crashed through the 14th Infantry Division. The 25th Infantry was hit by the 4th Panzer Division, but this division, having suffered a bloody nose at Mokra and another in careless street fighting in the outskirts of Warsaw, was unable to break or overrun the Polish infantry.

By the end of the fighting on 16 September, it had become evident to General Kutrzeba that any further offensive plans were out of the question. Drastic efforts would be required to save even a portion of the forces concentrated in the Bzura River pocket. That evening, he ordered his officers to begin plans to escape the pocket through the gap north of Sochaczew, which was weakly held by the 4th Panzer Division. On 17 September, the remnants of the Podolska and Wielkopolska cavalries, under Gen. Roman Abraham, and the 15th and 25th Infantry Divisions broke out. They began filtering through the Kampinos Forest northwest of Warsaw and into the capital. The remaining divisions were trapped and fought a two-day battle against the German forces closing the pocket. The small area held by the Poles was a ripe target for the Luftwaffe, especially since by this time the Poles had exhausted their supply of 40mm ammunition for their Bofors antiaircraft guns. The Polish lines finally collapsed on 18 September. For three days, the remaining regiments and isolated com-

THE POLISH CAMPAIGN OF 1939 (Situation on September 18)

panies were attacked and destroyed by German forces. By 21 September, the Germans had captured over one hundred thousand Polish troops and completely crushed Army Pomorze and Army Poznan. So ended the only major Polish counteroffensive of the war, and the largest single action, involving nine Polish infantry divisions and two cavalry brigades against nineteen German divisions, including two panzer divisions and three light divisions.

The Bzura River counteroffensive eventually resulted in the destruction of nearly a quarter of the Polish Army. Nevertheless, it derailed German plans along the central axis of attack. It is significant that the main German gains after the first ten days of fighting occurred on the northern and southern peripheries, not in the central region where the strongest German forces were concentrated. The counteroffensive on the Bzura assisted the remainder of the Polish Army, especially Army Warsaw and Army Lublin, in providing breathing space to concentrate forces and gather together the straggler units of divisions shattered in the frontier battles.

The merits of the Bzura operation have been the subject of much critical attention. German writers, especially officers involved in the fighting, are of the opinion that the counteroffensive would have had a greater impact on the German conduct of the campaign if it had occurred a few days earlier. Kutrzeba had proposed this, but Rydz-Smigly had been reluctant to permit it for fear that such an operation would play into German hands and allow the Wehrmacht to envelop and destroy a significant fraction of the Polish Army on the west bank of the Vistula without really upsetting the German timetable. Polish historians have been especially critical of the failure of the High Command to coordinate operations outside Army Poznan's region. Army Lodz and Army Prusy, in this view, could have been employed to relieve German pressure on the eastern and southern flanks of the Polish forces. However, this assumes that the forces south of the Bzura battlefield were in position to move against the much heavier concentration of German forces. Some Polish historians have also suggested that the initial focus of the Polish attack should have been placed further east to make a later breakout into the Warsaw area more feasible.

Nevertheless, the conduct of the Bzura counteroffensive highlights the two enormous handicaps of the Polish Army in 1939, its lack of operational mobility and its poor communications and control. In spite of the crushing attacks of the first two days of the counteroffensive, the Germans were easily able to move significant reinforcements into the area, in some cases from very distant locations, while the Poles desperately awaited the arrival of the haggard remnants of Army Pomorze. The Polish infantry fought as well as the German infantry when the odds were even, but it was repeatedly overwhelmed when the Germans brought their superior numbers and superior firepower to bear. While Western accounts of the September campaign have stressed the shock value of the panzers and Stuka attacks, they have tended to underestimate the punishing effect of German artillery on Polish units. Mobile and available in significant quantity, artillery shattered as many units as any other branch of the Wehrmacht or Luftwaffe. The lack of sufficient radio communication nets meant that the Bzura counteroffensive was conducted with virtually no contact with the rest of the Polish Army, and Army Poznan and Army Pomorze were left alone to their fate.

THE DEFENSE OF WARSAW

The lead elements of the German Tenth Army began to approach Warsaw in the afternoon of 7 September. In the lead was the 4th Panzer Division. The 4th Panzer had played a key role in creating and exploiting the gap between Army Lodz and Army Krakow, and though it was short about a quarter of its armored vehicles because of combat losses and mechanical breakdowns, it was still a formidable force. But it was also a force that was

The 4th Panzer Division suffered heavy losses when it attempted to launch tank attacks down the avenues of Warsaw's suburbs on 9 September 1939.

not very suitable for urban fighting. Polish plans for the defense of the city were not initially clear. There was some panic in the city in the evening of 6 September when it was announced that the High Command was departing for Brzesc, and this was compounded by radio broadcasts informing suitable age groups of men to leave the city eastward for mobilization into the army. This order was countermanded by the Warsaw Defense Command under Gen. Walerian Czuma. Mayor Stefan Starzynski's radio broadcasts assured the civilian population that the city would be held and urged civilians to assist in constructing antitank ditches and road obstructions. By the time the German tanks were approaching the capital, the city was already gearing up for a prolonged defense. Warsaw was acting as a magnet for retreating forces in the area, and the city defenses were gradually bolstered well after the siege began.

The tanks of the 4th Panzer Division began entering the southwestern suburbs of Warsaw in the early evening of 8 September. The Ochota section was not heavily built up and there were several rail lines and roads in the area which were very suitable for tanks. Around 1700, the tanks began to move into Ochota, but were repulsed by pointblank artillery fire. This foolhardiness continued the next morning. The 35th Panzer Regiment advanced down Zwirki and Wigury Avenues, and the 36th Panzer Regiment moved down Szczesliwicka and Grojecka Streets. These areas had been reinforced the previous evening and the streets blocked with tramway cars. More important, camouflaged 37mm antitank guns and 75mm field guns had been positioned at key street corners, supported by infantry. The German attack became a shambles. The tanks could not maneuver, even on wide thoroughfares like Grojecka Street, and suffered heavy casualties. The 35th Panzer Regiment suffered the heaviest losses to the guns of the 29th Light Artillery Regiment. The Germans also began attacks in the Wola district about 1000, but these attacks were no more successful.

The fighting in Warsaw largely abated after these initial attacks, as the German units were drawn off to counter the Bzura counteroffensive. Luftwaffe attacks continued in strength. The fighting did not resume in earnest until 15 September, when elements of the German Third Army began approaching the eastern suburb of Praga from the east. The main defense line was held by the 21st Infantry Regiment ("Children of Warsaw") and the 336th Infantry Regiment. The 21st was the only regiment of the ill-fated 8th Infantry Division to have survived the disintegration in the battles around Mlawa. It was heavily engaged with German infantry and armor trying to break into Praga. These attacks were repulsed, but at a very heavy cost. The 1st Battalion alone suffered 40 percent casualties through 18 September. German units gradually succeeded in isolating Warsaw from the other major defensive holdout at the Modlin garrison, and also from the ammunition dumps at Palmiry. There were attempts made by a group under Lt. Col. Leopold Okulicki to link up with Kutrzeba's forces during the Bzura fighting, but this was unsuccessful. Finally, on 19 September, the first elements of the Polish forces on the Bzura broke through the German lines and made it into Warsaw. These were the 14th Lancers, and on 20 September most of the remainder of Abraham's improvised cavalry group reached Warsaw after fighting their way through the Kampinos Forest.

German artillery fire and infantry probes continued, but the final assault on the city awaited the conclusion of the Bzura River fighting. The Germans amassed about a thousand artillery pieces for the final assault, and the city was gradually enveloped by thirteen divisions. Particularly heavy attacks were recorded on 23 September, building up to a massive air and artillery attack on the morning of 25 September, which went down in city legend as Black Monday. The land attacks came mainly in the Wola, Ochota, and Mokotow sections but gained little territory. The attacks on 26 September were far more successful, with the Germans overwhelming the three southernmost forts, Forts Mokotow, Dabrowski, and Czerniakow.

The defense of isolated Polish seacoast garrisons was undertaken by both Army and Navy units.

On the evening of 26 September, Gen. Juliusz Rommel, as commander of Army Warsaw, sent envoys to the German Eighth Army headquarters to discuss terms for surrender. Courier aircraft from High Command had made it clear that the position of the Polish Army was hopeless by this point, and the Warsaw commanders felt that any further fighting would be likely to involve substantial civilian casualties. Hitler had specifically ordered the Eighth Army not to permit civilians to leave the capital, correctly assuming that civilian need for food and water would eventually force capitulation. Hostilities officially ceased at 1400 on 27 September, and the 140,000 troops in the city surrendered. The following day, the Germans shifted their artillery and air support to the stubborn defenders of the Modlin garrison near Warsaw. Lacking water and food for his men, and with four thousand casualties, Gen. Wiktor Thommee ordered the surrender of his 24,000 troops on 29 September. The defense of Warsaw had been exceptionally costly. There were about 40,000 civilians killed in the bombing and artillery fire, and over 10 percent of the buildings totally destroyed. About 40 percent of the remaining buildings were heavily damaged. This would not be the last siege of Warsaw during the war, and the later battles would be even more bloody.

DEFENSE OF THE SEACOAST

The Seacoast Defense Force and the Navy were isolated from the rest of Poland in the first few days of fighting when the Germans crossed the Pomeranian Corridor. The Seacoast Defense Force was in fact divided into four major elements. To the far north, a KOP battalion as well as antiaircraft units and shore batteries defended the Hel Peninsula under Cmdr Wlodimierz Steyer. These forces numbered about 2800 troops. The largest force, under Col. Stanislaw Dabek held a defensive perimeter overlooking the Oksywie Bay, and numbered 14,000 men. It consisted of the Naval Rifle Brigade, the Naval National Guard Brigade, shore batteries, antiaircraft artillery, and various paramilitary formations such as workers' militias. The smallest garrison was the Polish Military Transit Depot under Major Henryk Sucharski at Westerplatte in Danzig with 182 men. The fourth element was the remainder of the navy and naval aviation units. With the departure of the Destroyer Flotilla to England immediately before the war's outbreak, the only major remaining ships were the destroyer ORP *Wicher,* the minelayer ORP *Grom,* and the five submarines. There were a number of auxiliaries, notably six minesweepers of the *Jaskolka* class.

The Westerplatte garrison was the first Polish position to be attacked during the September Campaign, when the old German battleship *Schles-*

The remains of the Westerplatte garrison after heavy shelling by German ships and artillery. Part of the city of Danzig (Gdansk) can be seen in the background. The frightful losses inflicted on the attacking German infantry led to them to refer to Westerplatte as "little Verdun" even though the Polish defensive works were of a modest, improvised nature.

wig-Holstein opened fire at 0400 on 1 September, starting World War II. The small garrison occupied a number of carefully concealed bunkers. The garrison was attacked by a mixed force of SS "Heimwehr Danzig," Danzig police units, and regular Wehrmacht troops. The attacks continued intermittently and without much success for a week, including pointblank barrages from the *Schleswig-Holstein* and frequent Stuka attacks. The Germans were forced to bring up 220mm mortars, and launched the main attack on 7 September. One of the Polish bunkers was obliterated by a direct hit from the battleship. Its ammunition soon exhausted, the garrison was obliged to surrender. It had suffered fifteen dead and twenty wounded, but had exacted a frightful toll of its attackers. The combined German forces, who had referred to the Westerplatte bunkers as a "little Verdun," had lost over 300 men in a week of fighting.

The fleet did not fare so well. The small Naval Air Detachment with about twenty-five obsolete light aircraft, was wiped out by air raids on the harbor of Puck. The *Wicher* and *Gryf* departed the base at Gdynia for Hel to begin minelaying operations, and the submarines took up war stations off the coast. Several small auxiliaries were sunk in German air attacks. On 3 September, the Kriegsmarine sent the destroyers Z.1 *Lebrecht Maas* and Z.9 *Wolfgang Zenker* to bombard the installations at Hel, but they were brought under fire from shore batteries and from the *Gryf* and *Wicher*. The *Wolfgang Zenger* was heavily damaged and both destroyers retired. This rebuff led to renewed air attacks that finally succeeded in sinking both the *Wicher* and the *Gryf*. The only remaining surface action by the fleet in Polish waters was the use of three minesweepers to provide gunfire support to shore operations until 16 September, when they were sunk by air attack.

The submarines had poor hunting. The Germans severely restricted merchant marine operations in Polish waters during the fighting, and rigid adherence to international law requiring prior notice before attacking merchantmen hampered any attacks. The only German ship sunk in Polish waters during the Polish Campaign was the minesweeper M-85, which struck an SM-5 mine laid by the submarine ORP *Zbik*. Some of the submarines had close brushes with German naval patrol aircraft, and damage and a lack of fuel and supplies finally forced the submarines to seek out

The Polish submarine ORP Sep *after it had been interned in Sweden.*

foreign harbors for internment. The *Rys, Zbik,* and *Sep* were all interned in Sweden. The *Orzel* sought safe harbor in Estonia, but when the ship was illegally seized, the crew overcame the Estonian guards and set out on a harrowing journey to England through the dangerous Danish Straits without maps or navigation gear. The *Wilk* managed to escape directly to England.

Besides the major sea elements, there was a River Flotilla with three assault groups; it was used in operations in eastern Poland. The assault groups were built around two monitors each and a gunboat as well as smaller launches.

The combined elements of the Seacoast Defense Force at Oksywie were opposed by an equally motley assortment of German units that outnumbered the Poles by about three to one. These elements were a corps under Gen. Leonhard Kaupisch with the 207th Infantry Division, and various Grenzschutz, Landwehr, and paramilitary units totaling about 26,000 troops. In addition, another 12,000 troops formed an improvised brigade under Gen. F. Eberhardt. This German force, heavily supported by both land and naval gunfire, was able to gradually constrict the much smaller Polish force. Kartuzy fell on 5 September when the 4th National Guard

The 100mm Canet Battery overlooking Oksywie harbor. In the background can be seen the old training hulk, ORP Baltyk, *which served during the defense of Gdynia.*

Battalion finally gave way before the whole 207th Infantry Division. This forced the Poles to fall back to a much tighter defense perimeter east of Rumia. Very heavy fighting continued through 14 September, when the Poles were finally obliged to evacuate Gdynia. Remaining resistance on the Oksywie peninsula was finally overcome on 19 September. Colonel Dabek committed suicide rather than surrender.

German attention turned to the garrison on the Hel peninsula. The area was heavily mined, and portions were fortified. The Luftwaffe had already lost over a dozen aircraft to antiaircraft batteries around the main base, and several German ships had been damaged while trying to bombard the garrison. There were a number of gun duels between the four 152mm Bofors guns of the Shore Defense Battery and the *Schleswig-Holstein,* with the battleship usually being forced to retire with additional damage. The main land attacks, backed by heavy artillery fire, were conducted after 21 September by a regiment of the 207th Infantry Division. It made very little headway, until 30 September. After intense hand-to-hand fighting, the Poles were pushed back to Kuznica, where they detonated some large mines that succeeded in partially separating the peninsula. Admiral Jozef Unrug, the commander of the Polish Navy, and present at Hel, had been radioed by Gen. Juliusz Rommel and informed of the surrender of Warsaw on 29 September. Unrug decided to continue fighting, but the situation had become hopeless. A ceasefire took effect at 1400 on 1 October, and the last garrison surrendered the next day.

The defense of the seacoast area was remarkable both for its duration and intensity. The shore batteries sank a number of German auxiliaries, and the antiaircraft batteries claimed thirty-six German planes. German troop losses were severe because of the tenacity of the Polish troops and their skillful use of modest field fortifications.

THE WAR IN THE AIR

Because of its small size and excessive dispersal, the Polish air force had only a modest impact on the conduct of the campaign. Its greatest success can be attributed to its fighter units, which, despite the obsolescence of their equipment, managed to down a surprisingly large number of German aircraft. The fighter units were allotted among the various armies and the Pursuit Brigade, which was devoted to the air defense of Warsaw. During the first six days of fighting, the fighter units had 105 confirmed kills, of which 42 belonged to the Pursuit Brigade. During this period, 63 Polish fighters were lost. On 6 September the fighter units attached to the armies were ordered to join the Pursuit Brigade in the Lublin area, where it had been ordered to move by the High Command. The sole exception was the

A flight of P.7s of the 111th "Kosciuszko" Fighter Squadron.

III/3 Detachment which remained with Army Poznan during the Bzura fighting. The fighter squadrons attached to the armies were experiencing severe difficulties in keeping their aircraft airworthy because of the constant moves between fields, lack of parts, and lack of fuel.

The shift of the fighter units to eastern Poland, as well as their losses in the first week of the war, drastically restricted their impact on further fighting. During the remainder of the campaign, the fighters accounted for twenty-one more confirmed kills of German aircraft, of which fourteen were credited to the fighters attached to Army Poznan alone. Much of the problem stemmed from the lack of fuel at the new airstrips in eastern Poland. With the intervention of the Soviet Union on 17 September, the fighter units were ordered evacuated to Romania, ending their role in the campaign. Although the Polish fighter units had 121 confirmed kills, later research into German records would seem to indicate that in fact the Polish fighters accounted for at least 160 aircraft. Nevertheless, the overwhelming numerical strength of the Luftwaffe made it virtually impossible for the small Polish squadrons to challenge Luftwaffe air supremacy, and German aircraft over Poland could largely bomb and strafe ground targets at will.

The Polish bomber aircraft such as the Los medium bomber and the Karas cooperation aircraft were few in number and did not have a significant effect on the fighting. The Bomber Brigade carried out about 225 bombing sorties, dropping about two hundred tons of bombs. The most significant of these raids was conducted against German mechanized units during the breakthrough along the Piotrkow-Warsaw road. The Karas and Los bombers made repeated low-altitude attacks on German columns, and claimed extensive damage to the German tank formations. The Los bombers were not designed for these types of attacks, but the High Command refused to use them against German industrial targets, ports, or other facilities where they could have had more effect. The Karas light bombers were better suited to this role, but suffered heavy losses to ground fire as they repeatedly pressed their attacks at low altitude. The attacks did not have any significant impact on the German tank columns, and probably caused few losses. Heavier losses were inflicted on unarmored vehicle columns, however.

The Luftwaffe was surprisingly ineffective in eliminating the Polish air force on the ground, contrary to the popular myth. Aside from several dozen derelict or obsolete aircraft destroyed on 1 September, the only substantial Luftwaffe success against actual operational combat aircraft

Air defense of many Polish combat units was limited to small arms and machine gun fire, as from this wz.30 ckm.

squadrons on the ground was the destruction of about seventeen Karas aircraft at the Hutniki airfield during two bombing attacks on 14–15 September. The Luftwaffe was far more successful in its attacks against the Polish Army, severely disrupting mobilization and concentration efforts, making many rail lines and roads impassable, and cutting communications. Polish antiaircraft units were too few in number to prevent this.

Of the 435 operational Polish combat aircraft, 327 aircraft were lost, 98 were evacuated to Romania, and 10 were unaccounted for. About 70 aircraft were lost in air-to-air combat and 30 to ground fire. A further 140 had to be written off as a result of combat damage, crash landings, and the like. At least 33 were lost to indiscriminate Polish ground fire. German losses were 285 aircraft totally destroyed and a further 279 heavily damaged, lost to strength and written off. Polish forces claimed 126 of these were destroyed by fighters, 7 by bombers, and about 87 by ground defenses. These claims are a historical rarity: the claims were considerably lower than actual performance, since the Poles used an extremely demanding system to account for kill claims. German aircraft losses, amounting to about one fifth of the total force committed, were quite heavy considering the short

A company of TKS tankettes prepare for a counterattack on the outskirts of Warsaw, 13 September 1939.

duration of the war and the very modest force opposing the Luftwaffe. These losses stand as a considerable tribute to the skills and heroism of the Polish aircrews who fought so well with so little. There were very few encounters between the Polish Air Force and the Red Air Force. There was one instance where a single P.11 fighter fought with three Soviet fighters, downing two before being shot down.

THE CAMPAIGN IN EASTERN POLAND

The decision to withdraw the main Polish forces behind the Vistula, Bug, and San rivers did not take into account the heavy disruption suffered by Polish forces in many sectors. In many areas of the front, German mechanized columns had already broken through, and were moving past the rivers faster than the Polish forces could withdraw. The Vistula front held because of the diversion of German forces to combat the Bzura River counteroffensive. But in the north, Army Modlin and Special Operational Group Narew were overwhelmed before they could establish an effective defense of the river line. In the south, the river lines were likewise lost before they could be manned.

On 10 September, Rydz-Smigly attempted to coordinate the increasingly confused situation east of the Vistula by forming the Northern and Southern Fronts. The Northern Front, commanded by Gen. S. Dab-Biernacki, consisted of Army Modlin and Special Operational Group Narew. The Southern Front, commanded by Gen. Kazimierz Sosnkowski consisted of Army Krakow and Army Malopolska. Gen. J. Rommel's Army Warsaw and Army Lublin remained independent, as did the forces engaged in the Bzura River counteroffensive. On 10 September, the German Third Army succeeded in breaching the Bug River defenses. The Northern Front was ordered to begin withdrawing under pressure with its aim being to hold the Polesie section of the country from Kock toward Brzesc. However, on 9 September, the German forces massing in East Prussia to form the Fourth Army had begun a rapid drive toward Brzesc against minimal Polish forces. By the end of 10 September, the 10th Panzer Division was far to the south of the Biebrza River, pinning the Suwalska Cavalry Brigade against the Kempf Panzer Division, and cutting part of it off. As the divisions of the Northern Front began their retreat, they were repeatedly forced to fight their way through German units already further south than themselves, rather than attempt to delay German forces north of themselves. The impending disintegration of the Northern Front marked by German penetrations over the Bug and the Vistula led Rydz-Smigly on 11 September to order the withdrawal of the whole army to the so-called Romanian bridgehead. His intention was to gather the remaining Polish forces in the southeastern extreme of the country where they might hold out until the launching of the French offensive that was expected in six days. The order bore little resemblance to reality. Army Pomorze and Army Poznan, already heavily committed to the Bzura counteroffensive, were expected to attack toward Radom and break through over the Vistula southward. These armies were barely capable of holding back the German forces concentrating against them, never mind breaking through, and the Germans were already in the process of enveloping scattered Polish forces in the Radom-Kielce area. In the north, virtually nothing stood in the way of German mechanized attacks toward Brzesc. The few reserves available in the Grodno area were already in transport by train along the Soviet frontier to reinforce the Southern Front's defense of the Romanian bridgehead. Nor was the Southern Front much more secure. The German 1st Mountain Division reached Sambor on 11 September, and the outskirts of Lwow the next day. Ominously, the Soviet Union announced a general mobilization, even though a secret mobilization had been going on since 7 September, when the Germans first announced they were at the gates of Warsaw.

Three wz.34 armored cars of a cavalry armored troop move into action in the outskirts of Warsaw in the second week of the fighting.

On 12 September, the bulk of Special Operational Group Narew had been bypassed by the German units driving on Brzesc and was unable to fight its way into Bialystok. Surviving remnants attempted to fight southeastward, but by 14 September, all that remained of Operational Group Narew were mangled and improvised groups attempting to continue resistance in the Polesie region. The shattered remnants of Army Modlin under Gen. Przedzymirski, consisting of the 41st (Reserve) Infantry Division, 33rd (Reserve) Infantry Division, and 1st Legion Infantry Division, were more successful in their withdrawal effort, although they suffered very heavy losses in the process.

Because of the proximity of German troops to Brzesc, the High Command began withdrawing to Mlynow on its way to the Romanian border. What little contact it had with the armies in the field became even more disrupted, and in many cases ceased. Many of the isolated units were setting up defensive positions in the isolated cities, notably at Lwow and Brzesc, but by this stage there was little organized control over the fighting in eastern Poland because the High Command was unable to communicate with its badly disrupted armies.

The Southern Front was in disturbingly bad condition. Army Krakow, unable to fight its way toward Lwow, was forced to move eastward toward Zamosc. The German 2nd Panzer and 4th Light Divisions had driven a solid wedge between Army Krakow and Army Malopolska, making it impossible for Sosnkowski's two main armies to coordinate their relief efforts toward Lwow. Moreover, the 2nd Panzer Division, which was virtually unopposed, began swinging northward, cutting Army Krakow off from the east and beginning its encirclement. On 14 September, elements of Gen. Tadeusz Piskor's Army Lublin, called the Central Front, began arriving from the north to reinforce Army Krakow. The 21st Mountain Division was engaged in heavy fighting with the German 45th Infantry Division in another attempt to join with Army Malopolska, but to no avail. Army Malopolska itself was nearly surrounded; its 11th, 24th, and 38th Infantry Divisions were engaged on its eastern periphery against the German 1st Mountain Division, which was besieging Lwow, and on its western and southern peripheries against the 7th Infantry and 2nd Mountain Divisions.

The fighting on 15 September did not relieve the problem. The German 28th Infantry Division drove a wedge between the 21st Mountain Division and the rest of Army Krakow, and Army Krakow found itself fighting a three-sided engagement as the German forces closed in on it. On 16 September, Piskor arrived to take command of Army Krakow, and the effort shifted to trying to break out of the closing German trap toward Rawa

Ruska further eastward. This was no more successful. By this time, Przedzymirski had withdrawn the Northern Front to the area between the Bug and Wieprz rivers. The front, now composed of several understrength infantry divisions and cavalry brigades, were formed into two groups, one to the north under Gen. Jan Kruszewski with the remaining cavalry and one under Gen. Jerzy Wolkowicki to the south. During the fighting on 16 September, Gen. Josef Kustron of the 21st Mountain Infantry Division was killed leading a bayonet attack.

THE SOVIET INTERVENTION

The Polish ambassador to the Soviet Union was informed in the early morning hours of 17 September that the Red Army was beginning to intervene in Poland "to protect its fraternal Byelorussian and Ukrainian population." The Red Army forces concentrated for the invasion were organized into two fronts, the Byelorussian and the Ukrainian Fronts, consisting of about twenty-four infantry divisions, fifteen cavalry divi-

Byelorussian peasants greet the arrival of Soviet BT-7 tanks of the 15th Tank Corps on 17 September near Grodetsk in Eastern Poland during the initial phase of the Red Army's invasion.

sions, two tanks corps, and several tank brigades. (See Appendix 2, "Red Army Order of Battle.") Each of the fronts was divided in turn into separate armies, each with a main objective. The Red Army did not foresee any major Polish resistance, as by this time even many of the KOP units had been drawn into the fighting further west. Indeed, when Soviet forces began moving across the Polish border on 17 September, they encountered very few Polish troops. Moreover, the troops encountered were frequently confused about the allegiance of the Red Army. Many were under the impression that the Red Army was intervening against the Wehrmacht, in support of the Polish Army, and so welcomed, rather than resisted the Soviet forces.

The intervention of the Red Army was not expected by the Polish High Command, and came as a great shock. The High Command was hoping for news of the promised French counteroffensive and instead was faced with the fact that the Soviet intervention would completely undermine its plans for the prolonged defense of the Romanian bridgehead. Rydz-Smigly decided to order all units still in the field east of the Vistula to withdraw into neighboring countries, primarily Hungary and Romania, with an aim to-

The crew of a Soviet BA-20 armored car look on during a discussion between German and Soviet field commanders along the German-Soviet demarcation line in Poland in 1939.

ward forming a rump Polish Army on French soil in order to continue the fighting. However, by 17 September, contact between the High Command and the many scattered units was nonexistent. Only the major groupings received these instructions.

Army Krakow prepared a major attack on Tomaszow Lubelski in an attempt to break out. All motor vehicles were drained of fuel and destroyed in order to collect enough fuel for the tanks of the Warsaw Mechanized Brigade and the 1st Light Tank Company, which were to launch the attack. Although the attack on the morning of 18 September was partially successful against the 4th Light Division, tanks of the 2nd Panzer Division intervened and halted the attack in this sector. The same was true of the infantry units participating in the attack. The attacks were repeated through 20 September, and were the largest tank vs. tank encounters of the campaign. Surrounded, badly outnumbered, and running out of ammunition and food, Piskor ordered the surrender of Army Krakow on 20 September. Although scattered elements of the forces under Sosnkowski filtered into Lwow, the remnants of his forces were captured by the Red Army on 20 September when they attempted to bypass German formations and enter the city from the east. There were some confrontations between

A Russian soldier stands by the wreck of a Polish PWS-26 trainer.

A rare view of a Polish Renault R-35 tank from the 21st Light Tank Battalion shortly after entering Romania in the last week of September.

the Wehrmacht and Red Army over the claim to Lwow, but the city and its ten thousand defenders finally surrendered to the Soviets on 22 September.

The main Polish forces remaining in the field after the defeats of Armies Krakow and Malopolska were the remnants of the Northern Front and Przedzymirski's forces around Komarow. The units came under Dab-Biernacki's command, and launched a southward attack toward Tomaszow Lubelski on the evening of 21 September. It was repulsed. Fighting against the German 27th Infantry Division and the 4th Light Division around Zamosc continued through 23 September, but proved fruitless. The Red Army reached the Bug River behind the Polish positions later that day, and that made any prolonged resistance impossible. Dab-Biernacki decided to surrender the bulk of the forces, but isolated groups continued their attempts to escape. On 26 September, about two thousand troops in one such group were surrounded and captured near Bilgoraj. On 27 September, parts of the 7th, 39th (Reserve), and 41st (Reserve) Infantry Divisions were surrounded and surrendered. A group of about two thousand troops under Col. Tadeusz Zieleniewski surrendered near Nisko on 2 October. A cavalry group under Gen. Wladyslaw Anders got as far as the region south of Przemysl, but was broken up by a Soviet armored unit.

Still remaining in the field was a variety of disjointed units. Special Operational Group Polesie under Gen. Franciszek Kleeberg had about 12,000 troops, the remnants of Special Operational Group Narew and various reserve formations. Aware that Warsaw had still not fallen, they decided to press westward to the capital. Further to the east, a KOP grouping under Gen. Wilhelm Orlik-Ruekemann had been formed from various KOP battalions and the 135th (Reserve) Infantry Regiment. These units had been in transit to the Romanian bridgehead when the Red Army intervened, cutting them off. The groups attempted to combine forces, but the KOP group was some 170–250 kilometers east of Kleeberg's group. Kleeberg's force began moving on 23 September when word arrived that the Soviets were at Brzesc and Kowel. There was some fighting with Soviet forces to the north, but the Germans were already in the process of withdrawing to their demarcation line with the Soviets and did not offer stiff resistance. The KOP unit was not so lucky; having fought its way to Wytyczne, it was surrounded and forced to surrender by the Red Army on 30 September. Kleeberg's forces fought against the German 13th Motorized Infantry Division for four days around Kock. Following the fall of Warsaw and other remaining bastions, Kleeberg ordered his troops to surrender at 1000 on 6 October, the last major fighting of the September Campaign. The Germans captured about 16,000 troops in the Kock area.

THE OUTCOME OF THE SEPTEMBER CAMPAIGN

The German armed forces lost 16,000 dead in the Polish campaigns, and about 32,000 wounded. Although troop losses were light, equipment losses were heavier. A total of 674 tanks were lost, 217 of them totally destroyed and the remainder damaged to the extent that they could not be repaired in the field by divisional recovery units. (Some of these were later rebuilt at German factories.) The totally lost tanks included 89 PzKpfw Is, 78 PzKpfw IIs, 26 PzKpfw IIIs, 19 PzKpfw IVs and 6 PzKpfw 35(t)s. This amounted to a quarter of the tanks committed to the conflict. The heaviest losses were suffered by the 4th Panzer Division, which lost 81 tanks, mainly at Mokra and in the Warsaw street fighting. In addition, 319 armored cars of various types were lost, as well as 195 guns and mortars, 6046 trucks, and 5538 motorcycles. The heavy loss of motorcycles is traceable to their widespread use for scouting, and their consequent heavy contact in combat. Soviet combat losses were about 900 dead.

Polish losses amounted to 66,300 troops killed, 133,700 wounded and 587,000 taken prisoner by the Germans and about 200,000 by the Soviets. Equipment losses were nearly total, except for small quantities of equipment accompanying the troops who withdrew into Romania, Hungary, and the Baltic republics. About 100,000 troops escaped into these countries. Historical studies estimate that 45 percent of Polish tank losses were attributable to combat and the remainder to mechanical breakdown, lack of fuel, or internment. Civilian losses were very high, approaching 40,000 dead in Warsaw alone. Several thousand civilians were killed in mass executions carried out both by the Wehrmacht and various security units. They marked the unhappy initiation of a five-year German reign of terror in Poland.

The roots of the Polish defeat are not particularly difficult to trace, though they have often been distorted. The outcome of the campaign was a foregone conclusion before it even began—so long as France and Britain had no serious intention of directly intervening on the Western Front. Without Allied intervention, the Wehrmacht could take the risk of committing the vast bulk of its strength against its much smaller Polish adversary. Although Western historians have been especially critical of Polish strategic deployment, the fact remains that the Polish Army could not have resisted the Wehrmacht single-handedly even under the most favorable circumstances. The task was even more hopeless after the intervention of the Red Army on 17 September. Correcting the shortcomings in Polish command decisions, troop dispositions, and tactical doctrine might have caused higher German casualties or prolonged the fighting by a few days or weeks, but it could not have substantially altered the outcome.

The most significant shortcoming of the Polish armed forces was in national command. Marshal Rydz-Smigly did not prove to be a particularly able war commander. He failed to delegate adequate authority to lower levels of command, and kept too many of the controls in his own hands. While this was acceptable practice in past wars, it proved inadequate in a blitzkrieg. The organization of the High Command was poor and should have contained an additional level of command, such as the later fronts, to coordinate the armies. The 3 September breakthrough between Army Lodz and Army Krakow might not have occurred so soon if a front commander in the field with better access to the army commanders had noticed the critical gap that was being created and so committed reserve forces in a more timely fashion.

Nor was the strategic disposition of Polish forces particularly skillful. While there were legitimate reasons to adopt a forward screening defense instead of initially concentrating the Polish Army behind the main river defense lines, particular aspects of the disposition were extremely faulty. Both Army Pomorze and Army Poznan were positioned much too close to the frontier. Had Army Poznan been allowed to concentrate deeper inside Poland, the counteroffensive in the Bzura region could have proceeded earlier and with greater control. The dispositions in Pomerania invited encirclement even by slow infantry formations.

Compounding these faults was the lack of an adequate command and control network. The command network in 1939 depended too heavily on existing civilian communication lines and on vunerable field telephone lines which were subject to relatively easy interdiction and lacked sufficient quantities of equipment. The High Command did not pay sufficient attention to developing modern radio links for major command headquarters. In view of the enormous sacrifice for modernization of the air force and, to a lesser extent, the armored force, the inept handling of both these resources in 1939 was particularly unfortunate.

In spite of these shortcomings, the Polish Army fought quite well in 1939, and certainly fought better than either the British or French Army in 1940. The Polish Army fought before blitzkrieg warfare had ever been demonstrated. It should not be forgotten that the Polish Army fought for nearly five weeks against the full weight of the Wehrmacht and later the Red Army, even though it was substantially outnumbered. In contrast, the British, French, Belgian, and Dutch armies, which outnumbered the Wehrmacht in men, tanks, and aircraft, and which did not suffer from a precarious strategic encirclement as Poland did, held out for only a few weeks more. The myth of the "eighteen-day war" is not borne out by German casualty figures. The German Army Group South, which bore 75 percent of the German casualties in Poland, lost more men killed in the final half of the war than in the first two weeks. The last two weeks of September saw the culmination of the savage Bzura River fighting, and the violent confrontations around Lwow, Tomaszow, Brzesc, Modlin, and Warsaw. While German commanders were frequently contemptuous of the Polish High Command, their opinion of the quality of the Polish soldiers, especially the cavalry troops was usually quite high.

The Polish predicament was not helped by the Soviet invasion on 17 September. Although there was little serious fighting between the Red Army and the Polish Army, the invasion shortened the duration of Polish resistance against the Wehrmacht and substantially reduced the number of Polish troops escaping into Romania and Hungary. Sandwiched between German and Soviet lines, many Polish units were forced to surrender rather than withdraw further eastward and continue fighting the Germans. The fighting in eastern Poland probably would have lasted several weeks longer but for the Soviet intervention. The Soviet intervention also closed off the southeast escape route of many Polish units.

The only factor that could have seriously prolonged Polish resistance would have been the French offensive promised for the second week of the war. It should not be forgotten that even as late as the third week of the war, the Polish Army was still fielding in excess of 250,000 troops. Had a significant fraction of Wehrmacht strength been forced to return westward, this force quite likely could have remained in the field, even with the Soviets occupying eastern Poland as far as Brzesc. Instead, the French occupied a few square miles of forest in the Saar, and settled down for seven months of Phony War. The British response consisted mainly of hard words and leaflet bombing. There was even some concern voiced in the British Parliament about the RAF bombing of German war industries since these were evidently private property!

The September defeat was not the end of the Polish Army. The troops who escaped to Romania and Hungary gradually slipped out to France. They were used to form four Polish infantry divisions, a mountain brigade, and a tank battalion which fought in Norway and France in 1940. Most of the trained personnel of the Polish air force escaped to England, where they were eventually incorporated into the RAF. During the critical weeks of the late summer of 1940, Polish pilots made up about one eighth of RAF fighter strength in the Battle of Britain, and a Polish squadron was the highest-scoring unit of that famous engagement. Polish units were re-formed in Britain after the French defeat, and Polish units later fought at Tobruk, at Monte Cassino, and elsewhere in Italy, and in the campaign in northwestern Europe. The 10th Mechanized Brigade commanded by Stanislaw Maczek fought in France first as a tank battalion, then formed the cadre of the 1st Polish Armored Division, and fought at the battle of the Falaise Gap in 1944 and along the Dutch and German coasts in 1945.

The Soviets also later formed the Polish People's Army in 1943, and it fought on the Eastern Front. During the Berlin operation in 1945, Polish units made up about one tenth of the attacking forces. By war's end, the Polish Army was the fourth-largest Allied army, after those of the USSR, the United States, and Britain.

Armed resistance in Poland itself never entirely ceased. A small cavalry detachment under the legendary Major "Hubal" (Maj. Henryk Dobrzanski) remained active in the Holy Cross Mountains until 1940, and as early as September 1939, the first underground cells of the Polish Home Army began forming. They would eventually number over 300,000 resistance fighters by the time of the Warsaw Uprising in 1944. Warsaw was also the site of the largest Jewish resistance groups, which in 1943 staged the famous Warsaw Ghetto uprising.

Although the conduct of the Polish Army was initially regarded with some embarrassment in Poland in view of the popular expectation that the war would last at least a few months, the equally rapid defeat of France and Britain in 1940 convinced most Poles that the root of the defeat was not simply the shortcomings of the Polish Army. Eventually, greater appreciation was felt for the accomplishments of their small but heroic army. Nevertheless, the September Campaign was the bloody prelude to the most tragic decade in Polish history. The September fighting was followed by over four years of brutal occupation by the Germans, and by an equally brutal year and a half of Soviet occupation. The Germans slaughtered nearly all of Poland's 3 million Jews, and a further 3 million Poles died in the German concentration camps, in the Siberian camps, in further fighting on Polish soil, or with the Army and the Resistance.

At the conclusion of the war, the Soviet Union refused to return the eastern territories it had seized in 1939, and instead gained the approval of Britain and the United States to the ceding of a portion of East Prussia and eastern Germany to Poland in recompense. In five bloody years of war, one out of every five Polish citizens died, the highest human loss suffered by any country in World War II. The crude Soviet efforts to impose a communist dictatorship after the war led to a little-known, but bloody civil war in which another 300,000 to 400,000 Poles died. A world war begun to guarantee Polish independence ended in a defeat-in-victory for Poland. Attempts to gain some autonomy from Soviet control have continued up to the present in a series of student strikes, workers' revolts, and other political actions.

It is not entirely surprising that the Poles themselves should have promoted the myth of the heroic Polish cavalry charge against German tanks in 1939. For many Poles, it is a metaphor for more recent confrontations. It hardly seems less plausible than student attempts at reform in 1968, the various attempts at economic reform in the strikes of the past decade, or the unlikely rise of the Solidarity movement in the early 1980s. Indeed, the odds in 1939 might have been a bit better.

6. Combat Chronology of Polish Units in the 1939 War

GROUP AND ARMY ACTIVITIES

1 September German offensive commences along the entire front, beginning at 0445 hours. Polish air bases and installations come under attack.

2 September to 5 September The Germans gain complete air superiority and advance on all fronts. The Danzig Corridor is cut. The Warta and Vistula Rivers are crossed. Britain and France declare war on Germany.

6 September to 9 September The Polish attempt to retreat behind the Vistula River fails. Krakow falls, and Germans reach the outskirts of Warsaw.

10 September to 12 September The Germans succeed in penetrating the Vistula, Bug, and San River lines. Encirclement battles begin. At Radom, 60,000 men are destroyed. The Kutno breakout fails. Warsaw is cut off as Polish forces begin a retreat to the southeast.

13 September to 18 September The cauldron on the Bzura is sealed, and the Russians launch their invasion (17 September).

19 September and thereafter Combat continues against German and Soviet forces. Warsaw and Modlin fall. Last organized resistance is destroyed at Hel and Kock on 6 October. Poland is partitioned for the fourth time in its history.

ARMY KARPATY ● Cmdr: Div. Gen. K. Fabrycy. ● Mobilized, 11 Jul 39. ● *1 Sep:* Defended against combined German and Slovak attacks. By evening, had been pushed back to the Jaworzyna-Jurgow-Nidzica line. Experienced heavy fighting in the Czorsztyn and Klodno areas. *2 Sep:* Reinforced with 11th and 24th Inf. Div. in order to hold Dunajec line and cover retreat of ARMY KRAKOW in northwest. By *4 Sep*, Group Boruta/Bielsko began occupying defensive positions on river from Zakliczyn to its mouth. Effective *6 Sep*, Army Karpaty was renamed MALOPOLSKA.

ARMY KRAKOW • Cmdr: Brig. Gen. A. Szylling. • Mobilized, 23 Mar 39. • *1 Sep:* Germans bypassed unfortified positions near the industrial area of Gory Slask and advanced to Mikolow against Group Slask. Group Bielsko's positions near Pszczyna came under heavy attack. In the Pogorze area, attacks from the Tatra Mountains toward Chabowka and Nowy Targ area proved even more threatening and required commitment of armored units (10th Mechanized Brigade). *2 Sep:* Engaged in heavy fighting in the vicinity of Wysoka-Gora Ludwiki-Jordanow-Chabowka-Kasina Wielka. Began retreat on night of 2 Sep and detached some units to ARMY KARPATY. *6 Sep,* failed to receive order to organize defense of Nida-Dunajec line and retreated toward Vistula. Heavy combat near Bronina, Stopnica, Otwock, and Gora Kalwaria. *10 Sep:* Heavy attacks near Baranow forced retreat across Vistula. *12 Sep:* Retreated across San River to concentrate in Janowski and Bilgoraski Forests. Received order (delayed from 10 Sep) to join with ARMY LUBLIN, and did so by *16 Sep.*

ARMY LODZ • Cmdr: Div. Gen. J. K. Rommel. • Mobilized, 23 Mar 39. • *Sep 1:* The Army was not assembled for action when the invasion came. The German Eighth and Tenth Armies made major advances and began driving a wedge on the southern flank, near Mokra, separating Army Lodz from ARMY KRAKOW, and threatening an advance through Radomsko and Piotrkow toward Warsaw. Advanced units engaged Germans despite lack of reinforcement. Army began retreating late on *2 Sep* under continuous pressure. Warta line broken, with defeats in Borowski mountain area. Through *6 Sep,* continued retreat toward Gora Kalwaria and Otwock. By *7 Sep,* commander had lost communications with his forces, and on *8 Sep* was ordered to assume command of the improvised forces of GROUP WARSAW. Army Lodz considered disbanded. Most units went to GROUP PIOTRKOW, under Brig. Gen. W. Thommee, which attempted to break through toward Warsaw as directly as possible. *10–12 Sep:* Group Piotrkow failed to penetrate toward Warsaw. Remnants of the 2d, 28th, and 30th Inf. Div. moved into Modlin area. (See also ARMY WARSAW.) Other units of the Army—10th Inf. Div. and KRESOWA and WOLYNSKA CAVALRY BRIGADES—crossed Vistula independently.

ARMY LUBLIN • Formed *4 Sep* to defend Vistula south of Warsaw under Gen. T. Piskor, initially held key positions between Karczew and Sandomierz while ARMIES LODZ, PRUSY, and KRAKOW retreated. On *6–7 Sep,* it reinforced defensive positions from Solec to Maciejowice, and prepared those from Annapol south to mouth of San River for destruction. It began a retreat behind Vistula to Michow-Baranow area. By *9 Sep,* it was engaged in vicinity of Gora Kalwaria, Maciejowice, and Deblin. Lacking 39th Inf. Div., the Army was only at division strength. On *10 Sep,* it took control of most units between Vistula and Bug rivers (except groups under J. Rommel, S. Dab-Biernacki, and S. Skwarczynski) in order to defend Vistula from Gora Kalwaria to Sandomierz. On afternoon of *12 Sep,* because of retreats in the north, Army began preparing to withdraw toward Tomaszow Lubelski and last defensive line. Initially occupied northern positions along Wieprz River to Lubartow and absorbed units from ARMY PRUSY on the same side of Vistula. German pressure continued. By *14 Sep,* Army was ordered to concentrate in Lublin region and prepare for further withdrawal toward Lwow. After taking over ARMY KRAKOW on *16 Sep,* both armies were encircled and advanced on Tomaszow Lubelski to break out, there beginning a series of battles. Remained heavily engaged northwest of Tomaszow Lubelski in breakout attempts, but encountered reinforced German defenses in the city. After exhausting their supplies, and taking heavy losses, the forces of General Piskor capitulated on *20 Sep.*

ARMY MALOPOLSKA ● Formed *6 Sep.* Heavily engaged on Dunajec River line and began withdrawal toward San River on *7 Sep.* Group Boruta took heavy losses in retreat and was disorganized. Defense of San River proved untenable as 2nd Mountain Brigade was destroyed and 3rd Mountain Brigade was thrown back on *9 Sep.* Counterattack not executed because of delayed orders. Army came under control of newly formed Army Group under Gen. K. Sosnkowski, who was in process of displacing his staff toward Lwow. Units were heavily engaged near Bircza on *12 Sep,* and Army was outflanked both north and south. After *13 Sep,* failed to avoid encirclement and Army Group Commander took direct control. Heavy battles near Przemysl and Janowski Forests. Remnants attempted to reach Lwow, but were destroyed on outskirts of the city as Russians approached.

ARMY MODLIN ● Cmdr: Brig. Gen. E. Krukowicz-Przedrzymirski. ● Mobilized, 23 Mar 39. ● In position on *1 Sep* to begin delaying actions, and engaged German Third Army. There was heavy fighting in the Rzegnowo and Mlawa areas, but line near Rzegnowo was broken and positions outflanked, causing retreat by *4 Sep,* with heavy losses from air attacks. The approach to Warsaw was partly opened as a result. Intensely engaged *6–7 Sep* near Rozan, Army began retreat behind Bug River. On *8 Sep* Army was attached to ARMY WARSAW. On *9 Sep,* Bug line was broken, causing retreat toward south. *10-12 Sep,* Army Modlin became part of Army Warsaw. Elements and command of Group Wyszkow were taken over by Gen. Krukowicz-Przedrzymirski and Army Group Dab-Biernacki. Reorganized, units began movement toward Tomaszow Lubelski. *13–18 Sep,* assembled near Tomaszow and encircled. From *21 to 26 Sep,* these units fought near Tomaszow, failed to break out, and after exhausting supplies surrendered.

ARMY POMORZE ● Cmdr: Div. Gen. W. Bortnowski. ● Mobilized, 23 Mar 39. ● Attacked on *1 Sep* along the entire line by German Third and Fourth Armies, including Guderian's motorized corps. The Polish line was penetrated and outflanked by seizure of the bridge over the Brda River near Sokole-Kuznica. Largely outflanked and partly surrounded between *2 and 5 Sep,* Army began retreat toward Warsaw behind ARMY POZNAN, with both armies ordered to march toward Warsaw and withdraw to region of Leczyca, Wloclawek, and Plock by *7 Sep.* Since motorized German units threatened encirclement, commander of Army Poznan proposed a unified command and delaying actions. This was approved on *9 Sep,* and Army Pomorze was attached to Army Poznan. Group Wschod was detached for combat near Lowicz on east flank of Army Poznan on *11 Sep,* effectively disbanding Army Pomorze. Other units conducted successful attack on Bzura, forcing four German infantry divisions to retreat with heavy losses, but halting themselves north of Lodz and breaking off attack late on *12 Sep.* Encirclement closed, and Army began attempts to break out. Final phase of battle on Bzura began on *16 Sep* with battle near Sochaczew. Only 15th and 25th Inf. Div. and a cavalry group reached the capital. Rest of Army was largely destroyed in Kampinos Forest area on *17–18 Sep* in the attempt to reach Warsaw.

ARMY POZNAN ● Cmdr: Div. Gen. T. Kutrzeba. ● Mobilized, 23 Mar 39. ● *1 Sep:* Feints from German Grenzschutz and Landwehr formations, with the most serious combat near Krotoszyn and in the Rawicz-Leszno area. Local German inhabitants also conducted diversionary actions. Army area came under heavy air attack, but there were no major land attacks. *2–5 Sep:* Elements launched attack into Prussia. Ordered to assist ARMY LODZ and then to retreat toward Warsaw. From *9 Sep,* joined unified command with ARMY POMORZE. Remnants destroyed at Kampinos Forest on *17–18 Sep.*

ARMY PRUSY ● Cmdr: Div. Gen. S. Dab-Biernacki. ● Mobilized, Jun 39 ● Only one division (36th Inf.) of Army was fully assembled on *1 Sep.* Remainder were in process of mobilizing or were still moving toward mobilization area. First group was ready by Piotrkow on *3 Sep* and launched counterattack on flank of ARMY LODZ and was repulsed toward Warsaw. Second group was concentrating near Gory Swietokrzyskie. Disorganized detachments then assembled in the Twarda area near Pilica. On *6 Sep,* defeat of 13th Inf. Div. opened road to Warsaw. To close gap, heavy battles took place in Kielce and Krasna areas, but second penetration took place in Konskie region, forcing retreat toward Vistula, which came under fire on *7 Sep.* On *8 Sep,* both 19th and 29th Inf. Div. were disorganized during fighting near Dobra Wola and Odrzywol. Remnants withdrew toward Radom and fought in Jedlnia and Maciejowice areas. The last major combat unit, the 36th Inf. Div., disbanded near Antonow on *10 Sep.*

ARMY WARSAW • Temporary Army Group formed *8 Sep,* mainly from command elements of ARMY LODZ, and designated Army Warsaw on *10 Sep.* It was to defend Narew-Vistula line with strongpoints at Warsaw and Modlin, but the capital was already outflanked. *13–18 Sep:* Advance by GROUP ANDERS led to heavy fighting in Minsk Mazowiecki area. Modlin was cut off from Warsaw, and siege of both cities began. Army Warsaw continued to defend capital. Thommee's forces held Modlin. After exhausting supplies, Warsaw gave up on *28 Sep,* surrendering about 100,000 soldiers. Modlin capitulated the next day.

OPERATIONAL GROUPS

GROUP ANDERS • Formed *11 Sep* as independent operational group around NOWOGRODZKA CAVALRY BRIGADE to attack Germans east of Warsaw near Wegrow to relieve the forces of Gen. E. Krukowicz-Przedrzymirski. Group Anders broke out of Warsaw near Minsk Mazowiecki on *13 Sep.* It was then ordered to Parczew region. Reached Deblin area by *17 Sep.* Came under air attack on *20 Sep.* By *22 Sep,* Anders had added to it Col. A. Zakrzewski's combined brigade, remnants of the 10th Inf. Div., and elements of MAZOWIECKA CAVALRY BRIGADE, and was attacking near Suchowola on *22–23 Sep* and Majdan Sopocki. Reached Ruda Rozaniecka by *24 Sep.* Fought near Krasnobrod and Ciotusza. Continued southeastward and fought near Broszki on *26 Sep.* Disbanded by *28 Sep,* with some elements reaching Hungary.

GROUP GRODNO • Cmdr: Brig. Gen. J. Olsyna-Wilczynski.

GROUP KUTNO • Completed mobilization *2–5 Sep* and reinforced ARMY KARPATY (24th Inf. Div.) & ARMIES MODLIN & POMORZE (5th Inf. Div.).

GROUP NAREW • Cmdr: Brig. Gen. C. Mlot-Fijalkowski. • Mobilized, 23 Mar 39. • Initially screened a front of about 200 km near the East Prussian border, where there were no significant German units. *2–5 Sep:* Began concentrating, with minor border engagements, and shifting forces westward to assist ARMY MODLIN. *6–9 Sep:* Failed to receive an order to prepare retreat. Attack of *8 Sep* on Narew and Biebrza resulted in protracted battles instead of withdrawal and caused heavy losses. On *9 Sep,* ordered to reorganize and fall back toward Siemiatycze. By *11 Sep,* encircled and attempted to break out, especially near Zambrow. Remnants of the 18th Inf. Div. surrendered on *13 Sep,* but some cavalry units escaped to join SUWALSKI CAVALRY BRIGADE and GROUP POLESIE.

GROUP POLESIE • Activated on *9 Sep* with Detachment Brzesc and Groups Kobryn, Drohiczyn, a KOP unit, and the Pinsk Flotilla. With improvised units, prepared a defense from Muchawiec to Prypec and Brzesc. In combat near Brzesc and then Zabinka on *14–18 Sep.* Began withdrawal toward Romania. On *22 Sep,* concentrated in the Kamien Koszyrski region. After hearing that the government and commander-in-chief had safely reached Romania, Polesie marched to assist Warsaw, through Krymno, Szack, and Piszcz. On *27–28 Sep,* concentrated on the west side of the Bug River near Wlodawa, joining with the ZAZA CAVALRY DIVISION from Ostrow Lubelski and becoming an independent unit (SGO). Group Brzesc departed, along with a KOP group. Besides Zaza Cavalry Division Polesie included 50th Inf. Div., 60th Inf. Div., PODALSKA CAVALRY BRIGADE, and smaller units. On *29 Sep,* it marched toward Parczew and Milanow, resting in Radzyn region before continuing march on *1 Oct.* It reached Kock region by *2 Oct,* where it successfully engaged German XIV Motorized Corps. Because of lack of supplies and the general situation, Group Polesie capitulated on *6 Oct.*

GROUP TARNOW • Was to have been reserve for High Command, but was disbanded to ARMY KRAKOW and ARMY KARPATY when war began. By *5 Sep,* 22nd Inf. Div. had been assigned to Army Krakow, and 38th Inf. Div. was not mobilized.

GROUP WYSZKOW • Cmdr: Brig. Gen. W. Kowalski. • Mobilized, 1 Sep 39. • Mobilizing on *1 Sep,* but only elements of 1st Inf. Div. assembled. Operated from *3 Sep* as part of ARMY MODLIN. Took over 33rd Inf. Div. on *6 Sep* instead of 35th Inf. Div.

DIVISIONS

1st INFANTRY (LEGION) • Cmdr: Brig. Gen. W. Kowalski; Inf. Cmdr: Col. W. Filipkowski. • Mobilized, 24–27 Aug. • *1 Sep:* Redeploying by rail from Wilno to forest between Bug and Narew Rivers. Assigned to GROUP WYSZKOW, northwest section, and still arriving until *4 Sep.* First engaged Germans early on *5 Sep.* Moved to Pultusk area and occupied defensive positions. Heavily engaged near Pultusk and Narew. Withdrew behind Bug, *7–8 Sep,* and defended Wyszkow area. Disengaged on *10 Sep* and marched to Katy Czerwonka region, reaching Jakubow-Rzadza River region by *11 Sep.* Continued marching southeastward that evening. Broke out of encirclement by Kempf Panzer Division, but took heavy losses. Withdrew toward Kuflewo and heavily engaged near Seroczyn, Wodynie, and Olesnia, Wola Wolynska, and Jagodne. Remnants assembled at Radzyn on *15 Sep,* moved to Parczew on *16 Sep,* and then west of Wlodawa. Reorganized with two regiments in Chelm Lubelski region, *18–20 Sep.*

Marched to Wozuczyn and attempted to break out to south on *22 Sep.* Destroyed near Falkow, Tarnowatka, and Antonowka by *23 Sep.* Some remnants went to 39th Inf. Div. and to GROUP POLESIE.

2ND INFANTRY (LEGION) • Cmdr: Col. E. Dojan-Surowka; Inf. Cmdr: Col. A. Staich. • Mobilized, 27–31 Aug. • *1 Sep:* Redeploying from Kielce to Pabianice region under ARMY LODZ, with some elements completing concentration near Czestochowa-Buczek-Zelow. *2–5 Sep:* Moved into Lask region. The 41st Inf. Regt. was detached to 28th Inf. Div. and then to 10th Inf. Div., taking heavy losses in Zapolice-Stronsko region. Engaged near Borowa Gora, on *5 Sep,* with heavy losses. The 31st Regt. was also in the Marzynek Forest and at Zygmuntowo. Retreating to Wronowice and Kalumn forests, division crossed Mroga River by *8 Sep* to defend Glowno-Kamien areas. Commander lost control of unit that evening. 146th Inf. Regt. joined the division; remnants of 2nd Inf. Regt. went to 30th Inf. Div.; 3rd Inf. Regt. reached Ruda, withdrawing toward Skierniewice on *9 Sep.* Units assembled in woods near Ruda on *9 Sep;* marched through Skierniewice on *10 Sep,* and fought near Rawka. Marched on Blonie on *11 Sep* and was engaged near there on *12 Sep.* Then unit continued march toward Oltarzew and Ozarow near Warsaw. On *13 Sep,* heavily engaged near Umiastow and Oltarzew, taking heavy losses, and forced to retreat. Marched to Modlin when unable to reach Warsaw. In Kazun area, *14–17 Sep.* Continued to defend Modlin until *29 Sep.*

3RD INFANTRY (LEGION) • Cmdr: Col. M. Turkowski; Inf. Cmdr: Col. J. Korkozowicz. • Mobilized, 1–3 Sep. • Completed mobilization at Zamosc, *3 Sep,* and was transported to Radom area. Heavily engaged, *6–9 Sep,* near Krosno area. Began fighting on morning of *8 Sep* and was ordered east on *9 Sep,* through Pilatka. Night attack failed; commander was wounded; and division became disorganized, no longer a viable unit. Remnants gathered, *10–12 Sep,* mainly at Antoninow-Czerwona and forest near Wola Dabrowska. Other elements joined units to east and west of Vistula River. Wounded were captured near Zwolen. Unit considered destroyed, though by *20 Sep* some remnants had combined with 1st Inf. Div.

4TH INFANTRY • Cmdr: Col. T. L. Lubicz-Niezabitowski (1–4 Sep, 11–14 Sep); Col. M. Rawicz-Myslowski (4–12 Sep); Col. J. Werobej (13–19 Sep); Brig. Gen. M. Boltuc (19–22 Sep); Inf. Cmdr: Col. M. Rawicz-Myslowski. • Mobilized, 24–27 Aug. • *1 Sep:* Deployed on southwestern sector of East Prussia under ARMY POMORZE, in the Brodnica-Jablonowo region. Redeployed to Radzyn region at night. From Radzyn, moved to Lake Melno region to support 16th Inf. Div., and heavily engaged. Forced back through Radzyn to Wronie Forest area. After losses of 20 percent, division reorganized during *4 Sep.* Marched to Dobrzyn and Torun area to prepare for defense. *6–9 Sep:* Continued withdrawal toward Kutno. *10–12 Sep:* Assembled near Brzesc Kujawski. Losses to air attack near Kutno on *10 Sep;* then marched southward toward Bzura. Heavily engaged, *11 Sep,* defending Bielawy-Rulice area, and took heavy losses. Reassembled, then advanced on Grodno late on *12 Sep,* and crossed Bzura River with intention of joining 16th Inf. Div. to attack enemy rear. Defending on *13 Sep,* then successfully advanced toward Dabkowice and Pilaszkow on 14 Sep. Heavily engaged on *15–16 Sep* near Zduny and took heavy losses. Withdrew to north near Osmolin-Kiernozia region. Underwent air attack at Ilow. Reduced to 4000 men by *18 Sep.* Remnants destroyed by *22 Sep* in attempt to reach Warsaw.

5TH INFANTRY • Cmdr: Brig. Gen. J. Zulauf; Inf. Cmdr: none. • Mobilized, 27 Aug–3 Sep. • *1 Sep:* Most of division still mobilizing in Lwow region. *2–5 Sep:* Only 19th Inf. Regt. entered ARMY POMORZE and was assigned to secure Vistula crossing for 16th Inf. Div. Other regiments were transported to Warsaw on *3 Sep* and unloaded in Praga and Zegrze areas. *6–9 Sep:* Disbanded as division. The 19th Regt. became part of Group Sadowski under Army Pomorze and was assigned to hold Wloclawek bridge for crossing by 16th Inf. Div., and fought near Plock on *8–9 Sep.* The 26th Inf. Regt. concentrated in Nowy Dwor region on *8 Sep* to defend Vistula-Nowa and repelled attacks near Karczew until *9 Sep.* The 40th Regt. was unloaded near Pradla and resisted attacks west of the Vistula on *8–9 Sep. 10–12 Sep:* The 19th Regt. was engaged on left bank of Vistula near Plock. The 26th Regt. took heavy losses in fighting near Karczew and Otwock. The 40th Regt. moved into Warsaw from Siedlce, defending Praga bridges. *13–18 Sep:* The 19th Regt. attacked on *13 Sep* and then withdrew to Lack region. It then moved to Gory, where it came under the 27th Inf. Div., and was largely destroyed in Gabin region on *17 Sep.* The 25th and 40th Regts. continued to defend Warsaw.

6TH INFANTRY • Cmdr: Brig. Gen. B. S. Mond; Inf. Cmdr: Col. I. Misiag. • Mobilized, 24 Aug. • *1 Sep:* Deployed under ARMY KRAKOW, defending Pszczyna region on a front of almost 20 km. Entered combat in the afternoon, halting enemy but taking high losses. Sustained heavy losses on *2 Sep,* with elements falling back toward Krakow and Skawa line on *3 Sep.* Reorganized, *4 Sep.* Repelled attack in Skawina area on *5 Sep* and retreated that night through Wieliczka. Losses over 40 percent. Reached Mokra-Jadowniki area on *7 Sep* after night marches. Retreated across Dunajec toward San River on *8 Sep.* Disorganized march toward San, reaching Bilgoraj by *12 Sep.* Continued retreat toward Bilgoraj on *13 Sep.* On *14 Sep,* ordered to attack northwestward from Tarnogrod. After crossing Tanew River, forced back to north by *15 Sep.* Ordered to break out of encirclement with remnants of 21st Inf. Div. toward Lwow. By *18 Sep* had arrived southeast of Tomaszow Lubelski. After encirclement in Cieszanow Forest, surrendered by *20 Sep.*

7TH INFANTRY • Cmdr: Brig. Gen. J. T. Gasiorowski; Inf. Cmdr: Col. K. B. Janicki. • Mobilized, 24–25 Aug. • *1 Sep:* Deployed on north flank of ARMY KRAKOW, defending Krzepice-Lubliniec area. Elements began delaying actions against German IV Corps. After defensive battle, retreated from Czestochowa on night of *2 Sep* to Janow region. Disorganized and encircled in Lelow region, on *3 Sep.* Attempted breakout toward Szczekociny resulted in heavy losses. Some units escaped toward Pilica on *4 Sep,* but 7th Inf. Regt. and most of division were captured in Zloty Potok region. Remnant battalion helped defend Kielce and Vistula crossings, and joined 36th Inf. Div.

8TH INFANTRY • Cmdr: Col. T. W. Furgalski; Inf. Cmdr: Col. L. de Leveaux, Col. W. Mlodzianowski. • Mobilized, 24 Aug. • *1 Sep:* Reinforcing 20th Inf. Div. near Mlawa, under ARMY MODLIN. On *2–3 Sep,* marched to Koziczyn area to reinforce 20th Inf. Div. Advanced toward Grudusk and Chrostow. Both 13th and 32nd Inf. Regt. repulsed, but 21st Inf. Regt. recaptured Chrostowo, then withdrew to Glinojeck area on *4 Sep* under heavy air attack. Elements scattered among Plock, Wyszogrod, and Modlin. On *7–8 Sep,* about 70 percent assembled near Modlin to defend city. On *11 Sep,* 21st Regt. near Warsaw and rest near Modlin and heavily engaged. Organized advance on Brzecin on *12 Sep,* but after some success was ordered back to city. *13–18 Sep:* Withdrew into Modlin to hold area from Kazun to Nowy Dwor with over 10,000 men, and continued to defend Modlin area until *29 Sep.*

9TH INFANTRY: • Cmdr: Col. J. Werobej; Inf. Cmdr: vacated 30 Aug. • Mobilized, 23 Mar. • *1 Sep:* Defending a front of about 70 km. under ARMY POMORZE on border of Danzig Corridor. Attacked along entire front by German II and XIX Corps (under Guderian). Division was split in two when Germans seized a bridge over Brda River. Counterattack that night failed to reestablish the front. On *2 Sep,* division attacked along Brda River in Klonowo region with heavy losses. That night, attack was called off, and unit began march toward Bydgoszcz, during which elements were mistaken for German unit and attacked by Polish units. Meanwhile, Germans attacked division rear, leading to encirclement in the Franciszkowo area on *3 Sep.* Air attacks destroyed division trains, and by *4 Sep* the division could no longer function as a unit. After *6 Sep* the 22nd Regt. was assigned to 27th Inf. Div. Other remnants were formed into Group Maliszewski under Army Pomorze.

10TH INFANTRY • Cmdr: Brig. Gen. F. Dindorf-Ankowicz; Inf. Cmdr: Col. J. Zientarski-Lizinski. • Mobilized, 24 Aug. • *1 Sep:* Defending a front of 28 km on Warta River, under ARMY LODZ, in the Sieradz region. Elements moved west to conduct delaying actions against German XIII Corps. Engaged in heavy defensive battles on Warta. Repelled heavy attacks on *4–5 Sep.* Forced to retreat to Szadek region where it assembled its elements after losses of 45 percent, and moved toward Ner River. Further retreat toward Glowno, and there, on *8 Sep,* was ordered to continue toward Vistula bridge by Otwock. By *9 Sep,* commander had lost control of units. Until *11 Sep,* after disorganized withdrawal toward Warsaw, the unit assembled in brigade strength to attack in Gora Kalwaria area, after which part of the unit joined GROUP ANDERS and the rest returned to defend Warsaw. From *13 to 18 Sep,* division in rearguard of Group Anders, withdrawing behind Wieprz River, adding two battalions from Lublinca for a total of five, plus four batteries. Until *21 Sep* continued march to Wojslawice-Grabowiec. Heavily engaged on *21 Sep.* Broke through on *22 Sep* to Ministrowka region, where it combined with Group Anders. Then joined Gen. J. Kruszewski's group on *23 Sep* near Komarow. Heavily engaged on *24 Sep* near Bozowol and Suchowola, then directed to Krasnobrod, where it fought until *25 Sep.* Remnants (1000 men) were unable to break out and destroyed heavy equipment. Most of unit was captured while attempting to infiltrate out of encirclement.

11TH INFANTRY • Cmdr: Col. B. Prugar-Ketling; Inf. Cmdr: None. • Mobilized, 31 Aug. • *1 Sep:* Mobilizing in the Carpathian region and allocated to ARMY KRAKOW. on *3 Sep,* one battalion of each regiment was detached to Bochnia-Brzesko area. Rest of division moved to ARMY KARPATY in Tarnow-Debica area. On *8 Sep,* concentrated north of Jaslo River and assigned to defend area Kolaczyce to Brzostek. Later, withdrew toward Barycz region, where it was heavily engaged *11–12 Sep.* Marched through Przemysl to Mosciska on *13–14 Sep,* under air attack. In Sadowe Wisznia on 15 Sep and ordered to attack at night to northeast in the Jaworow region, where it defeated SS Germania Regt., but took heavy losses. Remnants withdrew southeastward to Lelechowka by *18 Sep.* After *19 Sep,* remnants largely destroyed in attempts to reach Lwow.

12TH INFANTRY • Cmdr: Brig. Gen. G. Paszkiewicz; Inf. Cmdr: Col. S. Lancuski. • Mobilized 27–29 Aug. • *1 Sep:* Concentrating under ARMY PRUSY in the Konskie-Tomaszow Mazowiecki region. Some elements began westward deployment by rail. *2 Sep:* Unit transported to Skarzysko-Kamienna area. Moved to Kielce-Odrowaz region under Group Skwarczynski and conducted delaying actions until *8 Sep.* Withdrew behind Vistula on *8 Sep,* and resisted attacks from Ilza area. Marched toward

Michalow and Dabrowa on *9 Sep.* Division was disorganized by armor attacks, and remnants assembled near Piotrowe Pole and moved east on *11 Sep.* Heavily attacked and encircled near Borusk village and ordered to destroy its weapons. Remnants infiltrated across Vistula toward Jozefow. Remnants of 52nd Inf. Regt. became a battalion in 36th Inf. Div.

13TH INFANTRY ● Cmdr: Col. W. Zubosz-Kalinski; Inf. Cmdr: Col. W. Szalewicz. ● Mobilized, 14–15 Aug. ● *1 Sep:* Units located at railheads—Bydgoszcz-Fordon-Solec Kujawski. Ordered to ARMY PRUSY from ARMY POMORZE reserve. Transported, *2–5 Sep,* to Spala area of Army Prusy, and took heavy losses when rail cars were bombed near Tomaszow Mazowiecki; retreated south of Pilica on *7 Sep* with four weak battalions. Retreated under fire until *9 Sep* toward Dabrowka-Stawiszyn area, where the exhausted units were ordered toward Vistula. Occupied Glowaczow after combat on *10 Sep,* then ordered to Wygoda woods, leaving 44th Regt. After destroying crossings, remnants of division crossed Vistula and assembled in Podwierzbie region. Reorganizing on *12 Sep,* without heavy equipment. Formed new 43rd and 45th Regts., *13–16 Sep,* under Col. Szalewicz's 13th Brigade in Division WOLKOWICKI. On *12–15 Sep* elements under Col. Kalinski moved to Vistula and defended Maciejowice area. Pushed back to Samogoszcz on *17 Sep* and then began forced march to Warsaw, where it fought on 19 Sep near Falenica, and was destroyed, *20 Sep.*

14TH INFANTRY ● Cmdr: Brig. Gen. F. Wlad; Inf. Cmdr: Col. M. Lukoski. ● Mobilized, 24–27 Aug. ● *1 Sep:* Defending Poznan front in the towns of Rawicz and Leszno, and region of Zbaszyn and Miedzychod, as part of ARMY POZNAN. Moved toward Swarzedz on *3 Sep,* and in a series of night marches began moving toward Kutno. Arrived south of Kutno by *9 Sep,* joining Group Knoll-Kownacki, and began moving across Bzura. Reached Piatek on *10 Sep* after successful attack. In Pludwiny Forest and Osse-Kozle area by *11 Sep.* Heavily engaged *11–12 Sep;* then ordered back behind Bzura to Krzyanow-Stefanow region. Withdrew to Krzyzan region, then marched to Dabrowa Gora-Bakow. Advanced on Emilianow woods, *15 Sep.* On *16 Sep,* German armor and air attacks destroyed most of division in Jeziorko region and Wicie. General Wlad assembled remnants in Laziska Forest near Ilow, around core of 55th Regt. With his death, on *18 Sep,* this group collapsed in defense of Biala Gora.

15TH INFANTRY ● Cmdr: Brig. Gen. Z. Przyjalkowski; Inf. Cmdr: Col. A. Skroczynski. ● Mobilized, 24–27 Aug. ● *1 Sep:* Defending front west of Bydgoszcz, as part of ARMY POMORZE. On *4 Sep,* ordered to defend Bydgoszcz Canal and lower Brda River and engaged German irregular units in the city. Fought off German reconnaissance units on *5 Sep.* From *6–9 Sep,* successfully defended its positions, but withdrew toward Warsaw with rest of army. *10–12 Sep:* Withdrew with Army Pomorze along left bank of Vistula through Biskupin to Szczytno region. Ordered to defend Boniewo-Szczytno region; losses were heavy on both sides. On *14 Sep,* marched through Strzelno to Gabin region and took heavy losses. Ordered to secure crossings on Bzura near Budy Stare on *15 Sep.* Crossed river near Witkowice and took heavy losses in defensive battles north of Puszcza Kampinoska. Largely destroyed reaching Warsaw.

16TH INFANTRY ● Cmdr: Col. S. Switalski; Col. Z. Bohusz-Szyszko (from 2 Sep); Inf. Cmdr: Col. Bohusz-Szyszko; Col. S. Cieslak (from 4 Sep). ● Mobilized, 24 Aug. ● *1 Sep:* Assigned to Group West of ARMY POMORZE and defended the front on the Osie River from Grudziadz to the mouth of the Lutryna River. Fought mainly in Lasin-Slupski Mlyn region, but also along the rest of the front. Division repelled initial attacks. On *2 Sep,* pushed back by heavy attacks in the Lake Melno-Annowo area toward Grudziadz-Brodnica rail line. On *4 Sep,* began a series of night marches toward Torun, arriving on *9 Sep.* Reached Zychlin on *10 Sep.* Engaged in Lowicz on *11 Sep,* reaching Bzura and taking the city, *12 Sep,* then withdrawn north of river. Ordered to advance to Lowicz and Myslakow. Heavily engaged by *14 Sep.* Ordered back across Bzura and defended Malszyca-Strzelce region, and was heavily engaged until *16 Sep.* Withdrew and then moved toward Warsaw. Severely bombed en route. Only remnants of 64th and 65th Regts. (3500 men) reached Bialogora Forest on *18 Sep,* and arrived at Witkowice on *19 Sep* with additional losses. Largely destroyed by armor east of Bzura by *20 Sep,* except for small groups that reached Warsaw or Modlin.

17TH INFANTRY ● Cmdr: Col. M. S. Mozdyniewicz; Inf. Cmdr: Col. W. Smolarski. ● Mobilized, 24–27 Aug. ● *1 Sep:* Most of division had mobilized and was occupying the Gniezno and Wrzesnia regions, under ARMY POZNAN. No combat. Marched to Slupca region from *3 to 5 Sep.* After forced marches, searched Romartow-Witonia-Uwielinek area and entered combat late on *9 Sep.* Ordered on defensive, *10 Sep;* then marched toward Brzeziny and successfully engaged German 17th Inf. Div. Attacked, *11–12 Sep,* reaching southern part of forest near Katarzynow. Withdrawn through Mlogoszyn and Kiery behind Bzura. Regrouped in area south of Kutno on *13 Sep.* Advanced toward Sochaczew on *14–16 Sep.* Destroyed as division *16–17 Sep,* by armor and air attacks. After march through Puszcza Kampinoska, reduced to 4000 men by *19 Sep.* Defended Palmiry on *21 Sep* against 29th Motorized Division. Joined Group Boltuc by *22 Sep,* and largely destroyed breaking through to Warsaw at Lomienka. A small group finally joined 25th Inf. Div.

18TH INFANTRY • Cmdr: Col. S. Kossecki; Inf. Cmdr: Col. A. Hertel. • Mobilized, 24–26 Aug. • *1 Sep:* Defended a front of 70 km. under GROUP NAREW, along the Narew River from Pniewo to Kamionka. Fought delaying action and was heavily engaged near Ostroleka and Myszyniec through *5 Sep.* Concentrated north of Ostroleka on *6 Sep* to reinforce 41st Inf. Div., and resisted repeated attacks near Lomza and Nowogrod. Continued fight for Lomza and Nowogrod to *10 Sep;* then withdrew to Zambrow, *11 Sep.* Heavily engaged there and at Czerwony Bor, taking heavy losses. Withdrew that night. Remnants fought near Andrzejewo the next day, and were largely destroyed, finally capitulating near Letownica area on *13 Sep.*

19TH INFANTRY • Cmdr: Brig. Gen. J. Kwaciszewski; Inf. Cmdr: Col. T. W. Pelczynski. • Mobilized, 24–26 Aug. • *1 Sep:* Concentrating in the vicinity of Tomaszow Mazowiecki under ARMY PRUSY in readiness for action with either ARMY LODZ or ARMY KRAKOW. Most of the division completed rail movement to Lowicz area. Began moving, *2 Sep,* to Piotrkow, where it organized defenses. Heavily attacked on *5 Sep.* Retreated toward Kolo region, southeast of Piotrkow. Commander captured and unit disorganized by *9 Sep.* Commander of 77th Regt. assembled battle group, which became 18th "Brigade," and marched toward Chelm Lubelski, through *18 Sep.* Became part of Division WOLKOWICKI. On *21 Sep,* marched toward Tomaszow Lubelski, and attacked it unsuccessfully on *23 Sep.* Tank attack caused breakup into 77th Regt., which went north to Col. L. Koc's group, and 86th Regt., which went south to Col. S. Hanko-Kulesza's Dubno Cavalry Group and was destroyed *24 Sep* after battle near Rawa Ruska-Rzycka. Some remnants reached Hungary.

20TH INFANTRY • Cmdr: Col. W. A. Lawicz-Liska; Inf. Cmdr: Col. F. K. Dudzinski; Col. A. Epler. • Mobilized, 22–23 Mar. • *1 Sep:* Defended front of 31 km from Turza Mala to Rudno Jeziorowe area under ARMY MODLIN on East Prussian border. Resisted probing attacks by tank and infantry units of German I Corps. On *2–3 Sep,* repelled repeated attacks with heavy losses on both sides. Withdrew southward on *4 Sep* under heavy air attack. Some units encircled. Began reorganizing by *5 Sep,* after 40 percent losses. *6–9 Sep:* Reorganized and reinforced with Nowogrodska Cavalry Brigade, directed toward Modlin, near Beniaminowo and Nowy Dwor. *10–12 Sep:* Elements fought successfully near Rzadza River, but were forced back to Beniaminowo Forest. Defended Warsaw until capitulation.

21ST MOUNTAIN INFANTRY • Cmdr: Brig. Gen. J. Kustron; Inf. Cmdr: None. • Mobilized, Mar–Aug. • *1 Sep:* Defended front Olza-Istebna in the Bogumin and Bielsko Biala regions, under Group Bielsko of ARMY KRAKOW. German XVII Corps attacked along entire front. After heavy shelling and bombing, unit withdrew to Barwald-Witanow area. On *4 Sep*, ordered to Mogilany area; bombed. Withdrew again toward Bochnia and street fighting. Withdrew toward Radlow. Retreating and heavily engaged on both sides of Dunajec River, especially near Biskupice. Retreating toward San River on *9 Sep*. Then marched toward Krzeszow-Lezajsk above San. From there, on *11 Sep*, ordered to Tanew River, leaving behind 3rd Regt., but adding 1st KOP Regt. Division included only 3000 men. On *13 Sep*, marched south to Lwow, and broke through to Dachnow on *15 Sep*, but was forced back. Division commander died heroically in the defensive battles of Dzikow Nowy and Pierozki Forest area on *16 Sep*. One part of remnants withdrew westward to join 6th Inf. Div., and others joined cavalry group under Col. S. Hanko-Kulesza. Division thereby disbanded.

22ND MOUNTAIN INFANTRY • Cmdr: Col. L. Endel-Ragis; Inf. Cmdr: Col. L. Grot. • Mobilized, 27–29 Aug. • Originally intended for ARMY LODZ, but designated part of the High Command reserve on 28 August. On *1 Sep* it was moving by rail to concentrate in the Debica region. The 2nd and 5th Regts. still lacked the third battalions. *2–5 Sep:* On the move to Krzeszowice-Trzebinia areas, still short two battalions. Moved to defend Starczynow-Klucze on *3 Sep*. Moved toward Nida River through Czaple Wielkie-Wysocice. Cavalry engaged on *5 Sep*. Division engaged against tanks on *6 Sep* near Raclawice. Moved under artillery and bombing, continued combat. Crossed Nida near Wislica on *8 Sep*, and attempted to break out of encirclement on *8–9 Sep*, especially near Bronina, where desperate fighting occurred, leading to suicide of division commander. Attacked in Rytwiany and Sichowa by 5th Panzer Div. on *10 Sep*. In absence of concerted command, remnants broke into three groups, and division disbanded.

23RD INFANTRY • Cmdr: Col. W. P. Powierza; Inf. Cmdr: None. • Mobilized, 24–30 Aug. • *1 Sep:* Defended 45 km front from Swierklanca to Rybnik with 55th Inf. Div., as part of Group Slask under ARMY KRAKOW. Resisted attacks by German VIII Corps along entire front. From *2 Sep*, heavily engaged. Fought delaying actions toward Nida River defensive positions along axis Myslowice-Chrzanow-Alwernia. Assembled again in Krakow area on *5 Sep*. Continued withdrawal on left bank of Vistula above Nida, which proved indefensible. Retreated toward San River on *8 Sep* and fought near Nowy Korczyn with heavy losses. Successful meeting engagement on *9 Sep* in Sroczkow. Marched on Baranow region and crossed Vistula on *11 Sep*. Continued to Rozwadow late on *12 Sep*. Defended San crossings on *13 Sep*. Crossed by *14 Sep*. Heavily engaged on *15–16 Sep* in Puszcza Solska region. Then marched to Zwierzyniec region and assembled in Podklasztor-Borki area. By *21 Sep,* largely destroyed at Tomaszow Lubelski.

24TH INFANTRY • Cmdr: Col. B. M. Krzyzanowski; Inf. Cmdr: Col. B. Schwarzenberg-Czerny (to division, from 9 Sep). • Mobilized, 30 Aug. • Intended to be part of High Command Reserve Tarnow, but ordered to Karpaty region. On *1 Sep,* assembling in Jaroslaw area. *2–5 Sep:* Arriving in the Tarnow-Zakliczyn-Gromnik area. On *6–7 Sep,* retreating across Dunajec River with losses. Attack from south on *7 Sep* partly destroyed two regiments. Retreated toward Frysztak-Wislok region, then across San River below Dynow and prepared defenses. Changed commander on *9 Sep.* Marched toward Bircza. 39th Regt. destroyed on night of *10–11 Sep.* Defended region, *11–12 Sep,* with heavy losses. Engaged southeast of Przemysl on *13 Sep;* marched toward Lwow that night and again fought near Boratycze on *14 Sep,* reaching Chrosnica on *15 Sep.* Heavily engaged *16 Sep.* Then continued toward Janow on *17 Sep* and attempted to penetrate into Lwow on *18 Sep,* where it was reduced to remnants, some of which reached Hungary.

25TH INFANTRY • Cmdr. Brig. Gen. F. Alter; Inf. Cmdr: Col. J. Skokowski. • Mobilized, 24–26 Aug. • *1 Sep:* Assigned to screen the area of Wloclawek-Kolo in the Kalisz region, under ARMY POZNAN. Held defensive positions against German X Corps in the outskirts of Kalisz and Krotoszyn. *2–5 Sep:* Involved in border battles. Withdrew through Turek. Ordered to attack along flank of ARMY LODZ, then ordered back. Ordered toward Leczyca and National Guard Battalions transferred to Podolska Cavalry Brigade; crossed Warta on *7 Sep,* and fought German 30th Inf. Div. Marched through Dabie-Byszew-Grabow to region north of Leczyca and attacked Ozorkow. After successful *10 Sep* attack, engaged until *12 Sep;* then moved toward Czerchow and entered Skotniki. Withdrawn north of Bzura on *13 Sep* and Zychlin-Buszkowek region on *14 Sep,* followed by two-day forced march toward Sanniki. German armor attacked on *16 Sep* toward Rybnica, inflicting heavy losses. Remaining units crossed Bzura on *17–18 Sep.* Reorganized at Palmiry on *19 Sep* and marched to Borakowo and Mlociny by *20 Sep,* which it defended on *21 Sep.* After withdrawal to Bielany, it incorporated remnants of 14th and 17th Inf. Divs. Defended Warsaw until surrender.

26TH INFANTRY • Cmdr: Col. A. Brzechwa-Ajdukiewicz; Inf. Cmdr: Col. T. P. Parafinski. • Mobilized, 23 Mar. • *1 Sep:* Defended a front of 60 km from Naklo to Wagrowiec, under ARMY POZNAN. Screened flank of ARMY POMORZE and Army Poznan in the area between the Warta River and Notecia and defended against attack. *2–5 Sep:* In heavy defensive battle near Notecia. Occupied Notec line near Labiszyn on *6 Sep.* Came under

Army Pomorze on *7 Sep* and began withdrawal on *8 Sep.* Marched to Zychlin region to take defensive positions, then departed for Sochaczew region on *12 Sep.* By *14 Sep,* advancing with 16th Inf. Div. toward Skierniewice, then ordered behind Bzura to set up antitank defense. Heavily engaged in Garwolin region, *15–16 Sep,* and attacks on Kozlow and Emilianow. After air attacks, remnants reached Bzura on night of *17 Sep,* and were largely destroyed in crossing, near Brochow, on *18 Sep.* Remnants (500 men) were destroyed at Modlin.

27TH INFANTRY ● Cmdr: Brig. Gen. J. Drapella; Inf. Cmdr: Col. G. Kawinski. ● Mobilized, 14–16 Aug. ● *1 Sep:* Assembled in the Lubichowo-Osieczno-Ocypel region, southwest of Starogard, under ARMY POMORZE. Ordered to march in three columns toward Torun. Later received an order to counterattack the advancing Germans, from the direction of Sepolno, along with the 9th Inf. Div. After changing direction again, the division received a new order that evening directing it to the south. Elements encountered some German resistance. From *2 Sep,* heavily engaged near Swiekatowo and Tuszyny toward Bydgoszcz, losing 50th Inf. Regt. Moved toward Torun and reorganized. Marched from Torun area to Vistula on *6 Sep.* Disengaged on night of *7 Sep* and moved northwest of Wloclawek. Rearguard of army on *9 Sep.* After action in Wlocawek and Brzesc Kujawski region, moved to Kowal woods on 12 Sep. Defending Kowal area on *13 Sep.* With 15th Inf. Div., struck back at Plock on *14–15 Sep* with some success. Then ordered to Gabin region, and attacked en route. Continued east on *17 Sep.* Disorganized by air attack at Ilow and reduced to remnants by *18 Sep.* Destroyed by *19 Sep,* with small groups escaping to Modlin and Warsaw.

28TH INFANTRY ● Cmdr: Brig. Gen. W. Boncza-Uzdowski; Inf. Cmdr: Col. S. Broniowski (to division, 8–15 Sep); Col. A. Wacznadze. ● Mobilized, 24–26 Aug. ● *1 Sep:* Occupying delaying positions along the Wielun-Skomlin-Rudniki region, under ARMY LODZ. The 36th Regt. heavily engaged in Skomlin-Wierzbie area, and division took heavy losses from air attacks. On *2 Sep,* delaying actions near Widunca. Main defense along Widawka River on *3–4 Sep.* Outflanked and began withdrawal toward Ostrow-Gucin on *5 Sep.* Retreated to and organized defense of these towns, then to Kudrowice and Pabianice. Heavily engaged there *7 Sep,* with loss of 72nd Regt. Retreated toward Wola Cyrusowa. The 36th Regt. successfully attacked on *8 Sep,* but took heavy losses. Ordered to march toward Warsaw through Skierniewice and moved to defensive positions east of there with remaining three battalions. On *12 Sep,* ordered to break through to Warsaw after marching to Grodzisk-Brwinow. Heavily engaged on *12 Sep* and forced back to Modlin after heavy losses.

29TH INFANTRY • Cmdr: Col. I. J. Oziewicz; Inf. Cmdr: Col. J. Bratro. • Mobilized, 24–27 Aug. • *1 Sep:* Assembling in the region of Rawa Mazowiecka and Lubochnia, after movement to Skierniewice, under ARMY PRUSY. By *4 Sep,* organized defense near Pilica and Czarna Rivers, with initial battle by 76th Regt. on *5 Sep.* Heavily engaged on *6 Sep,* and 76th Regt. largely destroyed. Rest of division moved to Kolo, then east of Pilica. Heavily engaged on *8 Sep* defending Drzewiczka River and largely disbanded by *9 Sep.* After assembling in forest north of Ryczwol, elements attempted crossing of Vistula, taking heavy losses. Combined with remnants of seven battalions to form a 29th "Brigade" in Division WOL-KOWICKI. Elements also joined 39th Inf. Div. on *15–17 Sep,* near Rejowca.

30TH INFANTRY • Cmdr: Brig. Gen. L. J. Cehak; Inf. Cmdr: None. • Mobilized, 23 Mar. • *1 Sep:* Conducting delaying actions in the Warta area against German XI and XVI Corps, under GROUP PIOTRKOW in ARMY LODZ. Defended Warta line, then withdrew to main positions near Widawce on *3 Sep.* Successfully defended this area. On *6–7 Sep,* marched toward Tuszyn and Zaromin. Fought north of Brzeziny and retreated to Przylek region on *8–9 Sep;* suffered repeated air attacks. At 50 percent of strength, began combat there, and 83rd Regt. was destroyed. Remnants assembled in Karolinow Forest on *10 Sep,* including 82nd and 83rd Regts. with some artillery. Marched toward Warsaw on *11 Sep.* In combat, on *12 Sep,* near Zyrardow; retreated northward after heavy losses. Defended Modlin until surrender on *29 Sep.*

33RD INFANTRY • Cmdr: Col. T. Kalina-Zieleniewski; Inf. Cmdr: Col. S. L. Biestek. • Mobilized, 24–27 Aug. • *1 Sep:* Assembling in the area of GROUP NAREW. Remained there, but detached 135th Regt. and two artillery batteries to defend Osowca. After *4 Sep,* moved to Ostroleka area and Narew. On *6 Sep,* ordered toward Wyszkow region and took heavy losses from artillery. After confused march, reached forest northeast of Wyszkow on *7 Sep.* Marched to defend Bug River on *8 Sep,* but failed to reach positions in time. Withdrew toward Biala Podlaska through Majdan on *10 Sep,* and Sokolow on *11 Sep.* Diverted eastward toward Miedzyrzec woods by enemy action. Reached Slawatycze and Bug line by *16 Sep* and attacked Wlodawa with some success on *17 Sep.* Ordered back to Sobibor area. In Marynin region on *19 Sep.* Marched to Majdan Ostrowicki region on *20 Sep,* where it reorganized into a single regiment of 41ST INF. DIV.

35TH INFANTRY • Cmdr: Col. E. Zongolowicz; Inf. Cmdr: None. • *1 Sep:* Completing mobilization in the Wilenszczyzna area, deployed to GROUP WYSZKOW, though part of division had not assembled. *2–5 Sep:* Still assembling, with 205th Regt. split between Lwow and Warsaw. Concentrated, *7 Sep,* south of Bialystok. Ordered to Bielsko region, *8 Sep,* but after crossing Narew was directed to move by rail to Kowel region. *10–12 Sep:* Moved by rail to Lwow and began preparing defenses. Most of division then defended Lwow until surrender, *21 Sep.*

36TH INFANTRY • Cmdr: Col. B. A. Ostrowski; Inf. Cmdr: None. • Mobilized, 24–30 Aug. • *1 Sep:* Concentrating in the Opoczno region, under ARMY PRUSY. *2–5 Sep:* Elements (five battalions) unloaded at Szydlowiec and marched toward Konskie region; rest of division assigned to other units with no artillery. Prepared positions along Czarna River, west of Konskie. Defended Ruda Maleniecka area, *6 Sep,* and heavily engaged in Kazanow on *7 Sep.* Withdrew to Ilza on *8 Sep,* with rearguard destroyed under heavy fire. Absorbed 163rd Regt. after heavy losses. Assembled four battalions in forest near Opole. Moved toward Piotrowe Pole. Destroyed near Vistula by *11 Sep,* with remainder encircled in forest east of Zapusta. Commander of 163rd Regt. ordered elements attempt to reach other side of Vistula. Most remnants marched toward Lublin and Kowel, where they joined other formations. Considered disbanded.

38TH INFANTRY • Cmdr: Col. A. W. Konas; Inf. Cmdr: Col. J. Pecka. • *2–5 Sep:* Mobilizing and concentrating. Arrived at Lwow and assigned to ARMY MALOPOLSKA on 6 Sep. Directed to Przemysl on *7 Sep* and unloaded *8 Sep,* to march north of city on *9 Sep.* *10–12 Sep:* Marching through Mosciska region. From there moved to woods west of Janow; bombed there. Took heavy losses near Dobrostan and Kamieniobrod, and 97th Regt. destroyed. Other units ordered to defend Janow area on *17 Sep.* Heavily engaged on *18 Sep,* and remnants forced to retreat toward Lwow. After destroying heavy equipment, retreated to Lwow on *19 Sep* under heavy artillery fire. Ordered to reinforce 11th Inf. Div. at Holosko and advanced there. Division was destroyed in battles near Brzuchowice and Zamarstynow by *20 Sep.*

39TH INFANTRY • Cmdr: Brig. Gen. B. E. Olbrycht; Inf. Cmdr: Col. E. Duch. • *2–5 Sep:* Begin mobilization. *6–9 Sep:* Concentrated on Michow-Baranow region, under ARMY LUBLIN. *10–12 Sep:* Ordered to defend Deblin-Pulawy area and advanced to Vistula and Wieprz lines. Engaged some diversionary units en route. By *14 Sep,* withdrew to Chelm region and assigned to Group Kruszewski. Began fighting near Krasnystaw on *19 Sep.* Attacked Zamosc on *20 Sep.* Fought German 27th Inf. Div. near Czesniki and Barchaczow on *21–22 Sep.* Attempted to break out of encirclement on *24–25 Sep,* and finally capitulated in the Szopowe region on *27 Sep.*

41ST INFANTRY • Cmdr: Brig. Gen. W. Piekarski; Inf. Cmdr: Col. S. M. Raganowicz. • *1 Sep:* Mobilizing in the Lomza-Pultusk-Ostrow Mazowiecka region. *2–5 Sep:* Although only half mobilized (five battalions), received order to defend 25 km front near Lubie region. Heavily engaged near Rozan and withdrew, disorganized, *6–7 Sep.* After concentrating, ordered behind Bug River to defend from Tuchlin to Liwa. Occupied positions by *9 Sep* and heavily engaged. Withdrew from Bug line and was badly beaten en route, near Stoczek-Zulin and at Kaluszyn, assisting 1st Inf. Div. against Panzer attack. Largely destroyed, except for 114th Regt. By *15 Sep,* remnants assembled by Gen. Piekarski into a group of about 5000, and began march toward Chelm. On *19 Sep,* incorporated remnants of 33rd Inf. Div. in Chelm region. Marched to Tyszowice by *22 Sep.* Attempted to break out of encirclement during *24–25 Sep,* and after heavy fighting, capitulated on *26 Sep.*

44TH INFANTRY ● Cmdr: Col. E. Zongolowicz; Inf. Cmdr: None. ● *1 Sep:* Mobilizing in Wloclawek-Modlin-Piotrkow-Lowicz region. On *4 Sep,* ordered to complete mobilization and concentrate on Dlutow-Muta Dlutowska-Tuszyn; 146th Regt. already engaged near Borowskie Gory. On *5 Sep,* ordered to assume defensive positions east of Vistula, northeast of Warsaw. Elements of 145th Regt. incorporated into 10th Inf. Div. Most of division capitulated in Warsaw and Modlin.

45TH INFANTRY ● Cmdr: Brig. Gen. H. Paszkowski-Kruk; Inf. Cmdr: None. ● Mobilized, *1–3 Sep,* but not completed. Elements were attached to 1st Mountain Brigade, 10th Mechanized Brigade, and 24th Inf. Div. Rest were absorbed by ARMY KRAKOW and ARMY KARPATY.

50TH INFANTRY ("Brzoza") ● Formed from remnants and miscellaneous units under control of GROUP POLESIE. Capitulated at Kock on *6 Oct.*

55TH INFANTRY ● Cmdr: Col. S. Kalabinski; Inf. Cmdr: Col. J. Giza. ● Mobilized, 24 Aug, but not completed. ● *1 Sep:* Defended the Mikolow and Kobior areas under Group Slask. *2–5 Sep:* Withdrew through Katowice to Sosnowiec and Trzebinia. West of Proszowice on *6 Sep,* then marched to contact in Klimontow region, until *8 Sep.* Then marched to Stopnica on *9 Sep* and engaged German 27th Inf. Div. Joined with Col. W. Klaczynski's fortress group on *10 Sep.* Organized defense on Czarna River, then moved toward Vistula crossing at Baranow. Heavily engaged on *11 Sep* against German 27th Inf. Div. Disengaged and crossed river that night to assemble in Tarnobrzeg on *12 Sep.* Defended San River area by *14 Sep.* By *17 Sep,* withdrawing toward Lwow to break out of encirclement. Heavily engaged on *18 Sep* in Terespol and Jozefow region, and later advanced on Tomaszow Lubelski. Fighting near Ulow and Luszcyc on *19 Sep.* Encircled and destroyed near Pasieki by *20 Sep.*

60TH INFANTRY ("Kobryn") ● *2–5 Sep:* Began mobilizing, but not completed. *19 Sep:* Joined by miscellaneous units, reserves, and remnants, came under control of GROUP POLESIE.

WOLKOWICKI ● Formed, *13–16 Sep,* in Chelm Lubelski region from remnants of 13th, 19th, and 29th Inf. Divs. under Brig. Gen. Jerzy Wolkowicki. The 13th "Brigade" consisted of three two-battalion regiments (43rd, 44th, 45th). The 19th "Brigade" joined the division on *20 Sep* with the 77th and 86th Regts. and Col. M. Osetkiewicz's group. On *20–21 Sep* the division began march to Tomaszow Lubelski through Laszczow and Simno. Heavily engaged on *22–23 Sep.* After battle at Rawa Ruska and Rzyezkan, division command was destroyed, but both elements fought on until formal capitulation on *27 Sep* near Terespol.

MOUNTAIN BRIGADES

1ST MOUNTAIN ● Cmdr: Col. J. Galadyk. ● Mobilized, 23 Aug. ● *1 Sep:* Under heavy attack by German mechanized corps advancing toward Jablonka and Czarny Dunajec. Stopped enemy after reinforcement by 10th Mechanized Brigade, but was outflanked. Reinforced by 12th Inf. Regt. and Armored Train 51 in the Sucha-Makow area. Heavily engaged on *2 Sep* near Wegierska Gorka. On *3 Sep,* formed Group Strazyca, and other battalions went to 10th Mechanized Brigade and 21st Inf. Div. By *4 Sep,* considered disbanded.

2ND MOUNTAIN ● Cmdr: Col. A. Stawarz. ● Mobilized, 28 Aug. ● *1 Sep:* Defending Muszyna-Krynica-Krempa and blocking the valleys of Muszyna and Krynica. Brigade moved to Piwniczna to oppose German 4th Light Div. *2–5 Sep:* Heavily engaged near Kroscienko and Klodno, then retreated toward Grybow. Continued retreat toward Grybow under air attack, then to Jaslo region, reaching Jedlicze-Krosno by *8 Sep.* Heavily engaged in defense of Krosno and largely destroyed by Panzer attack by *9 Sep,* with remnants going to 3rd Mountain Brigade.

3RD MOUNTAIN ● Cmdr: Col. J. Kotowicz. ● Mobilized, ? Aug. ● *1 Sep:* Defending Lupkow, Cisna, and Dukla pass. Destroyed Lupkowski Tunnel and observed Slovak activities. No combat. *2–5 Sep:* Remained on Slovak border, with little activity. On *7 Sep,* engaged at Lupkow. Moved to Konty and Zmigrod. Heavily engaged, *8 Sep,* and ordered to delay Germans at San River, where it defended through *9 Sep.* Withdrew, *10–12 Sep,* to Kroscienko region, but was beaten en route in Starzowa region. Remnants moved to Turki area, where they combined with units retreating from San River battles. Defended St. Sambor, *15–16 Sep,* and after heavy combat managed to reach Hungary on *18 Sep.*

CAVALRY BRIGADES

ABRAHAM ● Formed *15 Sep* as independent cavalry group under Gen. R. Abraham from remnants of PODOLSKA and WIELKOPOLSKA BRIGADES.

After "miraculous" advance through Kampinos Forest, *18 Sep,* was heavily engaged on *19–20 Sep,* breaking into capital, led by 14th Regt. Defended Warsaw in Siekierki and Mokotow regions.

KRAKOWSKA ● Cmdr: Brig. Gen. Z. Piasecki; C/S: Lt. Col. T. Nalepa. ● Mobilized, 24 Aug at Krakow. ● *1 Sep:* Having concentrated in the region of Zawiercie-Ogrodzieniec-Myszkow, moved to defend the Wozniki region, after Germans occupied Kalety and Kosecin. *2–5 Sep:* Heavily engaged near Wozniki against tank units, then retreated to Pradel region. 8th Lancer Regt. destroyed near Szczekociny; after regrouping, began defense of Pinczow. In west part of Bogucice Forest on *6 Sep;* then ordered to defend Vistula from Nagnajow to Lipulk. Screened Vistula crossing near Nagnajow-Lipulk on *10-11 Sep.* Moved to Mokrzyszow-Wola Tarnowska with similar mission; then moved to Lipow area. Heavily engaged near Tarnogrod on *16 Sep,* then near Tomaszow Lubelski on *19 Sep,* and surrendered there with Army Lublin on *20 Sep.*

KRESOWA ● Cmdr: Col. S. Kulesza (to 4 Sep); C/S: Col. J. Grobicki. ● Mobilized, 27 Aug at Brody. ● *1 Sep:* Moving by rail to front. Germans bombed the 6th and 20th Regts. *2–5 Sep:* Bombed during unloading and concentration. Disorganized elements attached to group of Gen. F. Dinforn-Ankowicz in Warta region, retreating east of city on *4 Sep.* Counterattacked on *5 Sep.* Defended in forests near Szadek, and on *7 Sep* withdrew behind Ner, screening 10th Inf. Div. Withdrew toward Glowno, then Skierniewice on *9 Sep.* Its scattered units finally reached Suliszew region on *9 Sep.* Screened Group withdrawal near Karolinow on *10 Sep.* Split into two groups and defeated near Osuchow and Psary. Remnants under Colonel Grobicki defended Vistula near Otwock until absorbed by GROUP ANDERS.

MAZOWIECKA ● Cmdr: Col. J. Karcz; Asst.: Col. M. Wieckowski. ● Mobilized, 24 Aug at Warsaw. ● *1 Sep:* Attacked near Krzynowloga Mala by German Wodrig Corps. Retreated after being outflanked. *2–5 Sep:* Withdrew as rearguard. Defended Przasnysz-Pultusk area against tank attack and by *4 Sep* was pushed back toward Ciechanow. Assigned to GROUP WYSZKOW and occupied Narew River near Pultusk to Serock. By *7 Sep,* ordered to Bug line, where it occupied area from Wyszkow to Serock. Held line, then moved into woods north of Stanislawow on *10 Sep.* Ordered back to Bug on *11 Sep.* Heavily engaged on the road between Lochow and Minsk Mazowiecki and badly disorganized by *12 Sep.* Remnants withdrew to Chelma, reaching there by *19 Sep.* Fought at Lubelszczyzna and was encircled and destroyed near Suchowola by *21 Sep,* with some remnants of 1st Regt. escaping southward to join GROUP ANDERS in the Garwolin area.

NOWOGRODZKA ● Cmdr: Brig. Gen. W. Anders; Asst.: Col. K. Zelis-lawski. ● Mobilized, 23 Mar at Baranowicze. ● *1 Sep:* Left wing of ARMY MODLIN in Lidzbark and Dzialdowo area. Retreated toward Plock on *4 Sep,* and defended Vistula near Dobrzyn on *5 Sep to 8 Sep,* when it marched to Wyszogrod. By *11 Sep,* in Wiazowna region, where it came under GROUP ANDERS. Moving into Parczew region on *13 Sep,* continuing south and reaching east of Deblin on *17 Sep.* Marched south under Group Anders. Came under air attack on *20 Sep.* Joined by MAZOWIECKA elements and Col. A. Zakrewski's combined brigade (Warszawski Lancers, 8th Lancers, and WILENSKA remnants) by *22 Sep,* reaching Majdan Sopocki after repeated combat. Reached Ruda Rozaniecki by *24 Sep,* then moved southeastward through Broszki, where it fought the German 28th Inf. Div. Encircled by *28 Sep,* and disbanded, with some elements reaching Hungary.

PODLASKA ● Cmdr: Brig. Gen. L. Kmicic-Skrzynski. ● Mobilized, 24 Aug at Bialystok. ● *1 Sep:* Concentrated in the Stawiska-Korzeniste region. Only the 5th Regt. fought. *2–5 Sep:* Conducted successful reconnaissance into Prussia near Mielewo-Glinki region on *4 Sep;* withdrawn behind Narew River after losing fifty men. Until *7 Sep,* marched from Stawiski to Nadbory; then ordered toward Ostrow Mazowiecka, and Brok to prepare Bug River defenses. *10–12 Sep:* Retreated toward Zlotoryja-Zareby-Koscielna region. Directed near Ostrow Mazowiecka by *11 Sep,* and that night continued to Wielka Dabrowa region through Nowa Wies. Engaged near Domanowo on *13 Sep,* and reached Lapie-Mulawicze area by *14 Sep.* Stopped for rest at Bielowieza Forest on *16 Sep,* with some elements disorganized. By *18 Sep,* joined with SUWALSKA CAVALRY BRIGADE at Bialowieza Forest and units of both incorporated into ZAZA CAVALRY DIVISION.

PODOLSKA ● Cmdr: Col. L. Strzelecki; C/S: Lt. Col. W. Swiecicki. ● Mobilized, 27 Aug at Stanislawow. ● *1 Sep:* Concentrated in the Nekla Forest near Wrzesnia. Ordered to support the 14th Inf. Div. after moving west of the Warta. Marched west through Poznan on *2 Sep,* and east on *3 Sep* to Swarzedz region and joined with Poznan National Guard Brigade to form Group Strzelecki. Acted as army rearguard on *6 Sep,* near Sempono-Babiak, in series of night marches, then joined with remnants of POMORSKA CAVALRY BRIGADE to form Cavalry Group General Grzmot-Skotnicki. *10–12 Sep:* After heavy losses, 6th Lancers successfully stormed Uniejow to cross Warta; 14th Lancers captured Wartkowice; and both assembled east of Poddebice. Ordered to disrupt German rear area on *11 Sep* in the Zgierz area and east of Lodz. Heavily engaged against German 221st Inf. Div. on *12 Sep,* then ordered back north of Bzura to

Leczyca region. By *14 Sep,* moved to Brochow. Combined with WIEL-KOPOLSKA CAVALRY BRIGADE to form GROUP ABRAHAM on *15 Sep,* which became rearguard for Kutrzeba's forces. Marched to Modlin on *16 Sep,* and then to Palmiry area by *18 Sep* to begin battle near Sierakow. Heavily engaged there, then assembled at Smolarnia region, by *19 Sep.* Broke through to Warsaw at Weglowka Wolka and under heavy air attack on *20 Sep.* Defended Warsaw until surrender.

POMORSKA • Cmdr: Col. A. Zakrewski. • Mobilized, 23 Mar at Bydgoszcz. • *1 Sep:* Engaged along its entire front. At 1700 the 18th Regt. launched the first cavalry attack of the war and took heavy losses near Krojanty when surprised by armored column. Delayed and exhausted by long marches on *2–3 Sep,* elements scattered en route to Bydgoszcz, concentrating to fight near Poledno and Gruczno, with further skirmishes during march. Joined with elements of 27th Inf. Div. near Zatej Wsi region. Took heavy losses near Legowo including most of lancer regiment. Reorganized near Vistula by *7 Sep* into a regiment and attached to ARMY POZNAN near Bzura River, with PODOLSKA CAVALRY BRIGADE. Fought on *12 Sep* near Krakow. Remnants engaged near Bzura, where weakened 8th Rifles and 2nd Hussars marched toward Orla. Remnants destroyed near Izabelin on *18 Sep,* with some reaching Warsaw and Modlin.

SUWALSKA • Cmdr: Brig. Gen. Z. Podhorski (to 9 Sep); Col. K. Plisowski. • Mobilized, 24 Aug at Suwalki. • *1 Sep:* Assigned to defend Augustow area, under GROUP NAREW. After concentrating in Kurianki-Suwalki region, conducted raids into Prussia; then ordered to Zambrow region on *4 Sep.* On the march until *8 Sep,* from Sztabin to Tykocin; Lt. Col. W. Anders took control near Pruszki Wielki region. Late on *9 Sep,* moved into Glabosz Wielki Forest to prepare attack on Wodrig Corps. Panzer units advanced successfully on *10 Sep.* Withdrew to Koskowo Rzasnik region to prepare for breakout attempt that failed. On *12 Sep,* marched to Wielka Dabrowa region, then to Hodyszewo area. Heavily engaged until *15 Sep.* Reorganized after heavy losses on *15 Sep.* Then marched to Bielowieza Forest by *17 Sep.* Under air attack and in combat en route. Reached Bialowieza Forest on *18 Sep* and was absorbed into ZAZA CAVALRY DIVISION by *20 Sep.*

WIELKOPOLSKA • Cmdr: Brig. Gen. R. Abraham; C/S: Maj. T. Grzezulko. • Mobilized, 24 Aug at Poznan. • *1 Sep:* Concentrating. *2–5 Sep:* After two minor raids into Germany near Warta line, ordered to Wrzesnia-Slupca area on *4 Sep.* On *6 Sep,* moved toward Konin and Turek. Despite heavy air attacks and artillery fire, crossed Warta on *7 Sep,* near Dabie. Then ordered along the northern bank of Bzura to destroy crossing; reached Strzegocin late *8 Sep,* then crossed to Sobota region.

Engaged, *9 Sep,* in effort to establish contact with ARMY LODZ. Reached Glowno and took Walewice and Bielawy, but cut off on *10 Sep.* On *11 Sep,* despite local success, ordered back to north of Bzura and defense of crossing near Brochow region. In period *13–14 Sep,* heavily engaged defending Bzura River against SS-reinforced 4th Ranger Div. On *15 Sep,* formed an independent cavalry group under General Abraham by combining with PODOLSKA CAVALRY BRIGADE. Broke through German lines, night of *20 Sep,* and defended Warsaw.

WILENSKA ● Cmdr: Col. K. Drucki-Lubecki; C/S: Lt. Col. J. Skrzydlewski. ● Mobilized, 24 Aug at Wilno. ● *1 Sep:* Concentrating under ARMY PRUSY in Koluszki region. *2–5 Sep.* Ordered beyond Pilica to screen Sulejow crossings. Fought near Piotrkow. Crossed into Przysucha region on *7 Sep.* By *8 Sep,* defending in Jedlinsk region. Tank and air attacks forced brigade to retreat. Heavy losses occurred during Vistula crossing near Maciejowice. Disorganization resulted. 23rd Regt. cut off and disbanded east of Konskie. Between *10 and 12 Sep,* remnants assembled in woods south of Laskarzew, then were directed to Kurow. Joined Group Zakrewski and reached forest near Swidnik by *14 Sep;* then joined GROUP ANDERS, with elements of 4th and 13th Regts. marching to Chelm. Attached to MAZOWIECKA CAVALRY BRIGADE from *19 Sep.*

WOLYNSKA ● Cmdr: Col. J. Filipowicz; C/S: Maj. W. Lewicki. ● Mobilized, 13 Aug at Rowne. ● *1 Sep:* Concentrating in Radomsko area under ARMY LODZ and heavily engaged against 4th Panzer Div. in Mokra area. Despite heavy losses, resisted all enemy attacks and was credited with destruction of 50 armored vehicles. Withdrew to Ostrow line after Germans occupied flanking position at Klobuck. On *3 Sep,* heavily engaged near Ostrowarnia, losing 25 percent and forced back to Rozprza and Kamiensk. Raided 1st Panzer Div. Remnants withdrawn to Grabia woods, then ordered to Dlutow-Tuszyn area, screening southern flank of army. On *7 Sep,* west of Cyrusowa and distinguished itself there on *8 Sep.* Forced to retreat across Mroga, then to Przylek region after heavy fighting. Reached Puszcza Kampinoska on *10 Sep* and crossed Vistula near Nowy Dwor on *11 Sep,* reaching Sulejowek-Milosna woods on *12 Sep.* Fought near Minsk Mazowiecka with GROUP ANDERS, on *13–14 Sep.* Thereafter fighting near Tomaszow Lubelski at Krasnobrod on *23 Sep.* Fought toward Hungary and destroyed by Russians on *27 Sep.*

10TH MECHANIZED ● Cmdr: Col. S. Maczek; Asst.: Col. L. Michalski. ● Mobilized, 15 Mar at Rzeszow. ● *1 Sep:* Reinforced by 1st KOP Regt. in the Gora Ludwiki-Wysoka-Rokiciany area, resisted enemy attacks in the Jordanow-Chabowka area. Heavily engaged near Wysoka and screened withdrawal of ARMY KRAKOW on *3 Sep,* then withdrew with

KOP and fought, *4 Sep,* near Pcim and Kasina Wielka. Cut off from parent headquarters on *5 Sep.* Began preparing defenses near Dunajec and fought against units advancing on Bochnia. To avoid encirclement, withdrew to Radlowo region; then, on *7 Sep,* directed toward Radomysl Wielki region, but blocked by fall of Tarnow. Ordered to Rzeszow region and Group Sosnkowski, and then to defend San River line. Heavily engaged, *9 Sep,* near Lancut, and retreated toward Jaroslaw and Radymno. Retreated after heavy combat with 2nd Panzer Div. Ordered to block advance from Radymno to Krakowiec-Lwow. By *11 Sep,* Germans having crossed San River in force, attacked near Jaworow. Ordered to Solkwi region to defend Lwow. Reached Kulakowo region by *14 Sep* and attacked Zboiska on *15–17 Sep.* Then ordered to Hulicza region and crossed into Tatorow area by *18 Sep.* On *20 Sep,* crossed into Hungary.

WARSAW MECHANIZED • Cmdr: Col. S. Rowecki; C/S: Lt. Col. F. Stachowicz. • Mobilized, 1 Sep at Warsaw. • *1 Sep:* Concentrating in the Warsaw-Garwolin area. Ordered to block Vistula crossings on *3 Sep* in Pulawy, Deblin, and Maciejowice. Assigned to ARMY LUBLIN on *4 Sep.* By *5 Sep,* occupied line from Deblin to Solec. *6–9 Sep:* Defended from Deblin to Jozefow. First contact with Germans on *9 Sep* near Annopol. Ordered from Kurow-Markuszow area to Solec-Zawichost on Vistula. Marched to Chodel region, destroying bridges at Deblin and Pulawy en route, arriving *11 Sep.* Moved to Urzedow on *12 Sep,* where it was heavily engaged near Annopol and German bridgehead across Vistula. Withdrew to Krasnik region on *14 Sep,* then to Frampol on *15 Sep.* Broke through to Tomaszow Lubelski by *16 Sep.* Attacked near Rogozno on *17 Sep* and attempted to break line; temporarily held southeast part of city. Fought near Tomaszow Lubelski and took heavy losses near Rogozno by *20 Sep,* and forced to surrender.

ZAKREWSKI (GROUP) • Formed on *10 Sep,* under Col. Adam Zakrewski, near Garwolin as part of ARMY LUBLIN. The Grudziadz Cavalry School provided a cadre for the unit. By *12 Sep* the unit joined remnants of four cavalry formations and came under Col. T. Komorowski. After heavy losses at Krasnobrod on *21 Sep,* fought Russian units on *22–23 Sep* and some elements managed to escape to Hungary.

ZAZA CAVALRY DIVISION • Formed from remnants of SUWALSKA and PODOLSKA CAVALRY BRIGADES in GROUP NAREW area. New brigades formed—Plis (2nd Lancers, 10th Lancers, and elements of 5th Lancers), and Edward (1st Lancers, 3rd Horse, and 3rd Rifles)—and marched to Parczew area on *21 Sep.* Fought near Omalenc and Kalenkowicze on *22 Sep.* Then in the area of Wysokie Litewskie-Drohiczyn on *24 Sep.* It fought the German 4th Inf. Div. on the Wieprz River on *28 Sep.* On *29 Sep,* it joined GROUP POLESIE and marched to Czemerniki the next day, crossing the Tysmienica River by *1 Oct.* On *2 Oct* it defeated elements of the 13th Mechanized Division near Zerokomla. Fought alongside the 50th Inf. Div. from *2 to 5 Oct,* in the Kock area. After heavy losses, and lacking food and ammunition, it capitulated on *6 Oct.*

NATIONAL GUARD BRIGADES

CHELMSKA • *1 Sep:* Disbanded among various formations of ARMY POMORZE.

SLASKA-CIESYNSKA • *1 Sep:* Redesignated 202nd Inf. Regt. under 21st Inf. Div.

DABROWSKA • *1 Sep:* Redesignated 204th Inf. Regt. under 55th Inf. Div.

KALISKA • *1 Sep:* Disbanded among 25th and 26th Inf. Divs. and WIELKOPOLSKA CAVALRY BRIGADE.

KARPACKA • *1 Sep:* Mobilizing. Stationed along Hungarian border, defended "Romanian bridgehead."

LWOWSKA • *1 Sep:* Mobilizing. Part "Lwow I" defended Lwow. "Lwow II" fought on the Stryj as part of Group Dembenski.

MORSKA • *1 Sep:* Mobilizing. The 2nd Gdynia battalion ordered to march toward Koscierzyna and destroyed by German motorized formations en route. Other elements not engaged. *2–5 Sep:* Individual battalions suffer separately: 1st Gdynia destroyed on *1 Sep.* 2nd Gdynia is heavily engaged from *4 Sep.* 3rd Gdynia still mobilizing. 4th Kartuski heavily engaged in Zukow, then withdrew toward Kamionka region. Kaszubski not fully mobilized, but held positions in Warszkow region. *6–9 Sep:* Continued battalion actions. By *12 Sep,* brigade had lost almost half its strength. *13–18 Sep:* Began final defense of Gdynia area with remnants. Destroyed at Gdynia by *19 Sep,* with commander committing suicide to avoid capture.

NAVAL, see MORSKA.

PODHALANSKA • *1 Sep:* Converted to formations with the 1st and 2nd Mountain Brigades.

PODKARPACKA • *1 Sep:* Disbanded to 3rd Mountain Brigade.

POMORSKA • *1 Sep:* Mobilizing under ARMY POMORZE. Destroyed on *3 Sep,* with Starogard Battalion deployed near Tczew, then Chelmno, and Naklo Battalion attached to 26th Inf. Div.

POZNANSKA • Temporarily disbanded under ARMY POZNAN among 14th Inf. Div., etc., including air and naval units, *4 Sep.* Became rearguard for Army Poznan and divided into three regiments on western side of Warta. *6–9 Sep:* Moved across Warta. From *10 Sep,* defended Warta and screened left flank of Army Poznan with three groups: Kolo (Krotoszyn, Rawicz, and Leszno Battalions), Rudzica (Koscian and Kozmin Battalions), and Colonel Siudy (1st and 2nd Poznan and Grybow Battalions). Largely disbanded as unit.

SIERADZKA ● *1 Sep:* Disbanded. Kepno, Ostrzeszow, and 1st and 2nd Wielun Battalions assigned to 10th Inf. Div.; Klobuck Battalion to 7th Inf. Div.; and Lubliniec Battalion to Krakowska Cavalry Brigade.

SLASKA ● *1 Sep:* Disbanded. Battalions absorbed by 55th (Reserve) Inf. Div. (see Table 3–13). Destroyed near Tomaszow Lubelski by *20 Sep.*

WARSZAWSKA ● Mobilized *25 Aug* under ARMY MODLIN and 3rd Zegrze, 3rd Pultusk, Plock, and 1st Wyszogrod Battalions primarily assigned to defend Warsaw suburbs and bridges. 1st and 2nd Mazurski Battalions assigned to 20th Inf. Div. *2–5 Sep:* Concentrating and preparing defenses in Warsaw area. *6–9 Sep:* Continued battalion actions. *10–12 Sep:* 1st and 2d Mazurski Battalions took heavy losses. 1st Warsaw Battalion went to ARMY POZNAN. 2nd Warsaw went to ARMY WARSAW; 3rd Warsaw joined the 41st Inf. Div. and Army Modlin. Disbanded as brigade.

APPENDIX 1

German Army Order of Battle, 1 September 1939

ARMY HIGH COMMAND

Cmdr: Col. Gen. W. Brauchitsch; C/S F. Halder

ARMY GROUP NORTH

Cmdr: Col. Gen. F. von Bock

Fourth Army

Comdr: G. von Kluge

Corps	*Corps Units*
I Frontier Guard Corps	207th Inf. Div.
II Corps	3rd Inf. Div., 32nd Inf. Div.
III Corps	Netze Br., 50th Inf. Div.
XIX Mtz Corps	2nd Mtz Div., 3rd Panzer Div.

Fourth Army Reserve

II Frontier Guard Corps	
XII Frontier Guard Corps	23nd Inf. Div., 218th Inf. Div.

Third Army

Cmdr: von Kuechler

I Corps	Kempf Panzer Div., 11th Inf. Div., 61st Inf. Div.
XXI Corps	21st Inf. Div., 228th Inf. Div.
Brand Corps	Goldnap Br., Loetzen Br.
Wodrig Corps	1st Inf. Div., 12th Inf. Div., 1st Cav. Br.

Third Army Reserve

217th Inf. Div., Eberhard Br.

Army Group Reserves

10th Panzer Div., 73rd Inf. Div., 206th Inf. Div., 208th Inf. Div.

ARMY GROUP SOUTH

Cmdr: Col. Gen. G. von Rundstedt

Eighth Army

Cmdr: J. Blaskowitz

X Corps	24th Inf. Div., 30th Inf. Div.
XIII Corps	10th Inf. Div., 17th Inf. Div., SS Regt Adolf Hitler
XII Frontier Guard Corps	
XIV Frontier Guard Corps	

Tenth Army

Cmdr: W. von Reichenau

IV Corps	4th Inf. Div., 46th Inf. Div.
XI Corps	18th Inf. Div., 19th Inf. Div.
XV Mtz Corps	2nd Lt Div., 3rd Lt Div.
XVI Panzer Corps	1st Panzer Div., 4th Panzer Div., 14th Inf. Div., 31st Inf. Div.

Tenth Army Reserve

XIV Mtz Corps	13th Mtz Div., 14th Mtz Div., 1st Lt Div.

Fourteenth Army

Cmdr: W. List

VIII Corps	5th Panzer Div., 8th Inf. Div., 28th Inf. Div., SS Regt Germania
XVII Corps	7th Inf. Div., 44th Inf. Div., 45th Inf. Div.
XVIII Corps	2nd Panzer Div., 3rd Mtz Div., 4th Lt Div.

Fourteenth Army Reserve

XXII Corps	1st Mtn Div., 2nd Mtn Div.

Army Group Reserves

VII Corps   27th Inf. Div., 68th Inf. Div., 62nd Inf. Div., 213th Inf.
                 Div., 221th Inf. Div., 239th Inf. Div.; (later) 56th Inf.
                 Div., 57th Inf. Div., 252nd Inf. Div., 257th Inf. Div.,
                 258th Inf. Div.

AIR FORCE HIGH COMMAND (OKL)

Cmdr: Field Marshal H. Goering; C/S Jeschonnek

FIRST AIR FLEET

Cmdr: A. Kesselring

FOURTH AIR FLEET

Cmdr: Lohr

NAVY HIGH COMMAND (OKM)

Cmdr: Adm. Raeder; C/NO Schniewind

NAVAL COMMAND EAST

Cmdr: Albrecht

APPENDIX 2

Red Army Order of Battle, Invasion of Poland, 17 September 1939

Byelorussian Front

HQ: Minsk
Cmdr: Komandarm II M. P. Kovalyov
Byelorussian Front Horse-Mechanized Group
Cmdr: I. V. Boldin

Eleventh Army

Cmdr: N. P. Medvedev
(Units unknown)

Third "Vitebsk" Army

Cmdr: V. I. Kuznetzov
Objectives: Wilno

Corps	*Corps Units*
4th Rifle Corps	5th Rifle Div., 50th Rifle Div., 18th Tank Br.
Lepelska Army Gp	27th Rifle Div., 24th Cav. Div., 16th Tank Br.

Tenth Army

Cmdr: I. G. Zakharkin

24th Rifle Corps	29th Rifle Div., 139th Rifle Div., 145th Rifle Div.

Fourth "Bobruisk" Army

Cmdr: V. I. Chuikov
Objectives: Brzesc, Bialystok

6th Cav. Corps	4th Cav. Div., 6th Cav. Div., 11th Cav. Div., 16th Lt Tank Br.
16th Rifle Corps	4th Rifle Div., 13th Rifle Div., 33rd Rifle Div., 21st Tank Br.

| 15th Tank Corps | 27th Lt Tank Br., 45th Lt Bank Br., 20th Mtz Br. |
| 23rd Ind. Rifle Corps | 93rd Rifle Div., 109th Rifle Div., 152nd Rifle Div. |

UKRAINIAN FRONT

HQ: Proskurov
Cmdr: Komandarm I S. K. Timoshenko

Fifth "Zhytomier" Army

Cmdr: Komdiv I. G. Sovetnikov
Objectives: Lublin

| 8th Rifle Corps | 44th Rifle Div., 46th Rif. Div., 89th Rifle Div. |
| 3rd Cav. Corps | 7th Cav. Div., 11th Cav. Div., 27th Cav. Div., 3rd Lt Tank Br. |

Sixth "Vinnitsa" Army

Cmdr: Komkor F. I. Golikov
Objectives: Lwow

| 17th Rifle Corps | 72nd Rifle Div., 96th Rifle Div., 97th Rifle Div. |
| 2nd Cav. Corps | 3rd Cav. Div., 5th Cav. Div., 14th Cav. Div., 24th Lt Tank Br. |

Twelfth Army

Cmdr: Komandarm II I. V. Tiulenov
Objectives: ?

4th Cav. Corps	10th Cav. Div., 12th Cav. Div., 13th Cav. Div.
5th Cav. Corps	16th Cav. Div., 25th Cav. Div., 30th Cav. Div.
25th Tank Corps	4th Lt Tank Br., 5th Hvy Tank Br., 1st Motor Rifle Br. 23rd Ind. Tank Br., 26th Ind. Tank Br.
15th Ind. Rifle Corps	7th Rifle Div., 45th Rifle Div., 60th Rifle Div.

Bibliography

The September Campaign of 1939 has been generally ignored in English. Much of what has been written in general accounts has repeated hoary myths and distortions and is more reminiscent of German wartime propaganda than serious scholarship. There are a handful of English-language accounts which are far from adequate. The useful U.S. Army monograph on the subject by Maj. R. Kennedy looks at the campaign from a German perspective. Gen. Norwid Neugebauer's account was printed in Britain shortly after the 1939 campaign and is both dated and incomplete. A short popular history was printed in English in Warsaw as part of the Interpress series by Z. Bielecki. There were a number of English-language accounts of various units, including a good account of the 10th Mechanized Brigade. In the past few years, specialized magazines on military subjects have begun to examine some aspects of the 1939 campaign. The Polish air force has been particularly well covered in English both in books and articles. There are also a substantial number of articles on the Polish armored forces. Accounts of the political underpinnings of the war have flourished.

Although the subject has not been treated adequately in English, the September Campaign has been the subject of endless fascination in Polish-language accounts. One bibliography lists no fewer than 900 books and major articles on the 1939 fighting alone, and it is by no means complete. There have been several major works published on the subject, notably the London-based Sikorski Institute's excellent, but uncompleted, multivolume official history, and the studies published by WMON in Warsaw. The main shortcoming of the studies coming from Poland has been the sensitivity of the issue of the Soviet invasion of 17 September, which cannot be dealt with in any detail. Nevertheless, the focus of studies of the September Campaign has gradually shifted in the past decade from the emigre scholars in London to a new generation of scholars in Poland. A series of excellent monographs on such subjects as the various armies, the National Guard, the armored force and so on, continue to pour out of Poland along with many articles appearing in such journals as *Wojskowy Przeglad Historyczne*. Unfortunately, the language barrier has prevented most English-speaking military historians from becoming aware of the richness of these sources.

This short bibliography is intended to point out some of the major books in the field, both in English and Polish. Special emphasis has been placed on studies of the various branches of the Polish Armed Forces, such as the cavalry, artillery, and so on.

P. Bauer, and B. Polak, Armia Poznan *w wojnie obronnej, 1939* [Army Poznan in the 1939 Defensive War]. Poznan-Wyd. Poznanski, 1983.

N. Bethell, *The War Hitler Won, The Fall of Poland, 1939*. New York: Holt, Rinehart & Winston, 1972.

Z. Bielecki, R. Debowski, *In Defense of Independence, September 1939*. Warsaw: Interpress, 1972.

K. Ciechanowski, *Armia Pomorze*. Warsaw: WMON, 1983.

J. Cynk, *History of the Polish Air Force, 1918–68*. London: Osprey, 1972.

R. Dalecki, *Armia Karpaty, 1939.* Warsaw: WMON, 1979.

N. Davies, *White Eagle, Red Star: The Polish Soviet War, 1919–1920.* London: Macdonald, 1972.

S. Feret, *Polska sztuka wojenna, 1918–1939* [Polish military doctrine 1918–1939]. Warsaw: WMON, 1972.

K. Galster, *Ksiega pamiatkowa artylerii polskiej, 1914–1939* [Memorial book of the Polish artillery, 1914–1939]. London: KNOAPnO, 1975.

L. Glowacki. *Obrona Warsawy i Modlina, 1939* [The defense of Warsaw and Modlin in 1939]. Warsaw: WMON, 1975.

L. Gondek. *Wywiad Polski w Trzeciej Rzeszy, 1933–39* [Polish espionage in the Third Reich, 1933–39]. Warsaw: WMON, 1978.

T. Jurga, *Regularne jednostki Wojska Polskiego w 1939r.* Nr. 7 [Regular units of the Polish Army in 1939, No. 7]. Warsaw: WMON, 1975.

R. Kennedy, *The German Campaign in Poland.* U.S. Army Pamphlet 20–255. Washington: GPO, 1956.

I. Kolinski, *Regularne jednostki Wojska Polskiego (lotnictwo),* No. 9 [Regular units of the Polish Army (Aviation) No. 9]. Warsaw: WMON, 1978.

Komisja Historyczna Polskiego Sztabu Glownego w Londynie (Historical Commission of the Polish General Staff in London), *Polskie Sily Zbrojne w Drugiej Wojnie Swiatowej.* Tom I: *Kampania Wrzesniowa 1939* [The Polish Armed Forces in World War II. Vol. I: The September campaign, 1939]. (3 parts to date) London: Gen Sikorski Institute, 1959–.

E. Kozlowski, *Wojsko Polskie, 1936–1939: proby modernizacji i rozbudowy* [The Polish Army, 1936–39: attempts at modernization and reconstruction]. Warsaw: WMON, 1974.

E. Kozlowski et al. *Wojna Obronna Polski, 1939* [The defensive war of Poland, 1939]. Warsaw: WMON, 1979.

E. Kozlowski et al., *Wojna Obronna Polski, 1939, Wybor zrodel* [The defensive war of Poland, 1939, a selection of source documents]. Warsaw: WMON, 1968.

T. Kryska-Karski, *Piechota, 1939–45* [Infantry, 1939–45]. London: self-published, 1970–74.

W. Kucharski, *Kawaleria i Bron Pancerna w doktrynach wojennych, 1918–39* [The cavalry and armored force in military doctrine, 1918–39]. Krakow: PWN, 1984.

F. S. Kurcz (pseud. F. Skibinski), *The Black Brigade.* Harrow: Atlantis, 1943.

A. Kurowski, *Lotnictwo Polskie w 1939r.* [The Polish air force in 1939]. Warsaw: WMON, 1963.

T. Kutrzeba, *Bitwa nad Bzura* [Battle on the Bzura]. Warsaw: Czytelnik, 1957.

L. Mitkiewicz, *Kawaleria samodzielna rzeczypospolitej polskiej w wojnie 1939 roku* [The cavalry of the independent Polish republic in the 1939 war]. Toronto: ZKiAKwAP, 1964.

L. Moczulski, *Wojna Obronna Polski 1939* [The defensive war of Poland]. Poznan: banned on publication.

M. Norwid Neugebauer, *The Defense of Poland, September 1939.* London: M. I. Kolbin, 1942.

J. Pertek, *Wielki dni malej floty* [Great days of a small fleet]. Poznan: Wyd. Poznanskie, 1976.

S. Piaskowski, *Okrety rzeczpospolitej polskiej, 1920–46* [Ships of the Polish republic, 1920–1946], Albany: Sigma, 1981.

J. Piekalkiewicz, *Polen Feldzug.* Bergisch-Gladbach: Gustav Lubbe Verlag, 1982.

K. Pindel, *Obrona Narodowa, 1937–1939* [National Guard, 1937–39]. Warsaw: WMON, 1979.

M. Porwit, *Komentarze do historii polskich dzialan obronnych 1939r.* [Commentary on the history of Polish defensive actions in 1939]. Warsaw: Czytelnik, 1973.

A. Rzepniewski, *Obrona wybrzeza w 1939r.* [Defense of the seacoast in 1939]. Warsaw: WMON, 1964.

W. Steblik, *Armia Krakow, 1939.* Warsaw: WMON, 1975.

K. Szczepanska et al., *Bibliografia wojny wyzwolenczej narodu polskiego, 1939–45 (Materialy z lat 1939–67)* [Bibliography of the war for the liberation of the Polish people, 1939–1945 (Material from 1939–67)]. Warsaw: WMON, 1973.

R. Szubanski, *Polska bron pancerna w 1939 roku* [The Polish armored force in 1939]. Warsaw: WMON 1982.

J. Wroblewski, *Armia Lodz, 1939*. Warsaw: WMON, 1975.

S. Zaloga, *The Polish Army, 1939–45*. London: Osprey, 1981.

M. Zebrowski, *Zarys historii polskiej broni pancerne, 1918–46* [Outline history of the Polish armored force, 1918–46]. London: ZZKOBP, 1971.

M. Zgorniak, *Sytuacja militarna Europy w okresie kryzsu politycznego 1938r.* [The military situation in Europe during the 1938 political crisis]. Warsaw: PWN, 1979.